2020 | Volume 4

# U.P. READER

## Bringing Upper Michigan Literature to the World

A publication of the
Upper Peninsula Publishers and Authors Association (UPPAA)
Marquette, Michigan

UPPAA

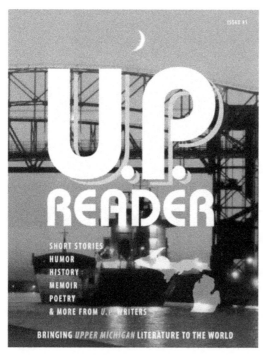

# U.P. Reader
## Volume 1 is still available!

Michigan's Upper Peninsula is blessed with a treasure chest of writers and poets, all seeking to capture the diverse experiences of Yooper Life. Now U.P. Reader offers a rich collection of their voices that embraces the U.P.'s natural beauty and way of life, along with a few surprises.

The twenty-eight works in this first annual volume take readers on a U.P. Road Trip from the Mackinac Bridge to Menominee. Every page is rich with descriptions of the characters and culture that make the Upper Peninsula worth living in and writing about.

Available in paperback, hardcover, and eBook editions!

**ISBN 978-1-61599-336-9**

## www.UPReader.org

U.P. Reader: Bringing Upper Michigan Literature to the World – Volume #4
Copyright © 2020 by Upper Peninsula Publishers and Authors Association (UPPAA). All Rights Reserved.

Cover Photo: by Mikel B. Classen.

Learn more about the UPPAA at www.UPPAA.org
Latest news on *UP Reader* can be found at www.UPReader.org

ISSN: 2572-0961

ISBN 978-1-61599-508-0 paperback
ISBN 978-1-61599-509-7 hardcover
ISBN 978-1-61599-510-3 eBook (ePub, Kindle, PDF)

Managing Editor - Mikel B. Classen
Associate Editor and Copy Editor - Deborah K. Frontiera
Production - Victor Volkman
Cover Photo - Mikel B. Classen
Interior Layout - Michal Splho

Distributed by Ingram (USA/CAN/AU), Bertram's Books (UK/EU)

Published by
Modern History Press
5145 Pontiac Trail
Ann Arbor, MI 48105

www.ModernHistoryPress.com
info@ModernHistoryPress.com

# CONTENTS

# Moving Up

## by Donna Winters

When I consider my father's life, three words come to mind—business, bowling, and boating. He clearly had a passion for all three. In reflecting on his accomplishments in those areas, I'd say he was always moving up.

Take business, for example. Before Dad was out of high school, he worked in his father's small-town business. Dad grew up in an Erie Canal town in western New York State during the early 1900s. It was the kind of place where, as a kid, if you heard a whistle blow, you ran as fast as you could to catch a ride on the lift bridge and watch the boat pass underneath.

At eighteen, Dad would have been working fulltime in his father's florist business except for one small problem: he had failed ancient history. He must have been disappointed when that failure prevented him from graduating from high school, but he was perfectly honest about the cause. He had been more interested in playing soccer than in studying.

So after his senior year, Dad went back to school part-time to get his diploma. Now normally, I would consider failure in academics to be a bad thing. But if Dad hadn't failed Ancient History, he would never have met Mom, who was seated right in front of him because of the alphabetical seating chart.

I think I know why Mom fell in love with Dad. He was a good-looking, dark-haired fellow of medium height. Dimples showed in his cheeks when he smiled, and his voice had a sweet timbre that hinted at his gentle-

ness. In the early 1930s, when the Depression was starting to take hold, a fellow with those qualities who had a steady job in a family business was probably considered a good catch.

Years later, when I was but five years old, Grandpa R. passed away suddenly of a heart attack. Overnight, the family florist business fell to Dad and his younger brother. I'm not sure what the division of duties was while Grandpa R. was alive, but after he died, Dad worked primarily in the hothouses.

Those glass hothouses always seemed bright, even on a cloudy day, and they smelled strongly of moist earth. If the sun was out and the temperature rose too much, Dad would crank a handle on a long shaft that creaked as the panes along the peak opened for ventilation. I remember looking up at the very top of the glass and asking Dad why all the windows were spattered with white spots. He explained that if he didn't put some whitewash on the glass, the plants would burn up.

One day when my older sister and I were about eight and six, Mom and Dad took us to work at the greenhouse. I don't remember much about the tasks we performed that day, but we felt pretty grown up to be helping out in the family business. Later, Mom asked us what we thought of working at the florist shop. I'm sure we said it was great fun and asked when we could do it again. Only years later did I learn that our parents had been trying to show us what hard work it was to be florists so we wouldn't want to

Main Street Looking South, Baraga, Mich.

Baraga street scene 1910

follow Dad's footsteps into the family business.

As I grew older, I gained appreciation for the growing cycles at the greenhouse. In fall, vivid yellows brightened the chrysanthemum hothouse, alleviating the dreariness of overcast days. When Thanksgiving was over, intense red poinsettias heralded the Christmas season. Dad always invited us to view the poinsettia house just before the first of the wholesale orders went out. He must have felt great satisfaction in the beauty he had produced from the thousands of cuttings he'd planted in July and August and repotted as the plants matured. When the holidays were over and the greenhouse benches were bare, Dad started filling them up with hundreds of white lilies. They would blossom just in time to grace the altars of local churches and the homes of retail customers for Easter.

Over the years, my dad's reputation as a successful florist caught the attention of the head of the State University Botany Depart-

ment in our small town. Dr. G. paid many visits to Dad's shop to discuss the details of growing ornamental plants. I don't know how Dr. G. did it, but he even convinced Dad, who had no college education, to teach a night class on flower arranging at the State University. In the world of ornamental horticulture, Dad had clearly moved up!

The family florist shop wasn't Dad's only passion in the business world. He took a great deal of interest in the way our village was run. Like his father and grandfather before him, he ran for office, being elected twice as a village trustee, and several years later, moving up to serve as mayor.

Because of the number of years Dad had spent in business and local politics, he knew almost everyone in town. When he walked along Main Street, shop owners would pause what they were doing and step out onto the sidewalk to greet him and shake his hand. As far as I know, everyone liked and respected Dad.

During Dad's tenure as mayor, infrastructure was a big concern. The local State University was rapidly expanding, putting more demands on the water and sewerage systems, and police and fire protection. Dad was even quoted in a *New York Times* article in June 1970 about the burden of college growth on the village budget, which had increased 25 percent in each of the previous two years. At that time, Dad and other mayors of small university towns in New York State were asking the State to allow the universities to be taxed to pay for services. In the years following, a system of PILOTs (payments in lieu of taxes) was instituted. On my last visit to my hometown, both the village and the university appeared to be thriving.

While Dad was very serious about business, he was equally serious about bowling. By the time I was in high school, he had accumulated more bowling trophies than could fit on the top of our large TV. He bowled in leagues at least two or three nights a week and on Sunday afternoons. If someone called him to sub, he'd be gone even more. And it wasn't unusual to find him at the local lanes on his lunch hour rolling practice games. By the time I was out of high school, his average was in the high 200s. Games of 283-289 were common. But as good as he was, he never hit 300. For a competitive bowler, that must have been a disappointment, but he found great reward (and more trophies) when his team(s) placed first at the end of the season. For as long as Dad bowled, his average was moving up.

When the bowling season was over and school was out for the year, Dad loved to head to our cottage, launch his motorboat, and spend time out on the lake. I remember his first runabout, a sixteen-foot wooden Penn Yan that he bought when I was about five. (That was in the days before fiberglass hulls.) Penn Yan boats were named for the Finger Lakes community in which they were built. The company no longer exists, but in its day, it was among the best of the boat builders out east. Over the years, Dad's boats (and motors) gradually increased in size and horsepower. He'd keep a boat and motor for a couple of years and then either trade up for a faster motor or buy both a bigger boat and larger motor. By the late 1970s, he was skimming across Lake Ontario in a twenty-four-foot cabin cruiser. He joined a yacht club and crossed the lake with several fellow boating enthusiasts.

It was obvious to me that Dad's yacht was his escape from the responsibility of caring for my mother, who had become disabled in the late 1960s. As Dad aged, the caregiver burden caused him to be an increasingly cranky and angry old man. I remember one time he and Mom drove several hundred miles to visit me and my husband. While they were with us, Dad began to criticize Mom harshly and unnecessarily. I wanted to tell him to stop speaking to Mom that way, but I was too intimidated by his controller-dominator personality to say anything. Later, in a conversation with Mom, I learned that she didn't think there was anything wrong with the way Dad had spoken to her. Evidently, she had accepted his verbal assaults as normal years earlier.

At the start of 1983, Dad placed an order at Penn Yan for a new, bigger cabin cruiser of thirty-some feet at the (then) whopping price of $70,000! Clearly, in the boating world, Dad was moving up. But before the boat was delivered, Dad's heart gave out, and at the age of seventy, he got his final call to move up. As I approach the age of seventy, I'm increasingly grateful for my memories of Dad, who despite his shortcomings, serves as an example of a life well lived.

**Donna Winters** is the author of over 20 books including the *Great Lakes Romances® Series,* and *Adventures with Vinnie*, a memoir of the most unpredictable shelter dog ever to join the Winters family. Donna lived her first sixty-five years in states bordering on the Great Lakes. Twelve of those years were spent in the Upper Peninsula, the setting for several of her historical romances. She is now developing memoirs about her ancestors. You can find her books at amazon.com/author/donnawinters.

# The Many Lives of Pierre LeBlanc (Based upon an old U.P. legend)

by Tyler R. Tichelaar

## Life 1

Chief Shob-wa-wa watched the canoe approach the shore. The old Ojibwa had seen it from high atop the ridge overlooking the bay where he had his wigwam. The rest of his tribe preferred to live closer to the shore and thought it odd he would live up on the ridge, but he knew his view of the lake would keep his people safe from being surprised should the Sioux seek to attack them.

However, this canoe did not bear Sioux warriors. Despite his advanced age, Shob-wa-wa's eyesight was as keen as an eagle's, and he soon saw that his sister's son was paddling the canoe. His sister had married into the Crane clan at Bahweting, the place the white men called Sault Saint Marie, and each spring Chief Shob-wa-wa traveled there with his clan to see her and fish the rapids. He recognized the other Ojibwa in the canoe also as men he had met at the rapids, but not the pale face in the middle of the canoe in a long black robe. He had seen other Black Robes at Bahweting, but never had one come to his bay. He had never spoken to a Black Robe, but he had heard good things of them from his relatives. More importantly, last night Nanabozho had sent him a dream, tell-

ing him a Black Robe would come, bearing great tidings of importance, so Shob-wa-wa knew this visit was a momentous event for his band.

As the canoe reached the shore, Shob-wa-wa rushed down the hill. By the time he arrived at the beach, the members of his band were gathered about the stranger. They were asking a great many questions of their cousins from Bahweting who had come with the Black Robe, but when they saw Shob-wa-wa coming, they quickly stepped aside and closed their lips out of respect for the old chief.

"Welcome," said Shob-wa-wa in Ojibwa, expecting the men from Bahweting to translate it into the white man's tongue for the stranger. Instead, Shob-wa-wa was surprised when the pale-faced Black Robe replied in Shob-wa-wa's native tongue.

"Thank you. I am Pere Marquette, and I have come to bring your people good news of the Savior of mankind so that they might believe in him, be baptized, and gain eternal life."

Shob-wa-wa bowed in acknowledgment of this kindness and then replied, "I am Shob-wa-wa, chief of these people, and your words make my heart glad for we have heard from our cousins of this savior and wish to learn more of him. You, his servant, are most welcome here."

"And I," continued Pere Marquette, "have likewise heard stories from your cousins of you, mighty Shob-wa-wa. You are a legend among your people for your intelligence and foresight. Even the white men have heard of you and are surprised you are not French like us because you are so wise."

Shob-wa-wa did not know how to reply to this, for despite knowing that these French white men had great ships and guns and the firewater, he was not always sure how wise they were. But he knew Pere Marquette's words were meant in kindness, so he said, "Let us be friends then and share our wisdom with one another."

To this proposal, Pere Marquette readily agreed, and that night, he feasted with Shob-wa-wa's people.

It is said that Pere Marquette stayed three weeks with Shob-wa-wa and his band. The Jesuit and the old chief spoke day and night about everything of any importance there was to know. Shob-wa-wa told Pere Marquette how his people had been led to the rapids, which the white men called Sault Sainte Marie, by a crane, and since then they had branched out all across this great peninsula between Anishinaabewi-gichigami and Ininwewi-gichigami. Shob-wa-wa also told Pere Marquette of the lore of his people, of Nanabozho and the creation of the world, and many another of their ancient stories. Then Pere Marquette told Shob-wa-wa of the Christian God who had created the world in seven days, and of how when man had fallen into sin, God had become a man, being born as his own son Jesus and dying so man's sins would be forgiven. Shob-wa-wa was so taken with this story that he believed Jesus set a very good example for his people and he agreed to be baptized, and when Shob-wa-wa's people saw how their leader loved the Black Robe and trusted in his teachings, they followed his example and were also baptized.

And then came the day when Pere Marquette said he must leave. "But remember, Shob-wa-wa," he said upon parting, "you

are now Pierre LeBlanc, for I have baptized you as such, causing your sins to be washed clean like the snow, and you are the rock upon which I have built the Ojibwa church here beside Anishinaabewi-gichigami."

"I will remember," Shob-wa-wa replied. "In fact, I will build a great city here named after you so that what you have taught us will be remembered long after we are both gone, and Nanabozho shall help me."

Then Pere Marquette and Shob-wa-wa smoked the peace pipe together. The next morning, they hugged one another goodbye and promised to meet again, if not in this world, in the next. Then Pere Marquette climbed back into his canoe and the men from Bahweting paddled across Anishinaabewi-gichigami until they were but a speck on the horizon.

Shob-wa-wa did not forget his promise. He built a church on a rock in the bay, and all his people built their wigwams around it. And for many years after, they met there and spoke of how the great Pere Marquette had brought them the story of Jesus, and they recited the stories he had told them from his holy magical book. It is said that Shob-wa-wa's church remained many years after he had gone to his rest; French fur traders often passed by it and told stories of how Pere Marquette had once visited that spot, and those memories did not fade, even after Anishinaabewi-gichigami had reclaimed the stones the church had been built from.

And that is how Christianity first came to the Ojibwa who resided along what would one day be called Iron Bay. But it is not the end of Shob-wa-wa's story.

# Life 2

Pierre LeBlanc had been born in France, but he had come to Quebec as a young man. He had found service in the employ of Antoine Laumet de La Mothe Cadillac, the sieur de Cadillac. The sieur's name was a fancy one, not at all like Pierre's simple one, but he and Cadillac got along nevertheless. Cadillac made Pierre the bowstroke in his canoe, and although history has forgotten it, they and their voyageur companions once made a long journey together along Lake Superior's shore.

One day Cadillac and his men passed a bay just east of the peninsula known as Presque Isle. Pierre LeBlanc was so struck by this bay's beauty that he said to Cadillac, "We should build a city here."

"It is too far from New France," Cadillac replied. "Who would live here?"

"I would," said Pierre, "and I would name it Marquette, after the great Jesuit missionary and explorer."

Pierre had grown up in France hearing stories of Marquette and Joliet and their famous journey down the Mississippi River. The story of their adventures had been what had inspired him to come to New France and travel beyond it to the Great Lakes. Ever since he was a boy, he had wanted nothing more than to explore these waters and to rub elbows with the Ojibwa whom Pere Marquette had known and loved, and now in Cadillac's canoe, he was doing so.

However, Cadillac just laughed at Pierre's dream of a city in such a remote wilderness.

And the laughter caused Pierre to smile at his own fantasy—it was a funny idea to build a city way out here. It would doubtless be centuries before any white people settled this land, and the Ojibwa were migratory, so they would not want to live in houses of wood or stone if he did build them.

Within a few days, Pierre and Cadillac had returned to Michilimackinac. It was there that Cadillac got in trouble for selling liquor to the Ojibwa. Pierre had warned him not to do it. "It is like poison to them for it drives them mad," he had said. But the Ojibwa dearly loved the brandy and whiskey the French often traded to them, and Cadillac wished to make money in beaver furs, and so Pierre's words fell on deaf ears.

Then one day, an already drunken Ojibwa got angry when Cadillac would not sell him more firewater.

Pierre tried to make peace between the men. He reminded the Ojibwa that Pere Marquette would have been against his drinking the firewater, but the Ojibwa was already too intoxicated to heed his words—he only knew

Statue of Father Marquette

he wanted more. When Cadillac continued to refuse to sell him more, the Ojibwa pulled out a knife. A scuffle ensued, in which Pierre, trying to protect Cadillac, was stabbed.

And then everything started to go black for Pierre.

*I guess I'll never get to build that city for Pere Marquette now*, was his last thought.

But Pierre did not know that Nanabozho had other plans.

# Life 3

It had been nearly fifty years since Peter White had come to Marquette. That first year of 1849, he'd been just a boy of eighteen when he'd sailed into Iron Bay with Robert Graveraet. On that day, he'd met his lifelong friend Charley Kawbawgam. Charley, in time, had become Chief of the local Ojibwa. And Peter, in time, had helped to found the town. Then Peter had served as mailman for Marquette, delivering mail by dogsled from as far away as Green Bay. It wasn't as prominent a position as being an Ojibwa chief, but Peter was a man of great abilities and determined to prosper. Soon he was made town clerk, and then he started an insurance agency and he began to sell real estate. He also founded a bank and accumulated great wealth, and then he became a great philanthropist. He donated a library to Marquette, he put roofs on churches, and he even bought an island he gave to the city for a park. Then he built a house at that park for his aging friend Chief Kawbawgam to live in. But that wasn't all. Peter got involved in state and national politics. President Cleveland offered to make him an ambassador to any country he wanted, but he turned it down because Marquette was home. Then Peter helped start a teacher's college in Marquette. He also invested heavily in the iron industry, organized the Michigan booth at the Chicago World's Fair, and did so much more that there just isn't space to mention it all.

But the most amazing thing of all he did—though no one else would ever realize how amazing it was—turned out to be something he had not wanted to do at first.

When Mr. Archambeau, a French Catholic, had suggested to him that they build a statue to honor Father Marquette, the town's namesake, Peter had not thought it a good idea because a depression was sweeping the country at that time. But after giving it some thought, he was won over by the project and became heavily involved in it. He even convinced the sculptor, Signor Trentanove, to use Kawbawgam as a model for one of the friezes on the statue's base. Some said Signor Trentanove also used Peter himself as a model, and so when the statue was unveiled, rumors spread that it looked more like Peter White than Father Marquette, but Peter, of course, denied this.

But just what was so amazing about that statue? Well, the night after all the big hoopla was held to unveil the statue, Peter decided to walk down the hill from his Ridge Street mansion just to look at it. He'd been so busy that day giving a speech, having his picture taken, and shaking hands with people that he hadn't been able to give the statue a good look, so now, on a moonlit night, he thought he'd get his chance when no one was likely to disturb him.

"It really is a fine piece of work," Peter said to himself, admiring the bronze figure in the still night air.

But then Peter blinked his eyes, thinking he was imagining things. Had the statue moved? It couldn't have. But sure enough, Peter saw the statue's arm reach up and scratch its nose. Stepping back in surprise, Peter was not at all prepared when the statue jumped down from its pedestal and there was Pere Marquette standing before him. As Peter watched, trying to find words to speak, the bronze finish seemed to fade from the statue and be replaced by living flesh and black cloth.

"We meet again, Shob-wa-wa," said Pere Marquette. "I see you've fulfilled your promise."

And then it all came back to Peter. He didn't know how Pere Marquette's spirit had come to embody the statue, or how it was that he instantly remembered events from past lives he had never known he'd had, but suddenly, he had knowledge beyond the ken of most men.

Smiling, and thinking it strange that this didn't seem so very strange after all, Peter said, "It's good to see you again, Pere." Then Pere Marquette gave Peter a wink. Peter blinked, and then there was just a statue before him again.

Peter was so astonished by all this that he didn't know what to think. "Maybe that Peter White Punch I mixed up this evening was stronger than I thought," he said to himself, scratching his head and turning to climb back up the hill to home.

•••

The next day, Peter took the streetcar out to Presque Isle Park where his old friend Chief Kawbawgam lived. Perhaps the old Ojibwa would know of some Native lore that could explain such a happening as a bronze statue coming to life.

But before Peter could even ask Kawbawgam about the statue turning into a person, he had a sudden insight into something that had never occurred to him before. Kawbawgam was a descendant of Shob-wa-wa. Peter didn't know how he knew it, but Kawbawgam was his own many greats-grandson from another lifetime. What were the odds?

"It took you long enough," said Kawbawgam when he saw the look of enlightenment on Peter's face. Of course, Kawbawgam said this in Ojibwa since he did not speak English, but Peter had long ago learned to speak Ojibwa. Now remembering his past life as Shob-wa-wa, he realized why learning Ojibwa had been so easy for him when most white men couldn't seem to tackle it.

Once Peter told the old chief about the statue coming to life, Kawbawgam explained that Nanabozho must be up to his old tricks again; after all, if Nanabozho could create the world, it would be nothing for him to bring a statue to life, or have a dead Jesuit's spirit embody it. Then Kawbawgam agreed to go with Peter that evening to visit the statue and see if it would come to life again.

Now Peter was a very smart man, so he knew what Kawbawgam said seemed logical, but he was also a white man. Even though he'd had that past life as an Ojibwa, his white brain just wasn't ready to accept everything he'd heard and seen, so that night when he and Kawbawgam went to visit the statue and it came to life again, Peter couldn't help but ask, "Pere Marquette, is this real, or do I need to lay off the Peter White Punch?"

Pere Marquette laughed so loud Peter thought he would wake up all of Marquette. Then the Jesuit said, "I wouldn't mind a glass of that punch right now."

And so the three of them, the two-hundred-plus-year-old Jesuit missionary, the near-one-hundred-year-old Ojibwa chief, and the Grand Old Man of Marquette retired to Peter White's mansion on Ridge Street and talked until the wee hours of the morning about everything from when Pere Marquette had first landed on the shore of Iron Bay to what Marquette would be like in the years and centuries to come. It is said they met regularly many a night after that, though I don't know who would have been there to know if that is true. Of course, the day came when both Chief Kawbawgam and Peter White left this life, and then once his friends were gone, Pere Marquette returned to his bronze sleep.

## Life 4

By the early twenty-first century, people in Marquette were getting concerned about global warming, and by the time Marquette celebrated its tricentennial in 2149, the water levels around Marquette were threatening to wash away the lakeshore because of all the arctic snow melting and causing Lake Superior's water level to rise. Meanwhile more and more people were moving to Marquette because the temperatures were much cooler than in most of the rest of the country. Even insects from the Deep South were moving north for cooler weather. Marquette's residents were starting to fear that if the killer bees didn't get them, they'd end up trampled to death by all the tourists.

"What will we do?" many a concerned citizen asked at the city commission meetings.

But they were all asking the wrong question.

The only person who thought to ask the right question was a young architect from Marquette named Rock Chawabeau. Rock's first architectural project had been to finally remodel the ore dock in the Lower Harbor, which had sat unused for more than a century and a half. He transformed it into a fabulous restaurant, botanical garden, and interactive history museum that had since become famous throughout the Midwest. But that had been an easy project compared to what lay before him now.

And to figure out how to face that project, Rock Chawabeau asked the question no one else in Marquette had thought to ask—not "What will we do?" but "What would Peter White do?"

It wasn't an easy question to answer, but Rock was determined to find out. He read everything he could about Peter White, even checking out dusty old books from the Peter White Public Library by people like Fred Rydholm, Russell Magnaghi, and Tyler Tichelaar that no one had read in decades. Most people in Marquette didn't even remember who Peter White was, despite the library being named for him. For that matter, most people didn't remember how to read—they'd all gone to audiobooks. But Rock had always loved history, and while the city commission had thought nothing about letting developers put up ugly skyscrapers in Marquette, he had always fought to preserve Marquette's historical sandstone look even in his newest buildings. And now he turned to Peter White for wisdom and inspiration.

One night, after reading a particularly dull tome that talked about old-time sports in Marquette, Rock fell asleep. Not surprisingly, that night he dreamed of Peter White. Peter White said to him, "I always helped to fund church roofs because there's no other way to keep out the rain."

When Rock woke, he pondered that dream for a long time. Then he remembered the book he had been reading. It had talked about a place called the Superior Dome that had once been part of Northern Michigan University. Rock had always wished he could have seen that dome, but it had been pulled down decades before he was born. Once too many head injuries had made football outlawed across the United States, the dome had fallen into disuse and dilapidation. After all, everyone just watched computer-generated sports now—they were safer. But Rock knew that dome had been an architectural wonder in its day — the world's largest wooden dome when it was built.

Then Rock had an idea.

"What if I could put a giant dome over all of Marquette?"

It wasn't an original idea. After all, it had existed in movies for years, but was it really possible to do? Rock didn't know, but he was going to try.

And so Rock set to work. After many months of trying to figure out how it would be possible, he settled on building a dome thirty stories high as the most practical and realistic result. That would mean some of the ugly modern skyscrapers in Marquette would have to be torn down, but the city commissioners were reasonable, and many were glad to be rid of those eyesores. Better be skyscraperless than succumb to global warming. The dome would also have very deep walls that would sink into the earth for twenty stories, and a great floor would be built beneath it, and beneath that would be engines and motors to make it float in case the earth beneath it caved in or the lake level rose so high that the entire dome needed to be projected onto its surface.

"A veritable Atlantis is what it is!" said the mayor, shaking Rock's hand once the decision to build it had been made.

"Brigadoon, eat your heart out," said the mayor's wife.

"Whoever would have thought such a thing possible?" asked the city manager.

But it was possible. It took a few years to complete, but when Marquette's protective dome was completed, it was named the eighth wonder of the world. It was built of beautiful sparkling see-through glass of incredible strength, the manufacture of which I cannot even describe since it hasn't been invented yet—this is, after all, a story set in the future. And grandest of all, on top of the dome, Rock had set a giant crown made out of iron ore so that everyone would know Marquette truly was the Queen City of the North. They say you could see that crown from as far away as Canada, the Porcupine Mountains, and even the Mackinac Bridge.

Of course, everyone now wanted to come live in Marquette, the Wonder City, but the city commission forbade it because overpopulation was exactly what it had been trying to avoid. Only current residents or people who could prove their families had lived in Marquette prior to its bicentennial were allowed in, although limited tourism was encouraged. The dome had been made with giant sliding glass doors, large enough for trucks and cars to drive through and even an ore boat to pass through on the lake side. Oh, yes, Rock had the dome stretch out a good three miles into Lake Superior just to make the yacht club happy. With all those wonderful features, how could the tourists stay away? But Marquette used the dome to help regulate the tourist industry so the city did not become overpopulated at any time. And most surprisingly, Marquette's tourism dramatically increased in the winter because the dome regulated the climate. Not that there wasn't snow in Marquette, but it was manageable and came down on an agreed-upon weekly schedule, which made the skiers very happy. But a couple of times a year, a good old-fashioned blizzard happened with only twenty-four-hour notice because, after all, Marquette without a snowstorm would be like a Cornishman without a pasty.

To make a long story short, Rock Chawabeau had saved the day for Marquette and made it a more desirable place to live than ever before.

The night after the dome was completed and the mayor gave Rock the key to the city, Rock decided he would celebrate by making up some Peter White Punch from a recipe he'd found in one of those old books.

He must have made that punch extra strong because he'd only had a few sips when two men unexpectedly appeared where he was sitting on his back porch overlooking the Lower Harbor. The first wore a long black robe and the other looked Native American.

"I'm Pere Marquette," said the first, in French.

"And I'm Charley Kawbawgam," said the second, in Ojibwa.

And the funny thing is, Rock understood them both completely.

"I'm so pleased to meet you," said Rock. "I've read a lot about both of you. I'm Rock Chawabeau. What can I do for you?"

"You've already done plenty," said Pere Marquette. "You're the rock upon which Marquette was built and saved."

"You're my old friend, Peter White," added Chief Kawbawgam.

"Why," said Rock, laughing at this revelation, "I guess I am. Well, what do you know! I wonder what I'll do in my next life."

Little did Rock know that Nanabozho already had his next life all planned out.

## Author's Note

Many years ago, I had the idea to write a story about the Father Marquette statue coming to life and walking about Marquette at night. Then recently, while doing research for another book, I looked through Peter White's scrapbooks at the Marquette Regional History Center and discovered that not long after the statue was dedicated in 1897, legends started to spread about the statue doing that very thing. I also came across a poem published in the *Detroit Free Press* on September 27, 1897 playing off the French Canadian legend that Peter White had been alive to greet Father Marquette when he first arrived in Iron Bay. "The Many Lives of Pierre LeBlanc" is based on these old legends with embellishments from my own imagination.

**Tyler R. Tichelaar** is the author of twenty books including *When Teddy Came to Town*, *Haunted Marquette*, and *The Marquette Trilogy*. His next book will be a biography of Ojibwa chief, Charles Kawbawgam, scheduled for release in November 2020. Tyler is also a professional editor and the owner of Superior Book Productions. Visit him at www.MarquetteFiction.com.

# Service Alert

## by Brandy Thomas

*(Archivist note: This is a selection of email from Margaret Decke, a quilter with her own business, over an approximate three-year period in the early 21st century.)*

September 29
Dear Sarah,

I am very sorry to hear of the loss of your husband. Cancer is a horrible disease that has taken too many people from this world too soon. I would be happy to make a memory quilt using a selection of his clothes.

Please send me clothing most representative of your husband. Anything I don't use as part of the quilt I will return to you with the finished quilt. Please see the attached document or my website for sizes, material requirements, and cost. You will receive a shipping notice and tracking number when the quilt is on its way to you.

Any questions or concerns please let me know and once again my deepest condolences for your loss.

Sincerely yours,
Margaret Decke

October 28
Dear Sarah,

I have finished your memory quilt but have not yet shipped the package to you. When I went to create a shipping label, I received a service alert that due to wildfires in California, there could potentially be shipping delays. I wanted to double check that you were safe and if I sent you the quilt it would make it to you.

Please let me know when you are able, what action you would like me to take. Obviously, you and your family's safety are the top priority but know that at least a small piece of the memory of your husband is safe.

Sincerely yours,
Margaret Decke

December 2
Dear MacKenzie,

I am so sorry to hear of the loss of your daughter. I would most certainly be able to make a stuffed teddy bear from your daughter's clothes. I know I advertise primarily quilts, but I can also make a wide variety of stuffed animals using similar techniques.

Please make sure to include a third more than the number of clothing articles listed for older children. Unfortunately, clothing that is smaller than 2T requires more items to provide enough material. If there is enough left over, I will include a small quilt as well, no extra charge.

I also wanted to make you aware that I received a service alert that items shipping to your area may be delayed in the upcoming weeks due to the measles outbreak that is affecting the region.

Sincerely yours,
Margaret Decke

January 11
Dear David,

I just wanted to make you aware that your package may be delayed due to snowstorms in the Northeast. I just received a service alert this morning after I had shipped your quilt. Although a new quilt would be nice to have in a snowstorm, it should, hopefully, arrive soon.

I hope you enjoy the quilt homage to your love of all things, Dr. Who. It was a nice change of pace to make something so fun. If you have any questions, please let me know.

Sincerely yours,
Margaret Decke

January 13
Dear Kina,

I am hoping you get this email. I received a service alert saying that shipping to Hawai'i will be delayed for the foreseeable future. Here on the mainland we have heard conflicting information on the events unfolding. We heard there was an emergency missile launch notification malfunction, aka someone screwed up, and sent out an emergency text signal in error. But then we heard it wasn't a malfunction but an actual attack! There is a lot of confusion and worry about what is going on.

No matter what is happening, I hope you and your family are safe. I will hold your quilt until I hear from you and where you would like me to ship it.

Sincerely yours,
Margaret Decke

April 30
Dear Harland,

I received a service alert that due to recent flooding along the Mississippi River, your package delivery will be delayed. I hope you and yours are safe and if you have any questions, please don't hesitate to contact me.

Sincerely,
Margaret Decke

July 3
Dear Amy,

I am writing to let you know that your quilts will arrive a little later than planned. I received a service alert this morning that shipments to the D.C. area will be delayed due to the protests happening throughout the city. If you have any questions or concerns, please let me know.

Sincerely,
Margaret Decke

November 12
Dear Donna,

I received a service alert this morning that due to the bridge collapse outside of Chicago, there will most likely be shipping delays once I finish your wife's quilts.

You mentioned in your last email that you had all the fabric and supplies of your late wife and were wondering where to sell all of it. I would like to propose a trade. In exchange for finishing the five quilts that were unfinished when she passed away, plus an additional twin sized quilt for your new granddaughter, I will take all of her fabric and sewing supplies. Please let me know if that trade would work for you.

Sincerely yours,
Margaret Decke

October 23
Dear Julia,

I wanted to reassure you that the memory quilt for your daughter will be finished in time for the memorial. I know you also received a service alert about shipping delays due to problems with the electrical grid. The rolling blackouts have been affecting everyone, but luckily, I have recently acquired a treadle sewing machine and this has allowed me to work even without electricity. I also do hand work as well, but the machine is much faster. Also, since you are located only an hour drive south of me, I will hand deliver the quilt at no extra charge. If that works for you, please let me know where you would like to meet.

Sincerely yours,
Margaret Decke

October 30
Dear Michael,

I normally do not give discounts on my quilts other than the occasional site-wide sale. However, I recently received a service alert about the disrupted shipping of international goods due to the earthquake and subsequent tsunami in the Pacific. This is delaying a lot of fabric shipments.

If you would be willing to send me various good quality cotton fabrics in addition to the material required for your quilt, I will make your quilt for no other cost. Since you are in a much larger city and are on the East Coast, the delays shouldn't affect your stores as much as remote areas, like where I live.

Let me know if this arrangement would work for you and I can give you an idea of yardage and color requests.

Sincerely yours,
Margaret Decke

January 2
Dear Sam,

With the latest service alert limiting nationwide shipping to essentials and emergency supplies only, I can no longer guarantee delivery outside of the Northern Great Lakes region where I live. I am going to be updating my website and other contact information to reflect my new limited area. I'm sorry I can't be of more help, but I wish you luck in finding someone to help you with your sewing needs locally.

Sincerely yours,
Margaret Decke

September 22
Dear Elyse,

Thank you for the email. I was very surprised to hear from you. With the continuing troubles, I am only able to check email once every couple of months. I'm not even sure how much longer that will even be possible.

Anyway, I hope you are doing well. I am so happy to hear that you received and loved your quilt. Too bad it took two years to get to you, but as they say, better late than never. They weren't lying in that alert when they said there could be significant shipping delays.

To answer your question, yes, I am still making quilts. Turns out people still need something to keep them warm even when everything is falling apart. I usually trade for what we can't grow in the garden or is hard to get locally. Older folk still want memory quilts, even more now than before, but the younger just want a practical excuse to have something beautiful.

Anyway, life goes on.

Sincerely Yours,
Margaret Decke

**Brandy Thomas** is a freelance editor based in Marquette, Michigan, who specializes in fiction but works and edits across the publishing spectrum. This includes working with indie and traditionally published authors in areas including mass media, non-fiction, doctoral dissertations and master's theses, science-fiction/fantasy, and other fiction. She is a graduate of Southern Illinois University and holds a Master's in Mass Communication and Media Arts. She has gained experience in writing and editing for public and corporate video productions, developing an adult continuing education class at Spokane Community Colleges, and editing a wide variety of fiction and non-fiction for local authors. When not at her desk, Brandy can be found drawing, painting, or sewing,

# The River of the Dead

## by Jon Taylor

The Dead River
Was given its name
Not because it has a slow
Or a listless current

But because
The spirits of the dead
Were thought to live in the spray
From its falls and rapids

And as one climbs
The length of its course
Where it comes down from the place
Of its headwaters

One gains an understanding
Of why the Indians singled out
What in English is called a lifeless stirring
As the river of the spirits of the dead

# How to Tell

## by Jon Taylor

A pair of basal leaves
And a lone flower atop the stem
The configuration of a dozen species
Of orchids, is it not?

Well, no, it is not –
The only orchid in the woods
Of that simple elegance
Is the pink lady's slipper

Others have a pair of basals
With multiple flowers up the stem
Or a single flower atop the stem
With one to several leaves below

But you can tell in spring
When the orchid is still in bud
Or in autumn when it's gone to seed
If it's a pink lady's slipper

**Jon Taylor** lives in Nashville, TN but gets up to Da Yoop as often as he can.

Escanaba logging sled and horses

# untitled symphony

## by t. kilgore splake

early sounds
passing through wilderness
light spring breeze
fierce summer storm
rattle of autumn leaves
loud blizzard winds
peaceful moments
before instruments
birth of music

# god's country

## by t. kilgore splake

escaping large city
busy noisy life
surrounded by
millions of people
racing here and there
leaving tired footprints
concrete sidewalk shadows
finding small village
quiet and free
with caring neighbors
frequent friendly greetings
post office and bank
grocery store checkout
personal emotions
coming from the heart
ex-pat poet
happy to belong

**T. Kilgore Splake** ("Cliffs Dancer") lives in Tamarack location, in an old mining row house in the ghost copper mining village of calumet in Michigan's Upper Peninsula. Splake has become a legend in the small press literary circles for his writing and photography. His most recent publication is *Beyond Brautigan Creek*. This collection of poems also includes a DVD attachment. Currently, Splake is working on a new poetry manuscript, the *Rosetta Café Ghosts*, which will have a cover photograph resembling Edward Hopper's "Nighthawks" painting.

# The Woundwort

## by Joni Scott

Helping my son Joel with his 5th grade leaf project kept my shattered soul from crumbling. I sometimes thought that without him, I would give up. I had four other children, but after what I had done, only my youngest, Joel, willingly and joyfully came to stay with me during the week.

Like hunters in search of elusive prey, Joel and I waded through the underbrush. We pursued his school assignment with zealous focus. The quarry we sought was twenty required local leaf and wildflower specimens common in our rural Upper Peninsula county. There were also a few unique plants and items that would guarantee my son an "A" on his Leaf Collection project.

"There!" I announced, victoriously pointing at a graceful wildflower amidst the foliage.

"Queen Anne's Lace!" Joel shouted, familiar with pictures of the slender plant. He bent over to admire the delicate white blossoms that feathered outward like an English doily. He plucked one, and, after admiring its intricacy, Joel placed the flower in the small bouquet I carried for him. It joined the tree branches and blossoms we already collected that day.

I shuddered from the damp breeze flowing through the woods. "Let's get going," I told Joel, noticing thick black clouds gathering. "It looks like rain."

We walked briskly along the riverside trail a few moments before Joel pointed at a cluster of small white petals popping out from the ditch alongside the trail. "Do we have that one yet?" he asked.

"Oh," I replied, considering the storm threat above. "That's Yarrow. It's super common. Let's get home to press what we have. We can get Yarrow later." As we passed the roadside abundantly flowing with Yarrow, I remembered something I had read about it. "Do you know what Yarrow used to be called by soldiers in the Revolutionary war?" I asked Joel.

"No." He replied, playfully poking the early fall leaves that decorated the sidewalk.

"Woundwort."

Joel squinched his nose in repulsion. "Wound*wart*?"

I had to laugh. Surely, he was picturing warts growing on wounds. "It doesn't hurt wounds! It's supposed to stop blood from flowing. If a soldier was injured, he would put Yarrow in his wounds to speed up the blood clotting."

"Oh," Joel mumbled in response, eyeing the flower suspiciously. Suddenly he was interested in climbing a nearby rock. I hurried on, knowing he would catch up quickly. *Woundwort,* I mused to myself. *I could use some woundwort.*

My wounds were not physical, but lethal nonetheless. It felt as though my heart was ripped out and my soul shattered, yet no one seemed to notice or care. Not so long ago, I was a pastor's wife and dedicated homeschooling mother. I was involved in every area of both our small churches' lives, and my children's as well. Our family was busy and happy. Yet something in me broke one day. I ended up having an affair. I left my family when they found out. In my small town it was scandalous and horrible. I went from being loved and admired to being hated and rejected.

Although I broke the relationship off, the loss and rejection continued. The internal wounds kept bleeding. Aside from three nights a week with my youngest son, Joel, I lived alone and completely exiled from my other four children and old church friends. My older children were too angry and hurt to visit. I missed them terribly. I barely slept, and could not eat much. I spent restless nights battling my tumultuous emotions. I would dream I heard my daughter singing, or wake up imagining I heard my older son's footsteps on the hard wood floor. It was an endless, terrible, nightmare.

*I deserve it...* I buried my face in the musky odor of the branches to hide my pain.

On cue with my emotions, drops of rain fell from the sky and interrupted my musings as Joel ran up. "It's raining!" he yelled, zipping by me and running to the car. I followed quickly as a damp breeze tugged at my jacket and rattled the leaves I carried. I tucked them next to Joel on the back seat and we hurried home.

Back in the warmth of my tiny rental house, we pressed our fresh leaves between thick books. This assignment was incredibly important to me. It represented a chance, not only help my son with his first big public school assignment; it also gave me a chance to be restored. I wanted to prove to my kids that I was the same woman they once admired.

*Who am I kidding?* I was trying to prove to *myself* I was the same person. Truth was, I wondered if the mother I once prided myself on being *was* dead. I hoped she was merely buried and waiting to be delivered. All I really knew for sure was that I made a tragic error and the consequences were appropriately brutal. I wanted to return to the vivacious, fun, and free woman I once was, but I didn't know how.

Raising my brood of five had given me purpose, but now only my youngest, Joel,

willingly and joyfully came to stay with me during the week. Joel was the one connection left of my happy past. I sometimes thought that without him, I would give up.

I attempted to explain my precarious new position to Joel. After a small dinner and a game of cribbage, I took a deep breath. Looking down at my nervously wringing hands I began. "Joel... I..."

Before I could express my thoughts, Joel sensed where I was going. He interrupted quickly and simply. "I forgive you," he said.

I raised my head and looked at Joel's face. A gentle smile beamed from under his mop of brown hair. He knew. His unmerited forgiveness touched me. My throat tightened as I choked back tears. I couldn't say another word.

That autumn, Joel and I continued to blaze nearby trails collecting our samples of broad leaves, needle leaves, and wildflowers. Simple things I once regularly enjoyed were now treasured like a rare plant species. I relished the evenings where I could work on homework with Joel, or watch cartoons together. Having even one of my children sleeping under the same roof as me kept at bay the despair which otherwise was threatening to drown me.

Whenever I was alone in town, I kept my head low. I avoided raising my eyes in case I met someone I knew. In the sparsely populated county where I lived, word of a scandal travelled fast. I was embarrassed to meet up with any acquaintances. I would have moved away, escaping the looks and whispers, but even though I had little communication with my other four children, I could not bear to be far from them.

In addition, the rumor mill busily churned out further tales, adding to an already sordid story. I heard I was the worst hypocrite who ever lived, that I was destined for hell, and that God had turned His back on me. I wondered if the whispers were true. Did God care about this fallen sinner?

Soon the autumn's breezes chased away the color and blossoms. With gloved hands and fuzzy hats, Joel and I scavenged a ditch.

Coal Dock, Escanaba, Mich.

Escanaba coal dock with schooner 1915

Shivering from the brittle cold we scurried to the warmth of the car. Joel checked his list of required finds. "Do we have Yarrow yet, Mom?"

"No," I sighed, blowing on my numb fingers. I glanced out the window I saw a few of the simple white flowers popping up from the ditch. "We have time. I promise to grab some later."

I was proud of our leaf project. It was progressing into what I considered a collaborative work of art. I took some great photos of Joel tucked into the branches of a flowing Weeping Willow. We chronicled an expedition into the thick of the woods to find an elusive White Pine. I scoured thrift stores for large books. Soon they piled up on every table, flattening leaves and blossoms. We bought specialty paper and spent hours designing our pages with craft scissors.

The leaf collection came together one piece at a time, as were the shattered pieces of my life. I began watching TV ministers in the morning, and reading the Bible with Joel before he left for school. I bravely attended my older son's football games. Although seeing old friends congregate to cheer for the team while I lingered alone in the shadows of the end zone stung like November's icy rains, my daughters began to respond. They meandered over to the edge of the field and watched a small portion of the game with me.

Soon Joel and I were removing all our dried plants and placing them carefully on each well-thought-out page. The flattened plants created delicate patterns that showed off God's creativity and imagination. As we sorted through our binder Joel noticed the empty "Yarrow" page.

"Mom, did we ever get Yarrow?"

*Yarrow?*

My hand paused above the colorful paper where I was about to glue a Silver Maple leaf. In that moment I realized how much I procrastinated when I had the chance to pick the most common of local wildflowers. I had completely forgotten about it! Despite all our extra-credit finds, Joel would not receive an "A" without one of the twenty required plants!

"Don't worry," I said with a cheeriness I was not feeling, "I'm sure there is plenty to be had." There would not be time to properly press the flower, but we could still add it in!

Determined to find Yarrow, I set out the next day to the trail where Yarrow once thrived. Instead of colorful foliage and white petals, I found lifeless sticks. A recent frost left behind nothing but dry, grey plants. My heart felt as crushed as a withered leaf. I refused to accept it. Somewhere I would find Yarrow! It had to be thriving elsewhere. Days of scouring river and roadside produced nothing but more drying twigs and lifeless stems. Yarrow was gone.

Distressed at my blunder, I printed a picture of Yarrow to add to the page. Even that failed. The picture was fuzzy and the plant indistinguishable. Once upon a time I would have prayed for God's help to find the lost wildflower. Thinking of that now, I only shook my head at such silliness. Prayers were answered for good folk. If I expected to ask a favor of the boss upstairs, I would have to somehow earn back His respect. *If that was even possible now...*

I gave up. Joel would not have Yarrow in his leaf collection. Like the brunt of our family's split, I knew I had to accept my responsibility and bear the guilt. I paged through the scrapbook the evening before it was due. It was still a respectable project. I admired Joel's hard work and handwritten notes. I lingered for a moment on the empty Yarrow page before closing the book and heading for bed.

Early the next morning, the leaf project was placed in the seat of honor up front as Joel wiggled into the backseat and snapped on his seatbelt. I pulled out of my driveway enjoying a blue sky after weeks of dismal grey clouds. A residue of frost sparkled as it clung to the grass. I admired the glittering roadside, suddenly stopping.

I spotted a lone wildflower peaking above the wet grass. *Could it be?*

I parked my van and walked over to the small, white flower. In all our searching, I had always seen Yarrow in clusters, never alone. It grew in roadside ditches, never on someone's front lawn. For that matter, I had never seen the plant in my neighborhood! I stared in amazement.

Joel would earn his "A" after all.

Like hope springing up from the cold earth, was one lone, flowering, Yarrow plant. I took a deep breath and whispered, "Thank-you," before reaching to pluck the precious, simple plant.

I dropped my youngest off at school, proudly toting his Leaf project. I smiled as he waved and disappeared beyond the heavy doors. I did not feel so alone anymore.

November passed quickly and soon the Upper Peninsula was covered with thick, cold snow. The grey stems and withered leaves were buried out of view. My own winter still lay ahead. The years would be difficult as I mended broken relationships with my children as painstakingly as I once helped Joel piece together his leaf project. Through it all, I held on to the memory of finding Yarrow one shiny morning.

The prize I once took for granted and lost could still be found.

**Joni Scott** adds a dash of humor and a sprinkle of meaning to her writing projects. She creates a concoction that both warms the heart and soothes the soul. She draws from her experiences serving in a wide variety of church ministries. Joni enjoys the Upper Peninsula's untamed beauty and loved raising her children in a little city in the big woods. Her writings have appeared in Upper Peninsula newspapers, as well as two self-published books.

# Cousin Jack Foster

## by Donna Searight Simons

My grandmother was born in 1903 and raised in Houghton. She lived on Pearl Street, where Jim's Foodmart is now located. My grandfather was a telegrapher for Western Union when they met. After she married, she and my grandfather moved to Detroit, but they took vacations every summer to the Copper Country for the rest of their lives. Their son, my father, loved the Keweenaw too, so he continued the tradition of taking his own family to the area every summer. As a child, I thought the U.P. was boring. Swimming in the cold waters of Lake Superior did not appeal to me like trips to Boblo Island or Cedar Point.

Everything changed for me during the summer of 1991.

Just graduating from Wayne State University, I traveled north with my father and his family. Of course, our destination was the Copper Country. I hadn't been there since my parents divorced ten years earlier. We drove to Calumet and decided to take a horse and carriage tour of the town. I was twenty-one years old with a journalism degree, no job, and no clue what to do with my life. My life was about to change.

I climbed on board the carriage. A man sat next to me and ended up being our tour guide. He handed me his business card that read, "W. John Foster, Retired Cousin Jack." The card also stated, "No business, no worries, no money, no prospects. This card will not get you anything, will not take you

Cousin Jack Foster

anywhere, but it's FREE." I appreciated his sense of humor.

As the carriage clopped along Sixth Street, Jack explained to our tour group that a lot of the copper miners originally came from

Escanaba river man on bank

Cornwall, England. The Cornish miners would send for relatives and friends from Cornwall to work the mines with them, calling them "Cousin Jacks." Since Jack was known as the town's local historian, he proudly took on the nickname Cousin Jack.

Jack was born in 1909 in Laurium and grew up at a boarding house in Calumet. Not only did he work at the Michigan Hotel, but also Calumet Theatre in 1926. He eventually worked for the police department where he became a Sergeant, Lieutenant, then Chief of Police, retiring in 1973 after forty-five years of service.

As the tour continued in Calumet's downtown area, Jack pointed out historical buildings such as the Calumet Theatre and St. Anne's church. He spoke about the 1913 labor strike and how copper miners demonstrated up and down the streets with picket signs throughout the Keweenaw. But when the carriage passed by Italian Hall, he stopped the horses so that he could tell us the story of a tragedy that took place on Christmas Eve in 1913. The miners and their families were enjoying a Christmas party

on the second floor of the auditorium when someone shouted "Fire!" People rushed to the stairwell, trying to flee the building as soon as possible. Someone tripped and fell on the stairs, which caused a chain reaction. Seventy-three people, mostly children, were killed in the stairwell, and there was never a fire to begin with.

Cousin Jack's stories about the Keweenaw were riveting. I thought the events in 1913 were so dramatic that I decided to write a historical novel. I quickly came to love the Copper Country for its people, history and scenery. I finally found some purpose in my life. I also became friends with Jack, who supported my writing dreams. In fact, I stopped by his house every year to hear more stories about the 1913 labor strike and Italian Hall. He welcomed me into his home with donuts and coffee, as he loved to talk about events that happened so long ago.

Jack's house could have doubled for a mining museum. He had collected mining equipment over many years, including tools, drills, carbide lamps and lunch pails. If you had walked through his house, you would have been transported to the early 1900s between all the mining memorabilia, along with Jack's wonderful storytelling.

In 2003, Jack sadly passed away. I miss his friendliness and passion about Copper Country history. Ten years later, I finally published my historical novel, *Copper Empire*. I believe Cousin Jack was smiling from heaven that day. If I had never met Cousin Jack, I would never have written a novel about the Copper Country, never had the courage to sell my book at stores, and certainly never would have given historical presentations at libraries throughout Michigan.

Thank you, Cousin Jack.

**Donna Searight Simons** is the author of *Copper Empire* and has given historical Copper Country presentations at numerous libraries throughout Michigan. She works at Oakland University (Rochester, MI) and looks forward to vacationing in the Copper Country every chance she can get.

# Mi Casa en El Paso

## by Terry Sanders

With Basic training completed, I arrived at Fort Bliss in Texas a day early. The gate guard checked me in and gave me a fat envelope with the name and location of my barracks.

The base bus stop was easy to find and got me to the barracks in ten minutes. This time, instead of taking the first bunk inside the front door, I went to the top floor and grabbed the farthest bunk from the stairway.

Before I had finished making up the bed, the First Sergeant came over to me and asked my name. He checked me off on his clipboard and said my squad leader would find me in the morning.

With my unpacking finished, I went down to the first floor to check out the bulletin board to get familiar with the map of the base. While I looked at it, a lieutenant asked me if I was assigned to this unit. When I said yes, he informed me that he was the officer of the day and he was making out the guard duty roster for tonight.

In the discussion that followed, the lieutenant explained that because of my rank, I would likely be the leader of the first watch. He arranged to meet me in the assembly room on the first floor at 1700. At the meeting, we were issued weapons and radios, were briefed and then driven to the duty site.

The building appeared to be a de-commissioned PX. It lay about 200 yds. from the eastern boundary of the City of El Paso. A chain-link fence went along the city boundary due north, disappearing from sight into the late afternoon haze.

I positioned two of the two-man sentry teams off the opposing diagonal corners of the building as instructed by orders. The other two teams had to check for any abnormal activity by looking through the glass entry doors at the front of the building and through the windows in the truck entry doors on the east side. Their passes were to be made four times per hour on an irregular schedule.

The first half of the watch went by without incident. After shuffling the teams to different positions, I overheard the discussion of one of the teams. The tone of it sounded a little anxious.

This team had looked through the windows of the truck bay doors. What they saw made them nervous. In the bays were parked four Brinks armored trucks. At the same time, the other sentry saw a calendar and realized tomorrow's date was October 1. They were looking at the payroll for the entire base. As I pondered what kind of cash we were protecting, another scenario began playing out.

Two speeding cars passed by on the road in front of us, slowing down when they were directly perpendicular to the building. In a few moments they resumed speed and drove 800 ft. to the main gate of the base but made a U-turn without entering.

Before the cars made it back to the front of the building, I called the watch officer, who dispatched backup that arrived just as the two cars stopped and three passengers got out. They were escorted off the base property. We were compleminted for following orders and were given the opinion of the Sergeant that we likely would not see those men again.

Finally, 2200 came and the last squad repositioning took place. There were five of us standing in a shadowed corner of the building. Two of us noticed a car with headlights off coming from the same place as the earlier ones. They did not, or could not, turn off the lights in the wheel wells.

•••

This time we followed night attack procedures. The red laser spotting sights were turned on and trained on the driver's window. I blew three short blasts with the gas operated air horn. As expected, spotlights from the base entry gate came on and found the car.

The escape attempt slowed down when the leaving car jumped the curb, turning to retreat. We watched as the MPs caught up to the car before it was out of our sight. The last thing I remembered about that night was one of the soldiers from guard duty saying that he prayed for us that none of us would ever again have to come that close to shooting anybody.

That weekend, some of us from my training squad decided to forgo a trip downtown in favor of checking out the base NCO club. We found the expected half-dozen lifer sergeants and maybe a dozen trainees like us. Female patrons we judged were probably contractor's secretaries.

One exception to the usual suspects was the hostess. She was professionally dressed and introduced herself with an engaging smile. We were asked if the club met our expectations. All agreed it did.

The topic of conversation then changed to what we hoped to see on our time off from training over the next three months. Everyone seemed to want to get over the border to see Juarez. Some to get Christmas presents for family, others to see the strip joints.

The hostess returned with our drinks during the discussion. Maria suggested a club in downtown El Paso might be an alternative to the ones in Juarez, if we didn't need to see undressed girls. She vouched for it by telling us her sister Josepha and her friends often went there after work. The club was called *Mi Casa.*

When training ended the next Friday, some of us were ready to see what downtown El Paso looked like. We took the city bus downtown and checked out the main street. In less than two blocks, we were in front of a building with a sign that read *"Mi Casa."*

The front door opened onto a landing with stairs that went up a half story to a big room identified as a dance floor. A smaller set of stairs went down to a restaurant pointed to by a large neon arrow.

All four of us went to examine the dance floor. It looked like it would hold two hundred or more people at two bars and more than two dozen tables. There were menus on the walls large enough to read from anywhere in the room. Another sign read: GIRLS UNDER 18 MUST BE ESCORTED. I was familiar with Texas liquor Licenses. That should not affect us.

It was near supper time so we went downstairs to see what the restaurant had to offer. There were people at three of the tables. The one nearest us had three younger girls eating.

After ordering, I looked carefully at one of them. She looked very much like Maria, the hostess at the NCO club on the base. The rest of my buddies agreed. Very much! I could not resist asking her.

"Te llamas Josepha?"

All three had puzzled looks on their faces.

Then I asked, "Es Maria su Hermana?"

All of the girls spoke simultaneously so fast I could no longer understand any of what they said. When they all stopped Josepha spoke clearly with no hint of an accent, "Are you Terry?"

Pausing enough to resume breathing I admitted I was. By means of informal introductions, we learned the girls all worked at the

Escanaba dog sled race to the finish

Farrah pants factory as seamstresses. Carmen and Maria Antonietta let "Josy" do most of the talking. Her sister had warned they might see us.

They were happy to have some of the higher paying jobs in El Paso. They admitted English skills were a big factor. Coming to this club gave them opportunity to strengthen that skill. In fact they all had landed second shift jobs as sales clerks between Thanksgiving and Christmas, enabling them to contribute more to their family's finances. I could now better understand why so many in the military had Spanish wives.

One discouraging thought crossed my memory. When I danced with the girls, I felt dry hard places on the skin of their hands. It was the same thing I had felt on my grandmother's hands. She had the same job they did sixty years earlier. The harsh sizing starch was the cause. For her, the end result was that work was a factor in later life arthritis. For me, that glimpse into a possible future for these consider-

ate young women was, to say the least, disheartening.

We did see those girls a few times when we were in downtown El Paso. They asked if it was OK to practice their English with us. We were happy to help and it usually turned into entertainment for both sides.

The next time I saw any of them was on a bus. I was on the way back from the Red Cross office downtown. My wife's doctor had petitioned for assistance from the Red Cross to get an early release for me because of difficulties in her pregnancy. About halfway back to the base, Josie got on the bus. She was on her way to Sears, her second job. I got up and went over to sit next to her. It was the first time she had seen me in uniform.

After she explained what she did at her job, she said the best part of it was she would make enough money by Christmas to buy presents for everyone in her family. Her last comment was there might even be enough left for her to get a warm winter coat. I had seen snow on the mountainsides from the base, even taken pictures of it on cactus and Joshua trees.

She seemed more excited than usual because while she talked her hand was on my leg. Then she asked me what I was expecting for Christmas. My reply was soon after I would get home, there could be an addition to my family. Her quick response was did I expect a brother or sister. My answer was, "No, a son or daughter." With that answer she moved her hand from my leg to my hand and squeezed it tightly.

Talk for the rest of the trip was about each other's family. Just before she got off to go to work I asked if the other girls knew that I was married. She said they guessed right away. As I stood up to let her get out at her stop, she hugged me before stepping off the bus.

The Wednesday before Thanksgiving my compadres chose to go to *Mi Casa*. The mess hall at the base was closed to prepare for Thanksgiving. We walked in to find Carmen, Toni and Josie there for supper.

They asked us if we knew someone called Gumby. We did. He was a member of our Company who had an infection in his jaw that necessitated all his teeth had to be removed. The replacements had not arrived and he was surviving on soup and oatmeal. Josie's sister Maria invited him to Thanksgiving Dinner so he wouldn't starve.

On a more positive note, Carmen asked if we knew what to expect for Thanksgiving dinner on the Base. When none of us could say we did, she told us. The tradition was it was catered, and best of all, the officers were the table waiters.

The high point of our evening came at the end of the night when the band upstairs played their last song. It was my favorite Beatles song, "La Vida Continua" (Life goes on). Here in El Paso, it was as pleasant as any place I had ever been.

We all collected at the bus stop ready to go our separate ways when Josie asked in a kind of whisper if I had seen everything I wanted to in El Paso. All but for one thing, I replied.

I read the city art museum had a portrait of St. Francis of Assisi, a rare one where he was not surrounded by animals. Josie told me she had seen it and offered to take me. She worked second shift on Saturday so that would be the day to go.

The dinner for Thanksgiving was exactly what we had been told to expect. That experience did a lot to raise our spirits. However, what I found in my mailbox had a near opposite effect. It was an emergency ticket voucher from the Red Cross.

Friday morning, I went to company headquarters to get a release from the captain. He said the base travel office had already checked on times of flights to Milwaukee. They found there were only two available connecting to Milwaukee today and if I didn't get on one of them, the next one was a week later.

The ticket I was issued allowed me to bump any passenger with a standby ticket. I took the latest one for that day when they told me the base was going to go on lock-down the next morning.

When the transfer paperwork was ready, there were only three and a half hours to board the flight. I packed in one and found the First Sergeant waiting at the front door with a car. After we got to the airport, he had to stay with me until I was on board the plane.

It was only when the plane began circling to a heading for Milwaukee that I thought of Carmen, Toni and Josie. If they had any feelings of abandonment caused by me, I hoped all were few and fleeting.

**Terry Sanders**, currently lives in Manistique, MI, after retirement from work as a mechanical designer, environmental technician, and contractor preparing operation and assembly manuals. He received a BA from the University of Wisconsin. Publications include: *High School Textbook for Mythology*, short works of fiction, and a modern novella version of *The Iliad*. He has presented workshops at the 2nd Saturday writers group in Curtis, MI.

# Catching the Butterflies

## by Ninie G. Syarikin

At your age, I can see that
you are still busy chasing the butterflies.
So many kinds of them, too,
colors, shapes, sizes, and splendors;
depending on what habitats they are nur-
tured from.
An urban park.
A green valley.
The rolling hills.
A palace garden.
A forest sanctuary.
A rebel's enclave.
A farmer's backyard.
Or a fisherman's porch.

Why haven't you settled on one?
It was time, past the time, was it not?
How old are you, may I ask?
70?
75?
80, maybe?

I noticed that your hair has become white,
from the pale gray that I used to gaze upon.
The delicate circles around your eyes.
The linings that mark your forehead.
The tightened stretch of skin on your cheek-
bones.
Have you used Botox, by the way?
Forgive me for being blunt.
Enver, Enver!
It pains me so to watch you running
around,
the other day,
with a girl at least half of your age,
if not one third,
young enough to warrant calling you
Grandpa!
What do you expect?

Until when?
Will you realize?
That trying to seize your youth
remains futile.
I am not really jealous, mind you!
Just a little disappointed,
and disturbed, perhaps,
for not having the flexibility and ability
of capturing the bees.
Like you and your social butterflies.
Yet, such is nature.
The youth that I once possessed,
now lost forever.
But I am still me, nevertheless.
I might not look fantastic at this moment,
but I feel beautiful, all right!

Slow down, Enver!
Stop, even.
Let those butterflies flap their wings.
You take my hand!
Let's sit on the bench
and enjoy the spectacular sunset.
Feasting our eyes on the flight of birds,
returning to their nests.
There will be the merry singing
of the tree frogs, too, soon,
welcoming the night.
And the fiery eyes of the owls,
reading at their pleasure.
Plus, the hungry bats eating bananas,
and the howling of the coyotes from afar.

Come, hold my hand!
Be my friend.
Let's tell each other stories
about our glorious past.
Now that we are equal
to each other.

# Love Is...

## by Ninie G. Syarikin

A parting at the CMX airport when a woman stands strong at the gate. Looking at a man and a boy about to board the big bird. Her eyes shining red like the tongue of a dragon. The father, crimson, containing emotion. The son, pink, sobbing softly, sulking and wiping tears. At times, stealing a glance at his mom through the glass door, then hiding his face again. Goodbye is never enough.

**Love is...**

when a mother climbing two flights of stairs up and down between her room at the attic and her three sons' in the middle floor, and the living room, admonishing them with a terse voice: "When your mother is going to travel, come out, don't hide. Ask, what can I help, Ummi? Don't just wait for me to leave you some money. I've none."

All the time, she's been complaining that they are lazy and slow. Yet, the tradition dictates that she leave an allowance for them while she's gone. So, as annoyed as she was, still she distributed $200 to each, albeit grown-ups. Then, like a troop, the oldest snatched her computer bag, the middle started the car, the youngest grabbed her luggage. Off she went to Quito, Ecuador, South America! To satisfy her love of traveling. Yet, after all the grumbles, goodbye is never enough.

**Love is...**

when you hide your fear, your worry, your shame from your child, who is about to depart for Africa to serve, that you actually have no money to spare. But the tradition dictates that you give her pocket money, to survive a possible uncertainty. You dig out your old jewelry pouch, and decide to let go few strands. No longer in their prime shape, true, but gold is gold, from the ancient time to the present. From Queen Sheba to Angelina Jolie. Putting on a brave face and waving a deprecating hand, you tell a white lie: "I no longer want to keep these bracelets. The hook and few rounds of the chains are already broken, so, I'm going to sell them."

When the heirlooms moved from your palm to the gold merchant, you whispered a painful goodbye. An arrow stabbed your heart. What you see in the modest sum of money that changed hands is a line of three generations, where you are caught in the middle: your mother and your daughter. It's too late now. At a split second, you straightened your stoic neck to look ahead. Inside, you weep, "May God replace what I've just lost."

Out of that damned store, you square up your shoulders and hold your head high. Then you sigh, "I've sold my unwanted gold," as if to convince yourself; but you know better. At the Union Station, you see your daughter off, like releasing a bird from your cupped hands, anxious for her to fly far away to seek her own fortune and not to sense your misery. Full of courage, you cover your face with all smile, as she grins at you with twinkling eyes. Yet, after all the kisses and hugs, still, goodbye is never enough.

**Ninie G. Syarikin** works as writer, translator and researcher. She translates/interprets from English to Indonesian and Malay languages and vice versa, and writes in both English and Indonesian. She holds an MFA in Creative Writing from The University of Tampa, Florida. Prior to managing her writing and translation business, US-SEA Strategy, in the city of Houghton, Ninie worked as a broadcast journalist for the U.S. Agency for Global Media's Voice of America Indonesian Service in Washington, DC for twenty-two years and now federally retired. A mother of three sons, Ninie enjoys cooking for them, reading, traveling, crocheting and playing with colors.

# Much Different Animal

## by Becky Ross Michael

Spring in Upper Michigan's Keweenaw Peninsula arrives late and is a whole different animal from other places I've lived. Harsh realities of winter recede, inch by inch, while signs of sprouting spring replace them in fits and starts. "Unpredictable" is the key word, and if the weather is pleasant for ten minutes, you should take advantage.

"Let's go for a ride out by Sand Bay," he suggested, as the two seasons collided on a clear Saturday afternoon.

Happy to make enjoyable use of weekend hours away from the classroom, I agreed. "Great idea. Let's leave the dog home," I added, glancing at our little, black Shih Tzu. "Boo Boo's muddy from our walk this morning, and I don't want him in the car before he's had a bath."

The drive along a two-lane, twisty road from Laurium toward the bay was relaxing, as always. I imagined the smell from clear, icy waters of Lake Superior greeting us as we turned northward. That day, unfortunately, the sky darkened as we neared the lake, and the view through the windshield became misty.

We passed a small waterfall and a bakery displaying a closed sign. I looked forward to when the monks would reopen The Jampot for the tourist season. Their delectable muffins often enhanced our trips to the beach.

Spotting the driveway to a house where one of my students lived, I knew we were approaching the turnout. By the time we ar-

rived at the graveled parking lot, the air was a thick, soupy fog.

We parked next to a lone car wearing an out-of-state license plate. Tourists didn't usually visit so early in the spring. Donning our jackets, we headed to the path. This was in the years before the posting of erosion regulations and construction of steep wooden steps for traversing the sand dunes. Our zealous beach-dog, Boo, had helped us blaze a trail during previous summers, and it headed west at an angle to avoid the steep decline of the bank. The winter's snow and ice were gone, but flattened grasses, bent bushes and cracked tree limbs attested to their recent occupancy.

Picking our way along the path, I envisioned warm summer days and wondered if we'd be able to see anything when we reached our goal. From the calm lake, I heard only a soft lapping when an occasional wave reached the shore. Toward the end of our descent, a male form materialized through the mist in front of us as we gained on him. *The tourist?* When the figure came to an abrupt halt, we almost ran into him, standing stock-still and looking toward the beach.

"Those your dogs?" the stranger asked, with a nervous edge to his voice.

Our gaze followed where his hand pointed, through a narrow expanse of underbrush and grasses. Slinking along the sand, their ghostly forms appeared out of the haze. As their sure paws wove around piles of stones formed from the scraping of winter ice floes, the two moved past us without a sound.

Escanaba smelt fishing

I held my breath.

"I don't think those are dogs," answered my partner.

Eyeballs widened, the stranger turned to face us for confirmation. Without missing a beat, he ignored the path and clawed his way straight up the steep embankment.

Relieved we hadn't brought Boo Boo along, we also decided to use caution and cut our visit short. With a bit more decorum, we stuck to the path.

Back in my elementary classroom on Monday, a typical indoor recess was necessary due to spring rains. During that wild twenty minutes, I overheard the student who lived near Sand Bay mention "dogs" while talking with a friend. With practiced nonchalance known to many teachers, I asked them if anything special happened

over the weekend. The child then recounted a story about their "hybrids" escaping the house and how they found them across the road at Sand Bay.

To this day, I picture the stranger telling anyone who will listen about his run-in with the "pack of wolves," in the untamed wilderness otherwise known as the Keweenaw.

**Becky Ross Michael**, a former Michigander, now creates stories for adults and children on her balcony perch in North Texas. Other literary pursuits include book clubs, critique groups, and freelance online editing. Becky's home in the blogosphere is Platform Number 4, and she welcomes visitors (platformnumber4.com).

# Dry Foot

## by Cyndi Perkins

Landing in the mangroves, Boot Key Harbor

D ry Foot hangs onto the sheared-off stump of piling. Her cuts sting in the saltwater. The barnacles here are rounded, uniform mini-crustacean circlets like those little oyster crackers you sprinkle on soup, each topped with a tiny blow hole. They scrape, but do not slash like the mussel shells, layer upon layer, coating the docks at home, razor blade slicing in a million places. These are paper cuts in comparison, only bleeding a little.

Still, sharks.

As if on cue, a barracuda glides into position at the piling base. She can barely see him in the ambient before-dawn when pelican wings and dolphin snorts are experienced most clearly, sensed unseen.

The light will rise as if on a dimmer switch turned in infinitesimal but ever-gathering increments. She made it once before, to shore. Through the mangroves onto a wave-rippled beach where, beyond the seaweed-braided wrack, blue umbrellas and striped blankets sheltered mothers and fathers and their ba-

bies. Couples in lust, strutting in loosely tied bikinis and baggy flowered low-slung bathing trunks. Sand volleyball. Beachcombers on holiday.

She came up on that finely-ground coral beach, Venus rising from the Atlantic, milking the seawater from her hair. There were twenty-six of them officially ashore. Catholic Charities provided broasted chicken dinners and dry clothes. Later, after processing, a FEMA trailer, brought south after the hurricanes. Some kind of job. Who cares where as long as it is not there?

Where he is. Where it hurt, all the time. Barnacles inside. Layered, permanent, strangulating. Cutting.

Clang of the bell buoy at the channel entrance. The light, a steel spider towering above it. You can see the beacon for fifty miles.

If a piece of the boat drifts her way, she will catch it and float to shore. It's hard to tell, yet, how far the mangroves are, in the wet January dawn settling in her dark hair, dampness in her head.

Cold-not cold. Cold enough. July is better.

The tide swirls deceptively, nearly indiscernible around the pole. Going out. If she lets go now it will carry her out to sea. The barracuda rocks, undulates, lets it move him.

He loved to watch her dance, he said. Made her dance. No more.

She'd come before in July when the weather was better, the seas not so rough. With her friend, Benita. Before Melissa. They were called "associates" at a Tom Thumb convenience store in Fort Lauderdale. Polo shirts—$9.13 an hour. Not enough. Not with the baby coming. She did not show. She danced. And the men and women who watched her made it rain.

She is wearing a striped t-shirt and cotton shorts. The tracksuit jacket and pants she stripped off when she saw how it was going to be. No clothes to drag her down. To be fast enough to get to Melissa. Help mama. Family, floating. The water is like a bath, in July. In January, 60 degrees. The kind of cold that stops your brain. Limbs sluggish in liquid ice.

Dry Foot shakes, the tiny muscles between her shoulder blades jump uncontrollably. Thin, wiry arms so strong, so tired, hug the pole. She adjusts, pulls in closer, elbows bent to a better angle. Recoils as brittle crustaceans graze her breastbone.

Tip of a hot poker, her thigh jerks. Again, searing the meat of her calf. Another, high on her left buttock. Now she sees the undulating, white, gelatinous flowers, expanding and contracting, dancing in the tide, stringers trailing, wispy skirts.

He loved to watch her dance. Made her dance, in black garter-belt and boned bustier that barely covered her nipples, long ebony hair cascading as she arched off the pole, gripped in her taut thighs, arms tracing arabesques. Now, this pole: thicker, splintered, spongy with saltwater, bleeding black-tar resin. Her feet are bleeding, too.

She can't go back. When the sun comes up just one tick lighter, but before the fishermen and the Coast Guard come out, she will swim for the mangroves. She remembers the safety of those sturdy root hammocks, bouncy, with give, footholds straddled above swamp, above the scrabbling blue crabs, diving iguanas, rosy rat snakes. She remembers the shady cover of leathery, elliptical, glabrous emerald leaves. Not these. Farther up, close to Miami. There, the dancing led to other things. Arrest. Deportation. They didn't arrest the men who wanted her to do things to them and who did things to her. Even though some of the men were Cuban, like her.

*The baby is safe.* With her mother. She is herself a mother, young, maybe not so wise yet, but her intuition is strong. Yes. She sees them at the center, draped in orange blankets, sipping something warm from Styrofoam cups. Her mother urges Melissa to drink slowly. Blows on the hot liquid so the baby won't burn her tongue. *If you are dead, Mama, tell me. Tell me so I can give up hope.*

Her arms are so heavy, an ache that locks her neck, a tightening steel string at the base of her skull that makes it difficult to turn her head. The piling from the old pier, or perhaps the wooden bridge that was here before the big bridge. She knows it is the Seven Mile. And directly before her, the Old Seven Mile, where wet-foot dry-foot was tested. The judge said they could stay. But it took many lawyers and years. *There is no dry foot for deported whores.*

She will swim in the light, toward the mangroves she cannot quite yet see, but knows are there. When the green-bean shaped seeds float by periodically, there are always mangroves. *The baby is safe. Mother is safe.* She prays. It was meant to be. Is better this way. Her mistake the last time will not affect their chances.

The Americans call them chugs, boats made of this and that—anything that floats. Buckets, plastic sheeting, blue or pink Styrofoam insulation sheets, inner tubes. Wooden pallets, duct tape. Lawnmower engines. Car bodies, car engines. The chug they rode on the ninety-mile trip across the Florida Straits a luxury yacht by comparison, with a marine diesel en-

Grand island - William's landing

gine and hard-chined aluminum sides. But these conveniences couldn't keep the fifteen-foot waves out or keep them on course when the north wind picked up and the current shoved them farther and farther south, trapped in the raging Gulf Stream, discernible by its distinct navy blue in the angry gunmetal sea. *Melissa has a life jacket. Mother is fine.*

She and mother wore theirs loose, un-buckled, and lost them in the first capsize. *Stupid.* They'd just reached a place of less current and were motoring steadily out of the stream when a wave slammed over them from the starboard side engulfing the fourteen-foot chug, riding low in the roiling water with ten immigrants aboard, four of them babies, three younger than five-year-old Melissa.

*She can handle herself, that one. After this trip, she is no longer a baby.*

She hears the low thrum of the engines before she sees the big gray inflatable with the flashing blue lights running out the chan-nel. The bell buoy clangs in the wake. She shoves off the pole. Panics in the sucking-out current. Clutches it again, like a lifeline. And then hears just the barest vibration of a cry.

*Mommeeeee.*

She swims, blindly, sloppy leaden-armed breaststroke, bloody feet kicking, toward the sound.

Writer and editor **Cyndi Perkins** is senior content specialist at Michigan Technologi-cal University, where the former Daily Min-ing Gazette managing editor and long-time magazine writer produces print and digital media, from Instagram stories to news fea-tures. The Lake Superior sailor's two 6,000-mile circumnavigations of Eastern North America inspired *More Than You Think You Know* (Beating Windward Press), a wild ride with three renegade women on a road (river) trip. cyndiperkins.com

# Called to the Edge of Gichigami

## by Charli Mills

In the beginning, lava flowed, followed by cooling in a copious silica environment that formed agates, followed by intrusions that formed copper and other minerals. Shallow inland seas followed: corals, and the silicification of fossils. Next was scouring glaciers, glacial melt, Great Lakes, and early humans who collected copper 9,000 years ago. More human migration followed: the First Fire that brought the Anishinaabe, the colonizers, traders, trappers, and tricksters. Then the miners came and dug for copper. Today, while prophetic fires on Turtle Island yet burn, people come to the Upper Peninsula of Michigan to pick agates and eat pasties.

Father Fredric Baraga left Slovenia in 1830 to minister where food grows on the water and raw copper courses through basalt. Black robe to the Anishinaabe, he ministered to the tribes of the UP, becoming their grammarian. For thirty years, he criss-crossed the region, often slogging through drifts on snowshoes or paddling a birch-bark canoe along the shores of Lake Superior – Gichigami. He was the first to write down her name in ink. No one knows why Father Baraga dedicated his calling to her shores. He tended to the souls of immigrant copper miners, too, but no stories speak of his interest in rocks.

It's true that he never left the region of Gichigami once he arrived, dying within the big lake's shadow in 1868. When an epidemic broke out in Grand Portage, Minnesota, he set out in his canoe to help. Gichigami erupted into rough seas, tossing the priest and his guide between heaves of rolling waves. Whatever happened during that trip between the lake and Father Baraga, he never forgot the relief of salvation when she dumped him unscathed on a sandy shore at the mouth of a river he Christened with a cross. Cross River. Father Baraga's cross still stands, erected in stone.

Gichigami speaks in stones.

It may seem a minor miracle for a priest's canoe to survive Gichigami's battle-fraught waves, but consider the *Edmond Fitzgerald*. Fully loaded with her region's iron ore in 1975, she seized that 730-foot-long vessel in a single storm. It's been sung before: Gichigami holds onto her dead.

The Keweenaw Peninsula has an edge, and I'm standing on its fault line. I'm no sailor and certainly no priest. It's my first UP winter, and I've come to witness the greatest of the Great Lakes. Snowdrifts sweep out in front of me, wind-sculpted and half-hiding the brown bones of dead trees. I'm alone on a beach endlessly carved by Gichigami, staring at the edge of land, tempted to walk on water, but knowing better than to give in to the urge. Her watery machinations don't favor the curious or ill-prepared.

Having walked as far as I can down the beach, I glance back and regard the devastation. Gichigami calls many of us, I'm sure. Today, she calls me to see what she has wrought. From the warmth of home in Hancock, I've enjoyed her town visits, her playful flurries of snow, her blinding, whirling blizzards. I've missed her on the days when she recedes into thick gray clouds over her lake but can always glimpse her denseness hanging gray over the distant shore. Winter is when you can see Gichigami walk on land. Call it lake effect snow if you like, but those of us living in the lee of the lake recognize her when she roams.

Today, she is atmospheric. Layer upon layer of gray lifts into the blue sky edged with lean white tips — her rib cage hovers over me. Gichigami gently blows, her breath reverberating through the birch on the hill. Somehow, I felt her call from the safety of my living room. It was a blue-sky day, *so why not*, I thought.

Like the awe Father Baraga must have felt during his thirty-year relationship with Gichigami, I gasped at my first winter glimpse of her, bare and exposed, her blue gown of summer sky and water discarded. Outside Calumet, where the road dips from the ridge toward the lake, white converged on white beneath a grip of gray vapor. When I saw it, terror frizzed across my nerves, and I heard the panic of the Father echo across time, *What the hell were you thinking, Fredric?*

Too late to turn back, enormous snowbanks make it impossible for me to turn around. I nearly missed the cut-off to Calumet Waterworks beach. Turning sharply, my car slid. Missing the drifts that loom like an Ice Age, I slowed down, heart pounding. I reasoned that I was only going to gander a peek. After all, with 132 inches of snow in less than three months, I figured I would not get near the beach. I found the parking lot plowed, so I pulled in, just to see from that distance.

Gichigami rose like a soul over her own frozen body below the plowed lot.

Snow buried birch trees on the ridge of the park to their lowest fork of limbs. Tops of picnic tables surfaced like slates in the drifts. Park slides and swings froze in time and snowbanks. Compacted snow formed a bridge to the wooden stairs that drifted snow like chutes to the beach below. And yet the clever wench hovering overhead had blown a small trail, exposing enough steps for daring feet. Gichigami invited me to venture down.

That is how I came to stand on the edge of the world, staring down the remains of a battlefield. Trees like soldiers had dropped from their banks during the gales of October and November. Violently the waves had spewed their denuded trunks against the cuts into the hillside. Like broken brown bones, they protrude through the snow and litter the beach. A smaller and less forcibly tangled line of littered driftwood forms a secondary barrier. Between the two, Gichigami has finger-painted ice as easily as if it where paste in a kindergarten classroom.

I stand on the edge, listening to a constant trickle. Gichigami has pruned back the water until it can barely ooze between grains of silica sand. In a display of force, piles of sand and beach rocks punch skyward through the crust of snow. She has sculpted these along the edge, freezing rocks into pedestals, altars to her name. From summer visits, I know I stand where waves lap to shore. No lapping now.

More fearsome yet is the battle raging between water and ice. Like brothers at war, ice versus liquid rips the lake bed. What might look like dunes or drifts of snow made by a runaway bulldozer are what remains of waves, sand, and rock transcending the space. Lake ice shatters into foot-thick shards upended and perpendicular to the shoreline. Gichigami circles overhead while a war rages in slow motion below — behold the power of Lake Superior in winter.

A party of parka-clad tourists interrupts my witnessing. They see me below and mistake me for Sir Ernest Shackleton or some other arctic explorer. The tourists, notably excited by winter wonders, have a single burning question: "Do you live here?"

"Yes." Not here as in on the frozen beach of Lake Superior, but here as in the UP, on the Keweenaw.

They whistle through frosted breath and shake their heads. Here is impressive to visit, worth the drive from downstate Michigan or out of state. Then the next question: "But why...?"

How do I tell them I'm captive to Gichigami, that I'm a snared wanderer and a minstrel of sand and snow? Would they think me crazy to say she speaks to me in stones and those who have lived and died here, yet remain, soul-siblings to me? Do they even understand that what they see is a battlefield as they stomp over the frontlines in high tech snow boots unaware that water undulates unforgivingly below them?

I want to say, *That's not a snowdrift but Gichigami's hip bone, and she's going to knock you to her watery depths if you don't take care. Look, her ribs fly exposed overhead, she's circling, circling. Do you belong to her? Don't wait to find out. Flee! The battles renew, surge when you least expect.*

But I give a less enigmatic answer: "Rocks. I like rocks."

"Oh." They sound disappointed, and inwardly I chuckle. No, these won't draw Gichigami's attention. She likes admirers, those who can read her signals. One tourist lingers, though.

"What kind of rocks?" he asks.

I look at this man before me, and his eyes show a snap of curiosity. I can tell he feels Gichigami's presence but doesn't know what it is. Asking about rocks is like asking for a sip of whiskey when you really don't understand what alcohol is all about.

Looking down, I see Gichigami has revealed stones for me as if she knew I'd take this chance to glimpse her domain. Okay, so I'll give the nice man a taste of firewater. "Oh, agates," I say.

"Ah, agates." He turns and walks away.

So, I say something more intriguing, wondering if Gichigami has me doing her bidding now. "Prehnite is my favorite though, especially copper inclusions."

"Copper inclusions?" This man has too much curiosity to be on this beach safely.

"Yeah. Prehnite is milky white, sometimes yellow like old peas, but sometimes it has copper and radiates hot pink and kale green bursts of inner crystallization."

"Oh! Are you a geologist?"

I want to tell him the truth — I belong to Gichigami; I am her siren's call. But I say, "No, but I raised one." My smile is meant to look innocent, motherly.

"Let's go!" His friends have reached the safety above on the hill over this battlefield. I can hear water trickling beneath us. I say

no more and turn to walk away. Wisely, he retreats to his friends but stumbles across another eruption.

"Hey! Hey–I found something. A rock! It's green!"

Overhead I watch Gichigami floating as clearly as the Lady of Shallot in her watery grave. I turn back, and the man approaches, holding out a rock in his now ungloved hand. It's the size of a tomato, steely gray, pocked with vesicles, filled with glittering pistachio green crystals. Oh, Gichigami, you are toying with him. "That's basalt filled in with secondary mineralization of epidote. Anything the color of pistachios is epidote."

"Cool!" He has no idea what epidote is or how common. But it is bedazzling, especially when the crystals aren't beach-pummeled smooth. He grins and pockets his find. "I see why you like living here."

She's snared another. From now on, he'll always want to come back to this edge. At work, likely an office job, maybe even as a CEO, he'll be in the middle of a meeting, taking notes or giving direction, and he'll think of that rock and how many others might be waiting on that beach. When the wind teases his hair, he'll look the direction of Lake Superior and not know why. As he drifts to sleep at night, he'll hear drums, miner's hammers, sails snapping, and the whispered prayers of Father Baraga.

**Charli Mills** relocated to the Keweenaw from out West. *Montana Outdoors*, *Living Naturally*, *Edible Twin Cities*, and *Sandpoint Magazine* have featured her writing. As a marketing communicator, she's penned columns, presented workshops nationally and managed writing contests. She's series editor of *Congress of the Rough Writers Flash Fiction Anthology* and her short stories have been featured in print, online, and on stage. Charli writes contemporary fiction about veterans, rocks, and history. In 2014, she founded CarrotRanch.com, hosting weekly 99-word story challenges. She provides literary outreach to libraries and veterans, leads writing workshops, and works on her MFA in Creative Writing.

# Your Invitation to join the UPPAA Today

# MEMBER BENEFITS:

- Annual **UPPAA Spring Conference** in Marquette with keynotes by breakout authors and publishing industry experts (attendance is FREE! for members)
- Access to exclusive UPPAA workshops, such as the NEW **Fiction Writing Workshop**
- Network and enjoy fun and fellowship (and good food!) with other UPPAA authors at our **annual Fall Picnic**
- Receive our information-packed **quarterly newsletter** *The Written Word*
- **Submit your author news** (about your personal experiences writing, publishing, marketing, selling your books) to *The Written Word* to be shared with membership and on our blog
- **Enjoy substantial discounts** on membership in national publisher associations (PMA and SPAN)
- Learn from other members via our **members-only email forum** discussion groups
- List your books in the **UPPAA.org online catalog** (membership required)
- Submit original short pieces to the **U.P. Reader** (membership required)
- Display books at UPPAA meetings and other U. P. book events
- Learn self-publishing *do's and don'ts* and share lessons learned

## WHAT IS UPPAA?
UPPAA is the Upper Peninsula Publishers and Authors Association.

## WHEN WAS UPPAA FOUNDED?
The organization began in 1998 when Sue Robishaw, Lynn Emerick and Michael Marsden joined together to produce the first UPPAA Conference with thirty people in attendance. Since the organization's founding, UPPAA has grown to more than 100 members, representing a diverse body of writers in the fields of fiction, nonfiction, history, children's books, science and many other fields. You can view our members' books at www.uppaa.org.

## WHAT IS UPPAA'S PURPOSE?
UPPAA was founded with the purpose to support and encourage networking and idea exchange among Upper Peninsula, and surrounding area, publishers and authors, and to promote books published and/or authored by UPPAA members.

## DOES UPPAA HAVE MEETINGS?
- An annual conference is held in the Spring in Marquette to provide convenience to members throughout the vast peninsula.
- The conference is divided into several workshops, focusing on such topics as writing, the mechanics of publishing, publishing cost-effectively, marketing, and publicity. UPPAA has also brought in internationally known guest speakers to its conferences, including Dan Poynter, Patrick Snow, Jerry Simmons, and Karen Dionne.
- Attendance at conferences is free to UPPAA members.
- Members are invited to join UPPAA Board meetings on the first Thursday of every month in person at the Peter White Library (Dandelion Cottage room) or remotely via ZOOM.US livestream or telephone call.

## HOW IS UPPAA ORGANIZED?
UPPAA is a non-profit organization with a Board of Directors. Board positions are open to any members and board members are nominated and voted in every two years by members.

## WHAT IS UPPAA'S FUTURE?
With a group of enthusiastic and innovative members, UPPAA continues to grow and seek new ways in the rapidly changing world of book publishing to promote its Upper Michigan authors and their books.

# Clark Kent Says It All

## by Tricia Carr

Police Chief Virtanen was behind his desk with a mug of hot coffee in front of him, and on his computer monitor, a replay of his favorite program, the "Westminster Dog Show." His young officer, Bob Makinen, came in, scraping sandy soil off his boots. It was spring in the Upper Peninsula of Michigan — finally — but the woods were still wet from the vanished snow.

"Anything, Bob?"

"Naw. Everyone's out at the bonfire, but no problems. Might get a little raucous later."

It was the weekend of the annual Lumberjack Festival. The poster on the door announced "Sawdust = Man Glitter," and flanked a huge drawing of Paul Bunyan and pictures from previous festivals. Lumberjacking was so woven into their history that this small Lake Superior island went all out. Men wearing plaid came from near and far to compete at old-fashioned tree chopping and pole climbing, and the kids had a ball trying their skill at log rolling. The day was ending with pasties, bratwurst, and pie at the village VFW hall.

"Well, just that one thing," Bob added. "I got the call from Bridget about the silent alarm at Edna Lutey's going off, but it was nothing. Why does she still have that?"

Chief Virtanen sighed. "Oh, she's always talking about her comic books. As if anybody would steal those. Why did the alarm go off?"

"Don't know. I met Sean Jurvi coming out of her circle drive. He came back for the festival and was on his way to catch the 7:00 car ferry when he heard that new dog of hers barking like mad, so he pulled in to see if there was a problem. I went all around with my flashlight but I didn't see or hear anything." He took off his jacket. "I had forgotten that she has a dog now, but she was talking about it at the festival earlier, how she adopted her Benji dog from the shelter."

Bridget Waino turned from the dispatch keyboard, smiling. "Is she still calling him that? I was volunteering down there when she got him and I tried to tell her he's not a 'Ben-ji' dog, he's a Basenji. It's a breed. Was she wearing that big Superman pin on her coat?"

"She was. She does love her Superman."

The door to the police station slammed open and Edna herself burst in, her little monkey face tense, her short gray hair on end.

"Chief!" she panted, "I've been robbed!"

Chief Virtanen came out of his chair. "Robbed! At our festival?"

Edna shook her head vigorously, trying to get her breath. "No," she gasped, "My comics! When I got home tonight they were gone!"

The Chief paused. "Okay, not robbed then. Burglarized." *Maybe*, he added mentally. "But your comics? They're gone?"

"My Superman comics! The ones my dad started saving for us when my brother and I were little, they're all gone!"

"Vintage comic books?" Bob said, startled. "Oh wow, those can be valuable! That must be why your alarm went off, and why Sean Juvi heard Benji barking up a storm! Somebody was robbing your house!"

Edna sank into a chair. "Well, go find that somebody! And his name isn't Benji," she said crossly, "it's Clark Kent. A Benji is what he is."

"Not a Benji, a Basenji!" Bridget said again.

"A Basenji," Chief Virtanen said. He looked down at his monitor where the dog show was still going on, and picked up his jacket.

"Bridget," he said briskly, "call Ooni at the ferry and tell him to delay. I'm going straight there. And if Sean Jurvi is there, tell Ooni to do anything to distract him, but make sure he doesn't leave the island."

Bob was staring at him, and the Chief looked up as he was swapping his comfortable office shoes for duty boots.

"Didn't you hear? That dog is a Basenji! Not a 'Benji' dog, a Basenji!" and was gone.

Bridget was rapidly typing into her computer. *A Basenji is a barkless dog* she read aloud. "Oh, Sean Jurvi couldn't have heard Clark Kent 'barking up a storm'! They don't bark!"

# Domestic Violence

## by Tricia Carr

B ack in the 80s, small Upper Michigan towns had their problems — teenagers breaking into sports shops or camps, prank calls, and the myriad of problems expected anywhere drinking can qualify as a winter sport — but this crime shocked the little mining community as few had. Indeed, it shocked the entire Upper Peninsula, which was, as the last part of that word indicates, an "insular" community.

A woman had been found in the woods behind the school, stabbed repeatedly, and next to her a note:

I'LL DO IT AGAIN.

Detective Maki turned quickly when Dr. Coppa came through the swinging doors of the tiny emergency room. "Well?"

Coppa fished change out of the gum pack tucked into the sleeve of his greens and dropped it into the candy machine.

"Well, she'll live. She's been sliced up pretty good but she was lucky, nothing vital was hit. Good thing it's cold, her coat probably saved her." He lowered his voice. "Whew! Can you believe this? I mean, we have our share of violence up here but it's usually domestic, or else guys getting liquored up and remembering old grudges. This kind of weirdness is something else. And Debra Marilek, too." He shook his head.

Maki looked up from his notebook quickly. "You know her?"

"Well, some. She used to work here, until the stress got to her and she left. Good E.R.

nurse. I know her husband a little better. We've both taught classes at the Community Center. God, he's really going to be shook by this."

He really was. He sat with Maki two hours later, in the small lounge across from his wife's room, waiting for permission to see her again. His hands dangled numbly between his knees, his face was drawn and gray.

"Mr. Marilek," Maki began, "who could have done this? Was your wife being bothered by anyone? Was she afraid of anyone?"

Marilek shook his head. "Not that I know about. She's been — nervy lately; a bit jumpy; but not like she's afraid of anyone. No."

"Any strange calls? Anything like that?"

The man looked vaguely surprised. He shook his head.

"No one at all she's had a problem with? I know it's hard to concentrate, but *think*, Mr. Marilek."

He shook his head again. He looked drained, exhausted.

Maki strummed his fingers on the table thoughtfully. Then he pushed the cuff back from his watch.

"Well, I think I'll look in on your wife again now; see if she's awake yet."

Dennis Marilek stood up. "Okay."

Maki lifted an eyebrow.

Marilek said heavily, "They say she really hasn't come to enough yet to even realize what's happened. I don't want her to wake up and have you be the first thing she sees, a strange man. I'd like to be there, to reassure her."

There was a bare pause before Maki nodded.

"Sure," he said agreeably. "Come on."

Dennis Marilek pushed his wife's hair gently back from her forehead. "Debra? Deb? Wake up, hon. Wake up." He took her hand and softly kneaded it.

Debra Marilek's eyes opened. She looked blankly up at her husband. He said, slightly stressing the words, "You're all right, Deb. You're at the hospital. You're *all right.*"

She stared up at him for an uncomprehending moment, then her eyes cleared and memory and despair and great fear flashed.

Maki said quickly, "Mrs. Marilek, I'm Detective Maki. Can you talk with me? Tell me what happened? And why?"

She waved a hand weakly. Tears slipped into her hair from the corners of her closed eyes.

Maki was silent for a moment, looking at her. Then he moved closer and said quietly, "Do you know who it was?"

She opened her eyes quickly and for a moment surprise was plain. There was a perceptible pause — one heartbeat; two; three — and Maki felt something shift in the atmosphere.

Debra Marilek seemed suddenly smaller, as if her body had shrunk into itself under the bedclothes. She lay very still. Her husband's fingers stopped kneading hers and a current seemed to pass between them. Then he stood, looking past Maki's eyes, and took a step to the window. With his back turned he said, "Can you tell him who did this, Deb?" His voice had an odd vibrating tightness.

Her head moved slowly from side to side on the pillow. Her eyes closed again.

Maki paused, trying to assess the change.

There was despair, and wariness, in this room. And an aura of unhappy fierce protectiveness.

He glanced from Dennis Marilek's rigid back, at the window, to the slight woman hunched in the bed.

He didn't like this. He didn't like this a bit.

On his way to the elevator he stopped at the desk. A nurse looked up from the telephone. "Can I help you, Detective?"

He smiled at her. "Well, you're using what I need. Is there another phone close?"

"Pay phone, in the lounge."

"Gee thanks."

The elevator doors opened and Dr. Coppa got out with a small group of nurses arriving for midnight shift. He stopped when he saw Maki.

"Talked to her yet? Where's her husband?"

"I just left her room. She still wasn't able to say much. Marilek was helping her with some ice chips."

In the tiny nurses' locker room off the hallway, one voice was suddenly raised above the others.

"If that isn't just like her! Of all the people in this town, naturally the one attacked would be Debra. When we were kids at Grandma's, she was always the one who fell out of the tree and got fussed over! Honestly, I think she just loves the attention!"

"God, Julia!"

"I mean it! Or else she led some guy on and then wouldn't deliver, so she got what she deserved. It's just like her!"

Someone slammed a locker in disgust, briefly drowning out the voice. Maki whispered to Coppa, "Who in the world is that?"

"Julia Bruce. Practical nurse. Terrible woman. Mind like a puddle — about four inches deep, with a lot of muck at the bottom. Related to the Marileks, I think."

"Oh?" Maki remembered her now. *Beige.* Beige hair, eyes a faded pale brown, eyebrows and lashes blending into a thick beige skin, flushed now to an unbecoming, excited mauve.

Coppa shook his head. "I hear Julia is known as the family embarrassment, always blurting stuff out at the worst time. Not very socially adept."

Julia Bruce was coming out of the locker room, still talking in a loud shaking voice.

"She's made Dennis miserable. And anyway, I met him first, it was me he liked—"

Another nurse looked past her at the two men and rolled her eyes.

"He wishes he'd never married her! I know!"

The charge nurse came hurrying from the medication cubby.

"What on earth — Julia, don't you have anything to do?" She hustled the woman off, whispering vehemently, "The idea, standing around in the halls talking at the top of your lungs!"

"Honestly," the other nurse said with disgust. "She's always been strange, but if she doesn't watch it, she'll go completely around the bend. Imagine being mad at Debra for being in that bed all bandaged up! Whoa," she added, as the charge nurse appeared again, frowning, in the doorway of the little office. "Gotta go."

"Me too," Maki said to Coppa. "Need to check in."

Dennis Marilek was sitting in the lounge staring bleakly toward the television screen. He turned his head when Maki came in.

"She was sleepy," he said in his slow quiet voice. "I told her I'd wait. You need me?"

Maki shook his head and dug out change. "Nope. Need the phone."

The number was busy. Maki fished his change out of the return box and propped himself against the wall.

The medication nurse was making her final rounds before the shift change, checking patients with I.V.s. She came out of Debra Marilek's room looking puzzled. She caught Dr. Coppa's eye and gave a faint jerk of her head. He followed her swiftly into the room.

Maki shifted himself to see past the partially open door. Coppa seemed to be examining the tiny wheel on the I.V. tube that controlled the rate of flow. The nurse was talking in a low voice. Coppa shrugged but came out of the room, frowning. He stopped when he saw Maki and started to speak, then looked beyond him to Dennis Marilek and paused. His mouth went grim.

Maki raised an eyebrow.

After a moment, Coppa came across the hall and spoke abruptly. "Dennis, why don't you go home?"

The man looked startled at the brusque tone.

"I thought I'd wait—"

"No more visitors tonight. We've given her something to make sure she rests. You might as well go home."

After a moment, Marilek stood up. Coppa walked with him to the elevator, punched the 'down' button, then unwrapped two sticks of gum and stood chewing until the doors closed.

Maki made his call and left. The eyebrow was still up.

The next noon when he came to the hospital to speak to Debra Marilek, she had a roommate, an older woman with ferociously permed hair whose permanent expression seemed cranky. Maki went past her to Debra's bed with a pleasant nod.

Debra went home after ten long days. Coppa had gone down to Detroit to visit family but Maki made a point of being at the hospital, propped against the wall of the lounge across the hall while a staff person eased her into a wheelchair. She was a small woman, ordinary looking except for huge dark-lashed hazel eyes. Bambi eyes, Maki thought. Mercifully, the attack had left her face untouched; for a woman especially, that could be so important.

She had taken longer to heal than Coppa had expected, but then she didn't look as if she'd been eating right for quite a while. Wisdom said going home was probably the best thing for her. Maki hoped wisdom was right.

The transporter pushed the chair carefully down the hall and onto the elevator, a sullen Julia Bruce following with a cart loaded with the cards and flowers Debra had received, many from shocked strangers. Dennis Marilek walked beside his wife, looking straight ahead, his hand holding hers tightly.

Throughout the community, the attack had ignited a mixture of horrified speculation, paralyzing fear, gossip and excitement. Women borrowed dogs to take with them jogging. High school boys walked girls everywhere, making loud jokes but underneath with a tingle of pleasure at being asked. In stores, bowling alleys, libraries, and especially in lonely areas, the public was on the lookout for "one of them psychos."

At the police station Maki was doodling and pondering.

A weirdo slasher?

Or — something closer to home?

If someone crazy...

The nature of the crime, the savagery of the attack, and the note, all raised the question.

Maki groaned. The last thing they wanted to deal with was a horrible series of crimes like those that had plagued other parts of the country too often. Right here in Michigan it had happened sometimes — look at that string of child murders around Detroit some years ago. No one ever caught, either. And if there had been, you could bet you'd hear a chorus of "You're kidding, not him! He's such a nice guy!" Look at the murders in Ann Arbor in the late sixties; Michigan's version of Ted Bundy.

Maki shuddered. A retired state police officer he knew had worked with the Ypsilanti police department at that time, and he had told Maki of working frantically against a psychopath's mind, of the warnings to women not to hitchhike, not to be out by themselves or alone with new acquaintances — and of the sense of sickness and fury when yet another girl's body was found.

Maki shook his head sharply. It wasn't just his dread of that kind of situation that kept bringing the thought of domestic violence to him. He had been brought up short by that strange sense in the air the first time he had been able to talk with Debra Marilek, and her husband's quiet maneuvering to be present...

Of course, the problem was that these things might have nothing to do with the attack. Maybe the oddness in the atmosphere had been because of a spat earlier in the evening. Of course, both of them said that there had been no quarrel, but if there had been, maybe they felt that if they hadn't quarreled she wouldn't have been out that night, wouldn't have been the woman attacked.

Maybe, maybe. You could think up a thousand maybes.

Dennis Marilek was a tall, strong man. A big man. A quiet man. One who seemed to love his wife.

Maki sighed. Love could be such a funny word. He couldn't count the men he'd locked up over the years for knocking their wives around and most of them would swear, with tears in their eyes, that they "loved" their wives.

The note.

His present pondering was the result of the report received late this morning on the printer used for the note.

Tracing it had been almost too easy; it had come at some point off the public machine at the Community Center.

Marilek and his wife had taught classes at the Community Center on Tuesday nights. Marilek had access to that printer.

Maki shook his head. So did everyone for miles around. Lots of people with an evening to kill dropped by and shot a few baskets, swapped hunting lies and gossip, or just sat for a while and watched television in the lounge. This meant that if their man was a psycho he must be someone local, someone whose presence at the little Center would not stand out. That really was an unpleasant thought, and no mistake.

There was something else — another possibility that had flashed across his mind once — what was it? He shut his eyes and leaned back in his chair and gave himself up to thought. The memory of a face came —a spiteful, beige-mauve face. And a voice — a vicious woman's voice — "Probably led some guy on — she's like that, you know."

Malicious, unreliable, of course; that stuck out a mile. Still, it did raise points of speculation.

Another man? Someone rejected? There had been no hint of such a thing from anyone else he'd talked with, but still. And even if her husband only thought it might be true, it could provide motive. One of the oldest motives for violence: jealousy.

There were many kinds of jealousy.

Maki opened his eyes and stared at the ceiling.

There were many kinds of jealousy. And Julia Bruce was a big woman.

Maki moved his head sharply. A *woman?*

They had automatically been referring to the attacker as "he," but actually there was no evidence that it had been a man. The attack had not been in any way sexual, which was perhaps unusual in itself, in these times.

He sat for a long time at his desk and absently drew battleships on his blotter and thought.

Leaning Rock, Gros Cap Drive, St. Ignace, Mich.

Gros Cap leaning rock and carriage

A psychopath.

Domestic violence.

Or...?

Then he stood up, glancing at his watch and jingling his car keys. He needed to talk to a few people.

Maki looked speculatively at the man sitting across the table from him in the small interrogation room. There was no doubt that in the short time since the attack, Dennis Marilek had gone rapidly downhill. He looked shrunken; guarded. He'd hesitated when Maki stopped him on his way home from work and asked him to come by the station, then reluctantly nodded, obviously because he felt he had little choice.

Maki sat silent for a moment. What he wanted was to get a feel for this man, and if Marilek was annoyed at being waylaid on his way home, so much the better. It would be instructive to see what he was like when upset.

A young part-time officer tapped and opened the door a crack. "Someone to see you, Detective."

"Right." Maki nodded to Dennis Marilek. "Be right back."

In the other room Dr. Coppa was pacing. "I just got back," he said quickly. "I called someone to meet me here. I think you need to talk to her — oh, here she is."

The outer door opened and a woman came in; a woman who looked familiar; a woman whose face was no longer cross but whose hair was still ferociously permed.

Maki looked from the newcomer to Coppa and sat down on the edge of his desk. "Well Coppa," he said slowly, "what's this about?"

Coppa rubbed his eyebrows. "Well, first I'd better explain..." He glanced at the partially open door, at Dennis Marilek hunched over the table in the interrogation room. Maki turned his ear as Coppa leaned in, saying something in a low rapid voice.

The Detective's swinging foot stopped. He interrupted the doctor abruptly. "Just a minute. She's a witness?" He looked at the woman and back to Coppa. "You would both testify?"

The woman's eyebrows went up. "Well yes, but..."

"Maki..."

"You two just wait here. Ben," he jerked his head at the young policeman across the room. "Get them some coffee."

Dennis Marilek was still sitting at the table, turning his hands over slowly, looking intently at his fingers, as though he had never seen them before. He looked up when

Maki closed the door, and straightened a little in his chair.

Maki sat down opposite him, his mind focused and hard, seeking rapidly the best way to use the information Coppa had brought him.

"Mr. Marilek," he began, "you remember that I read you your rights when you came in today? You remember signing the form?"

Marilek nodded, his eyes widening a little.

Maki was silent for a moment. "Well," he said finally, and his voice was oddly gentle. "I've just had a visit from the doctor who took care of your wife in the hospital, and from the woman who was your wife's roommate. The staff was a little puzzled, because your wife's injuries were taking longer to heal than it seemed they should. And it was noticed that often after a visit from you her bandages were disturbed, or her I.V. not working right, or her wounds — bothered."

Dennis Marilek had gone suddenly gray.

"All right," Maki said quietly, "why don't you tell me about it?"

Marilek looked at him mutely. Maki suddenly lost his temper.

"Come on, man!" he shouted. "And what about that note? What about other people, other women? TALK!"

Without warning the man's face crumpled.

"There's no other people, no other women!" He began to sob, a horrible guttural sound. "Only her. Only her!"

Maki stared at him. Unexpectedly there came back to him an earlier half-formed thought.

*Only her.*

The skin along his spine prickled, and then suddenly in his mind all the facts shifted and clicked into place and he saw.

"Tell me," he said urgently, but his voice was gentle again.

The police car swung rapidly into the driveway of the Marilek bungalow. The sun was low in the gray sky. Everything was very silent.

"Detective," the young officer with him said, but Maki shook his head sharply. They quickly got out of the car and went up the porch steps.

The front door was unlocked. Inside, no lamps were on and no one answered Maki's call. They stood for a moment, listening, then through the ticking stillness they heard a muffled scrabbling sound beneath the floor.

"Oh, God in heaven," the young officer breathed.

They found her there, in the basement, the red seeping through the slashes in her clothes, showing dark in the gloom. They turned her gently over, and the beautiful eyes opened.

"Thank God, she's not dead," the young officer said fervently, and went leaping up the stairs to the phone.

Thirty minutes later the paramedics were bringing the gurney rapidly in through the hospital emergency doors. Dr. Coppa, alerted by Maki, was waiting. He made a quick, gentle check of the paramedics' work and nodded. His eyes met Maki's.

"Like before. She'll live. Lucky she's a nurse. She wasn't meant to die."

The young officer was looking down at the woman. "But which is it?" he asked Maki in a low voice. "Someone with a mental quirk? Or domestic?"

"Actually," Maki said quietly, "it's a form of both."

As the gurney went past, Debra Marilek's eyes opened and she looked directly at them. Her pale mouth smiled faintly.

"Told you — I'd do it again," she whispered.

**Tricia Carr** was born in Detroit, but grew up on stories from her mother and grandparents about life in the Upper Peninsula of Michigan. She moved her new family to the U.P. just a few years after her marriage. After raising her children and being a Jill of all trades, including a short stint publishing a regional magazine and a long stint at her local library, she went back to her real love, writing traditional short fiction. She cut her teeth first on Trixie Belden and then on Agatha Christie, so a mystery is what comes naturally to her. Her three cats, a Pomeranian, and her daughters and husband cheer her on.

# The Truck

## by Raymond Luczak

Its paint chipping from rain and rust, the truck
sits there, bloated in the yard where in dusk
among uncut grass and corn's ripe husk
left whole to rot in the November muck.

At one time the truck carried families
and picnic baskets filled up with harvest
for warm days on the shore for games and rest.
Flies buzz about its seat of memories.

Its tank long emptied and its tires gone flat,
the truck holds up a creaky steering wheel.
The doors, if they can be pulled open, squeal.

Sometimes it harbors a pregnant stray cat
alone with her thoughts set on warm pasture.
Abandoned trucks that reek have no future.

# Independence Day

## by Raymond Luczak

As I strip for the shower, I catch a glimpse of myself in the mirror. The bathroom walls have a swirl of pink and white with opaque chains of copper. The linoleum floor has a mixture of lime with undercurrents of gray and white with sprinkles of gold on top. Two columns of vanity bulbs are soldiered next to the mirror above the sink. That mirror silently recorded how I grew.

At first, when I was a little girl, I didn't care to look because I was too short. When I saw how my older sisters Lizzie, Patty, and Colleen stood in front of the mirror, fixing their hair and applying their makeup, I became curious. They didn't invite me in the way that they did with our youngest sister, Fiona, and there she laughed with them when she tried on a bit of lipstick.

It didn't help that I couldn't follow the boisterous conversations around the dinner table. There were nine of us—five girls, two boys, and Mom and Dad. I had to keep asking why they were laughing. They said, "I'll tell you later," and continued with their carrying on. They were having oh so much fun!

Later, when it was time for them to tell me what I'd missed, they'd forgotten. It wasn't really that important, anyway. Besides, they were too busy.

My needs weren't important at all. It was all about survival of the fittest.

I began dreaming of suicide.

Each time I took out Dad's razor blades from the uppermost shelf containing aspirin and the like, the look of concern in Jobby's brown eyes stopped me from going any further. My dog had the annoying habit of having to be in the bathroom with me. How could I abandon him? He wagged his tail when I took a deep breath and put away the blades. Another night he kept jumping on me when I was trying to get a bottle of aspirin from the uppermost shelf in the bathroom. I was annoyed by his interruptions, but when I finally closed the cabinet door, he plopped himself right in front of me and rested his head on his paws. His eyes were full of sorrow. Sometimes, late at night, he leapt onto my bed where I could muffle my tears into the fur of his meaty back.

When I was alone in the bathroom, I experimented with lipstick, rouge, and powder. I found I didn't like the look. I didn't want to be phony. It seemed that with the exception of my speech therapist, Mrs. Gates, everyone who wore makeup were fake. I didn't see the point of spending money on makeup anyway. I brushed my dull-looking hair until it shone. I tried using barrettes to keep the bangs out of my eyes. I took to combing the top of my hair and pulling it back into a ponytail. It meant that the earmolds I'd wanted to hide would stick out, but I didn't care. Why hide them if everyone knew that I was deaf? Later, when I was in Marquette for my annual hearing test, the audiologist showed me a pair of behind-the-ear hearing aids. I couldn't believe that at sixteen, I was finally allowed to wear them. With no cords coming out of my ears, I felt more like everyone else around me.

Freshened, I step out of the shower and find Jobby suddenly standing up with an expectant look on his face, wagging his thick tail. He doesn't care that I'm dripping naked; he wants me to scratch behind his ears right this minute. I laugh. Even though I'd never lived with a Labrador before, he is already my favorite Lab in the world. He is all chocolate with warm eyes.

Moments later, as we step outside the house, the chilly winds jolt me awake. I grip Jobby's leash, knowing full well how he will pull hard from excitement at being outside at a strange hour; it's five o'clock in the morning. "Wait," I say.

As I close the outer door, he turns around to sit and looks up into my face in shadow. He doesn't seem to understand that I won't be seeing him for five months. Or maybe he does. It's hard to tell with dogs. Calendar dates mean nothing to them, but I'll always remember today's date: July 18, 1984.

In less than two hours I will board the bus for Minneapolis, where my sister Patty lives. I will stay overnight with her and board my first plane for Washington, D.C. I feel as if I've waited my entire life for this one day.

•••

Some years ago, many streetlamps stayed lit overnight in our neighborhood. Each light opened its arms wide enough to connect from each circle to the next as we walked on the sidewalks home.

Now, because of budget cuts, there is only one remaining lit on the corner down the street. It is awaiting me. Even though I'm wearing a hooded sweatshirt and jeans, I feel bathed in warm light. I've sometimes wondered, as I do now, what it must feel like to be a moth gone light-mad. Would I still flutter crazily knowing that I could die from so much exertion and disappointment from not breaking through the glass of light's divinity?

The streetlamp stands near a rusted fire hydrant right in front of a blue-and-white house where a retired priest lives. Father Tom's manner is often abrupt with the initial appearance of patience. I used to know his aging mother who lived in that house, but not very well. When she died, the house stayed vacant for a long time with lights inside turning on promptly at eight every evening. Any burglar could have peered inside to see that there was no flicker of television.

I dreamed of seeing her peeking at us kids through the gauzy curtains overlooking the yard where we played. The question of her was answered when her son, bald and overweight, reappeared. He hunched with a baseball cap on his head on a small riding mower when he bounced up and down long rows of grass. He nodded at me whenever he caught me watching.

I don't know his story. All I know is that he used to be a priest and has moved into his mother's house. Even though I live right next door, we've never spoken to each other. He has been living next to us for five years now.

Jobby lifts his leg at the fire hydrant and lets loose.

•••

In the daytime, the houses in our neighborhood are occupied by men and women deeply comforted by the familiarity of loneliness. Their lives, once filled with the racket of their children not yet aware of their own mortality, echo the wax cylinders ceaselessly spinning in their Victrola of memory. Each time they recall a line from a song they wish to sing again, the needle skips sideways to a different groove. The song is supposed to sound the same, but it doesn't. The song's already changed, but they've stopped listening to it. They prefer what they'd learned when they were young with not a care in the world. Each time I see them sitting on their porches and working in their opened garages, something about them has changed. I can never pinpoint precisely what, whether in their faces or from the way they move, but something *has* changed. Nevertheless they wave as before when I walk past.

Seeing everything clearly in daylight isn't the same as sensing everything differently at night. The colors of shadow are many, and they are all cut from the same fabric of black.

Details intimately familiar in the sun turn mysterious and calm as in dreams when Jobby and I walk past beyond the midnight hour. The grass looks blotchy with scuffs of jagged black. There is no mesh of bark among trees. The sidewalk cracks look severe as glass.

The guilloché of constellations shines brightly through the enamel of midnight blue. The moon is a telescope-eye of light. She is watching every movement we make. She powders the footprints in our wake, but we never look back.

•••

The other corner house right across from Father Tom's is smaller, and painted hunter green with an eggshell-colored enamel trim. Mrs. Weiss used to live there, but she's now in a nursing home. I remember her face filled with both bewilderment and exasperation as she tried to herd all of us babbling siblings in her house when Mom needed a babysitter at the last minute.

The hardwood floors shimmered underneath its veneer. The intricate woodwork that framed the doorways fascinated me. The wallpaper in the dining room repeated a tiny bouquet of wildflowers over and over again. The thick lacquer that covered the wooden table shone like glass. It reminded me of the pews in St. Michael's where we went every Sunday for Mass.

I do not comprehend then that her last name is a typically Jewish surname, or that once upon a time there was a small thriving Jewish community living on the other side of the river where they had their own cemetery. Since the house is empty, it doesn't feel filled with anything but silences. I am not even sure if the Weisses ever had children. I do not know their story. I wonder if I ever will.

•••

In class, I was condemned to the first row where I was to pay full attention to the teacher. My scholastic excellence was singled out on my report cards. As a deaf person who could talk quite well, I was considered a smashing success, but no one thought to ask if I had any friends. I was not a cool kid. I didn't know how or why at the time, but my hands felt so lonely. In the absence of love and understanding, I felt my veins throb with rage.

By the time puberty took hold of me, I didn't know what to do with my body hearing aids. I had a pair of them strapped to my chest, and now I had to wear a training bra. I came to hate riding the school bus home from Ironwood Catholic Grade School. This time I chose to sit near the front of the bus because I knew how some of the boys would gesture at my bosom, topped off with a rattle of laughs. Then they shouted, "Double boobs! Double boobs!"

I kept my face straight ahead, wishing that at least one of my female classmates would tell them to just quit it. Not even Fiona, who was on the bus, said anything. I couldn't believe the bus driver didn't try to shush them. Hadn't he heard them saying those words?

I wanted to shout back something, but two things kept me in check. I was a *girl*, and they'd imitate anything I said with their version of my deaf speech.

I came home full of tears.

Mom was washing dishes. "What happened?"

Fiona said, "They were making fun of her on the bus!"

Mom said, "Well, if they're laughing at you, you should laugh *with* them."

I tried to explain that no, no, no, this was different, but my nose was stopped up with mucus. I grabbed a Kleenex tissue from the other kitchen counter and blew my nose.

"Oh, no, you just laugh *with* them," Mom said. "That's how the world works."

"So I should laugh at my double boobs? My *double boobs*?"

Mom looked away in shame.

"Well?" I wanted her to hug me, to tell me that I was indeed all right. "What do you say to *that*?"

Instead she looked down and continued washing dishes.

I went upstairs and sobbed on my bed. Jobby kept trying to lick my face so much that I had to laugh when he finally had his way. Dogs are the best. They somehow intuit exactly what you need, and they give it to you, no questions asked.

I decided to make-do with a pair of strong rubber bands and strings to attach my body aids to the waist of my pants. The boys finally stopped taunting me. I think they realized that shaming me was causing the other girls to lose interest in them.

Mom never apologized or mentioned our conversation again. Her silence on the matter felt like a complicit approval of how the hearing world had treated me. I wasn't human enough. Wasn't I her daughter?

I began to drift away from her.

I dreamed often of running away. Maybe dropping out of school wouldn't be such a bad idea. It was such a miserable place anyway.

I decided that I would avenge my family with silence. I wouldn't talk much. They never asked what I thought of anything anyway. I would sit there and daydream of my future. I would do my homework and read books and watch TV. I would take Jobby on long walks where there weren't people.

I swore never to be like Mom with my own children. Maybe I'd never bring them to Ironwood. *How about that, Mom?*

The woods across the street became my sanctuary. I lay down on a blanket and looked up into the mottle of leaves above where the sun flickered through. Jobby lay down with his body against mine, but sometimes he suddenly shot up, his ears keening toward a suspicious sound. I never knew what those sounds were, but he never scampered off for a chase. After a few moments he settled down again, and I fell back into my lazy dreaming. There is nothing like the deep sleep of a dog against your body.

In winter, I turned to my notebook and wrote whatever popped into my mind. I had no one to talk to. On the page I held conversations with myself.

When I started attending Ironwood Catholic High School, I didn't need to take the bus anymore. I could easily walk there.

As I watched my siblings move out of the house one by one after graduation, I discovered to my surprise that having fewer people at the dinner table made conversations easier to follow. Even then, that still didn't take away the sting of not being included for so long. My hearing aids had certified me as a non-person. I dreamed again of suicide, the ultimate lesson that my own family would need to *fucking* learn.

Jobby has saved me again and again. He is the closest thing to an angel on this planet. I don't want to think about how much I'm going to miss him for five months. I pray that he'll somehow understand that I will come back in December. In fact, he'd be the only reason why I'd return to Ironwood. The very thought makes me wipe my eyes again. I can't bear to leave him, but I must.

•••

Jobby and I go south on Spruce Street, which is full of potholes and deep creases. The constant batter of winters has made its mark, but having navigated around these dangerous spots with my bicycle, I know all its landmines in the map of my memory. Jobby waggles happily, quickly sniffing here and there to see if he should pee or wait, and gallops after me.

The house on my right is white with a pale tan trim. An older couple lives there, but I don't know their names. They hate it when any of us uses their huge side yard as a diagonal shortcut to our backyard. Their garage is wide enough for two cars, and on one side are a power lathe and an electric saw, and a wall hung with power tools on hooks. The man is always working on a piece of wood. I never see any of his projects come together, and then he is suddenly varnishing and staining a rocking chair or a side table. Their house must be overrun with pieces of wooden furniture. The woman? I have no idea.

Right now, their house is silent with a dim lamp trying to stay awake above their front door. We stroll on by.

•••

My only friend was Mrs. Gates, a speech therapist who dyed her hair a copper red and worked me hard with her lip-reading exercises. She even had me learn how to read lips from the side. She covered her neck with a scarf so I couldn't tell if she was making a "b" or "p" with the movements of her Adam's apple. It was difficult, but she said that I was her best lip reader. She knew that Mom and Dad were against me learning sign language, but she said that when I turned eighteen years old, they couldn't stop me if I wanted to learn it. She was the one who discreetly slid a copy of the Gallaudet College catalog across the table facing me on the second day of my senior year. She mouthed, "Don't tell anyone you got this from me."

I nodded and slipped it into my backpack. There in the privacy of my bedroom I read the entire catalog from cover to cover. Its pictures of deaf students and teachers signing made me tingle all over. The idea of going to a college full of deaf people gave me hope. I never applied anywhere else. Mom and Dad weren't happy that I'd chosen Gallaudet, but I didn't care. I had never felt so elated. I knew I wouldn't miss getting up early to join Mom for the annual three-hour ride to Marquette, where the only audiology clinic in the entire U.P. was, so I could have my hearing tested. As Marquette was the largest city in the U.P., I wondered naturally just how much bigger Washington, D.C. would be. No matter, though, because Gallaudet has a New Signers Program happening three weeks right before the New Student Orientation. They would teach American Sign Language because all of the classes on campus were conducted in ASL. I liked the idea of not having to wait until August to leave for college. *College? Washington, D.C.? Oh, wow. How could anyone* not *go?*

•••

Still on Spruce Street, Jobby and I cross Tamarack Street.

The yellow ranch house on my right has a family of four living there: a short, gnarly-faced man in a white undershirt marked by car grease stains and never without a cigarette perched on his lips, a tall and slender woman with large round curls and glasses, a tall bow-legged boy whose furtive looks at me while he hung out with my brother Louie had always made me wonder if he was attracted to me, and a pretty, short-haired girl with a vivacious smile. Sheila is good friends with Colleen, but I don't really know her family at all. Their brown skin makes them stand out in a town that's all white. Because it's usually difficult to lip read anyone on a pixelated TV screen, I have no idea whether it's acceptable to ask about one's skin color even though I've watched shows like *Good Times* and *What's Happening!!*

And because I can't overhear conversations, it will be years before I learn the names of all those neighborhoods in Ironwood. It turns out that we've been living in the Ashland Location; it'd been named after the mine then in operation. Jobby and I have walked many times through the unkempt property across the street to the edge of a huge cave-in where the water swells. The saplings encircling the cave-in seem to be bystanders, waiting for something to happen. All I know is that a mine had collapsed there, but I wouldn't learn until later that it was the Ashland Mine, the first in Ironwood to go dry back in 1926. The only history I can glean there is the broken cement floor littered with pastel bricks, the only remnants of a building that once housed a shower room for the miners. The land that sits between Bulinski Boulevard and South Lowell Street belongs to the power company on the corner where they've set up fat cement poles and steel beams to hold piles of wooden utility poles. Electricity slithers inside the thick black cables that hang like clotheslines between poles.

I've never given these landmarks a name but I always describe them in this way: the green house on the corner next to the Vega house. The gas station up the street from the *Daily Globe* building. The rundown hotel across the street from the police station. Only a few landmarks have names that everyone uses: the Memorial Building, the Hiawatha, Luther L.

Only recently have I seen Ironwood's future as a quicksand of uncertainty. Growing up, I had never grasped this feeling. I was more concerned with survival of a different kind.

•••

When Jobby and I reach Birch Street, we turn left. The blue and white house on the corner opposite me always stops me as if by instinct. There is a huge pothole right in front where one summer I'd tried to ride across with my bike but flipped over its handlebars only to land on my butt on the gravelly shoulder next to the lawn. A nurse who'd lost her husband to a car accident and her son to a group of bullies happened to see me from her driveway and helped me. Such a nice lady. She knew how to gesture and communicate with me. She must've dealt with many patients who couldn't hear as well.

I stay to the left of the street as I gaze ahead at Norrie School on my far right. A single eye of light glows below its tall and wide chimney and above its sloped parking lot. The building is a monster waiting to awaken. Even though I still have an hour left

before breakfast, I hurry Jobby along until we come to Balsam Street. I glance to my right at the green house in the middle of the block facing the east side of Norrie School. A lone light above the garage door illuminates the black Corvette with flames hand-painted on the side flaring from the wheels. I've always hated the boy who lives in that house. Because Nils lived right across from the school, it was easy for him to hop on his banana bike to chase me and call me names and make fun of my hearing aids. More than once he'd made me cry, and I hated him even more when he laughed at my reaction. For a long time, I stopped riding my bike along Balsam Street. The fact that he didn't attend my school was the best thing about enduring those long days at Ironwood Catholic.

Nils hasn't chased me in a long time, but I give his house the middle finger anyway. I walk over to the front of his house and glance both ways for traffic. No cars. I lean forward and spit over and over again until his Corvette, clearly his pride and joy, is pockmarked with saliva. I suddenly wish I'd thought of bringing a carton of eggs so I could bless his car with my venom. But spit would have to do. I pray again that he rots in Hell. When I realize that once I'm in *Washington, D.C.*—I still can't get over saying the city's name!—I wouldn't have to see him again. I smile.

I look down when Jobby unexpectedly lifts his leg to unleash a fire hose of pee at one of the wheels. I cover my gasps of laughter with my hand, but I don't pull him away. "Good," I say. "Good boy!"

Done, he trots along with me north on Balsam. He seems mighty pleased with himself.

•••

Sometimes I hear a staticky murmur even when my hearing aids aren't turned on. I glance around to see where the noise is coming from, but I inevitably see nothing out of the ordinary. I always think that someone's trying to talk to me, but I see no one. If ghosts do exist, they don't seem to understand that I can't always make out a person's voice unless I can lip read them. Their urgent voices, filled with proclamations and questions, don't sound familiar to me. As I'm not one to read books about the occult, I don't know if I believe in ghosts. Maybe I won't ever hear them again when I leave.

The worst part of today will be leaving Jobby behind. *Five months?* The thought still fills me with dread. I pray that he doesn't die while I'm gone. *No, he can't!*

Yet three years later I will get a letter from Mom saying that he's died of a heat stroke. I will weep for weeks afterward, and then, when the crying jags stop, I will feel his panting breath against my leg. He will be the one to make me believe in ghosts with certainty and carry the weight of all my stories till the day I die.

•••

I don't remember the faces of anyone in these few houses on the next block; surely I'd seen people come and go out of these places. They always seemed mysterious, as if full of secrets. I wonder what their stories are.

When I reach the corner of Tamarack and Balsam, I look up at the wooden building on my left. It used to be a convenience store with a huge table of penny candies, which was very popular with the kids at Norrie. Then one day its glass windows were boarded up and painted over with white. The owner's family still lives above the store, though. I remember the owner's first name: Johnny. I haven't seen him in years. Perhaps he'd died? No one in my family ever tells me anything like that. I usually find out such things years after the fact.

Even if I read the obituaries in the *Daily Globe*, I don't recall the names of my neighbors. Mom has probably told me all their names, but I don't remember them. I need to *see* a name to remember it. People don't understand this about me, how visual I am. I suspect that I'd remember everyone's name once I see it in Sign.

I can't wait. My hands are alive with anticipation.

•••

As Jobby and I walk past the corner of Spruce and Oak, and about to go up the hill to my house, I sense that if I turn my head to my left quickly enough, I'll catch sight of all those doors opening out on the streets everywhere and revealing in a blare of light their silhouettes, outlined by pajamas and nightgowns, waving farewell to me.

Each house I pass in the dark has a story or two. I do not know it yet, but my entire being is slowly awakening to the many stories I do not know about the people I know here in Ironwood. The hours of loneliness spent with my pen on paper are about to turn into a lifetime of stories. The family who should've been mine has long dissipated like dandelion whiskers swept away by wind. I am left with a forlorn stem in my hand.

No one in my family has ever sat me down and explained those stories freely shared in the air around me. I do not know the popular anecdotes about my grandparents, aunts, uncles, and cousins; they're just names and faces to me. The only past I know is the one that I've experienced daily.

I'm so tired of feeling like a vacant motel room. I feel like I have been living out of a suitcase my whole life. Now it's time to pull the zipper shut and check out.

Today I am leaving to find a new family where orphans like me will learn a whole new language and forge a new home in each other's arms. We will create new stories that are clear and easy to follow, and they will be cherished from generation to generation.

That house, intimately familiar as my own body, is not mine. It never was. It is bottled with memories, but I will uncork them one day. They will fizzle like fireworks. I will whittle words out of the pulpy fibers of paper. My pen is the sharpest knife I own.

I will outlive this town.

**Raymond Luczak** grew up in Ironwood and Houghton, Michigan. After living in Washington, D.C. and New York City for over two decades, he now lives in Minneapolis, Minnesota where he is the author and editor of twenty-two books, including *Flannelwood* (Red Hen Press) and *Assembly Required: Notes from a Deaf Gay Life* (Handtype Press). He remains a proud Yooper.

# Coyote Pups

## by David Lehto

Atmospheric conditions in every family are different. Some parents believe in *free range*, others are physical abusers. Some children are put up for adoption, others run away from home.

My three brothers and I had a *"figure it out on your own"* childhood. Dad was always busy doing hard physical labor at his tree removal business, while Mom groomed her cuticles and dreamt of tummy tucks. Dad had one simple rule for the four of us boys: "KEEP YOUR SHIT TOGETHER." Whatever the situation, it was our responsibility. No excuses. It wouldn't have mattered if we were struck by a meteorite coming in from the heavens. He would've said, "What the hell were you thinking, standing in the flight path of a cosmic rock? Don't you know those things can kill you?"

Even as grade schoolers we became remarkably self-sufficient, learning to solve problems on our own. It did no good to cry to Mom and we all knew better than to piss off the old man. We learned to survive like coyotes, creating rules to fit our environment and satisfy Dad, old *Iron Balls*, the brick wall of reality.

One January, the pipes froze at our elementary school, creating an unexpected day off. Mom wasn't used to having us home during the day, so with all of us tearing the place apart, she began to feel the pressure. When Will, who was six and Karl, eight, asked to walk to the convenience store for candy, she quickly gave in. They wanted to bring Mugsy, our little Dachshund, but the idea was quickly shot down. It was only by chance that Mugsy survived as long as he did.

The mid-day temperature was frozen hard around zero. The boys were bundled against the cold, puffed up in their snow suits and as long as they kept moving they'd be fine. If they took the shortcut, which consisted of going through a construction site, cutting across the back of a farmer's field and around a swamp, it was less than a mile to the party store. That's exactly what they did but they never made it.

In the summer, we'd follow a path around the edge of the swamp. But in the winter we'd cut across on the ice, a bad habit we should have never taught Will. Anything his older brothers were doing had to be okay.

An Artesian spring fed the swamp, creating a slightly warmer spot with thin ice. Perhaps attracted by the smother, shinier surface, Will walked onto it, broke through and sank to his chest. The feeling of icy cold water flooding his clothing and stabbing his nerve endings caused him to let out a panicked scream we would've heard if the windows were open. Karl was only twenty feet away when Will went in and acted with surprising common sense for an eight-year old. He found a long branch, slid one end of it out to Will, told him to grab hold, and bracing himself on a patch of frozen cattails, pulled his little brother out. Using a large piece of found cardboard, he dragged him off the ice, across the field, towards the construction site. Will was quickly freezing to the cardboard so Karl forced him onto his feet and ordered him to march home. Will's crying was blurring his vision and with several gallons of water soaked into his clothing he was beginning to stiffen up. But Karl stayed on him and they made it home.

Will was alright once we got the frozen clothing off and wrapped him in warm blankets. Karl, on the other hand, suffered some damage in the ordeal. He'd lost a mitten on the ice, while he was sliding the branch out to Will, and the tips of his fingers were badly frozen. As they thawed the pain was unbearable and he began crying loudly. Mom called Dad, who was across town, ninety feet up an oak tree. Zero degrees Fahrenheit couldn't stop him from working. He was almost indestructible. When he walked in, Karl immediately stopped crying. Karl's hand could've been severed off at the wrist and he would've stopped crying.

But Dad didn't even raise his voice; his mere presence commandeered the situation, like a tough marine sergeant appearing in the thick of battle. Karl was actually glad to see him. And since he brought Will home safely he knew he was in good standing with old *Iron Balls*.

He inspected Karl's hand and said, "It's borderline. Tough it out until morning and I'll look at it again."

Karl never went to the doctor. He lost two fingernails and I remember the skin peeling off the tips of his fingers. But in the long run he was alright and the lesson was never forgotten by my brothers and I: KEEP YOUR SHIT TOGETHER.

# *The Shepherd*

## by David Lehto

We are influenced too heavily by first impressions. I was digging for antique bottles, in a heavily wooded ravine, down the road from my grandmother's house. Long before people became concerned about the environment, before curbside trash pickup, they'd throw their garbage down a hillside behind their farm. To a ten-year-old boy, the possibility of finding a rare, unbroken, antique was like unearthing a cache of money.

Oblivious to my surroundings, except for the growl of an approaching thunderstorm, I concentrated on the hole I was digging. Then I heard a sound like someone dragging their feet, unevenly, through the dry leaves. Scanning the area, seeing nothing, I resumed digging. I figured it was a squirrel or chipmunk foraging for food. The second time I heard it, I spun around and scanned the bushes carefully. Then I saw them. Two sets of eyes will find each other. I was locking vision with what appeared to be a Timber wolf, dried blood caked around its mouth as though having recently gorged itself at a deer kill. It sat, idling in neutral. Partially obscured by the bushes, I couldn't tell if it was in lunging mode. Maybe its stomach was full and it wasn't interested in dining on my organs. It hung its head low as it silently stared at me. I held the shovel in front of me but it felt like having a gun with no bullets. A strong adult might have been able to fend it off with a shovel but I was a skinny, little, runt dripping fear. Then I noticed its right front paw; it was a bony, bloody mess. Clutching the shovel as I backed away, I climbed out of the ravine. The creature stalked me with its uneven stride. Not wanting to turn my back on it or try running, I walked backward down the shoulder of the road towards Grandma's house. It was then that I noticed it was wearing a large choke chain, obscured by its ruffled fur. I climbed the steps to the back porch. The creature surveyed the elevation, then hobbled up, keeping its mangled paw in the air. Being too nervous for rational thinking, I let it follow me into the mudroom. I would have let it follow me into the living room, thinking that Grandma might miraculously defuse the situation.

Grandma was home alone. My three brothers and our Dachshund, Mugsy, had gone to town with our Uncle Henry.

"Nick, is that you?"

"Yes," I answered, entering the kitchen. Just then, the creature made a noise in the mudroom.

"What's that sound?" she asked. "Did you let a *tramp* into the house?"

I pushed open the mudroom door. The creature sat on its haunches, raised its damaged paw and stared at Grandma as though some unseen force had guided it to our door. Grandma returned the stare, her face turning pale, possibly from fear or maybe the animal was stirring some long-ago remembrance. I stared too, but they had forgotten I was in the room. The trance was broken by the sound of Uncle Henry's car pulling up the driveway. The gang unloaded and came barging in.

"Everyone, stay calm," said Grandma. "Injured animals are unpredictable."

Uncle Henry spoke next, "That's Emil Glare's wolf-dog hybrid. She got her foot caught in a coyote trap."

The half-breed panted heavily, as though still tired from trying to chew through the steel jaws, her gums torn raw.

"Emil was going to shoot her," he said. "But when he went inside to get his gun she disappeared."

At that moment, Mugsy wiggled out of Will's arms and darted at the creature. By himself, Mugsy was timid. But when he was with us brothers, his courage elevated, he was anxious to charge into danger. Before anyone could grab him, the two animals examined each other and came to a canine understanding.

"She'll probably wander into the woods and die of gangrene," said Uncle Henry, grabbing her firmly by her choke chain.

"Is she friendly?" asked Jack, my oldest brother.

"I'm not sure," Uncle Henry said. "Emil was training her to be a guard dog. He'd beat her with a steel pipe until she'd fight back."

"Put her outside," said Grandma. "I have to make dinner. And stay away from her. We can't afford a trip to the emergency room."

As he led her out the back door, she let out a throaty moan as though resigning herself to another beating.

That evening, as we ate baked chicken, she sat in a soaking downpour, the pain of gangrene creeping up her leg. Looking out the window, into the backyard, I could see her silhouette through the gray storm. Waiting.

After dinner, when the storm passed, Grandma took a bowl of chicken broth outside. Only giving the creature a sniff, she then led her across the field to Otto Saarinen's place. Otto was a childhood friend of Grandma and Grandpa's. After Grandpa died, they saw more of each other. He was a farm-taught rural doctor, not a doctor of any formal training. His skills were born from the necessities of the Great Depression. He could set a broken bone or stitch up a farm wound.

First, they put drugs in her chicken broth to knock her out. Nothing happened for ten minutes. She went outside and peed. When she came in, she seemed disoriented and soon collapsed on the floor of the shed. Otto, who stood six foot three, could sling a deer carcass over his shoulders while snowshoeing through a mile of swamp, easily cradled her into his arms.

"Come on girl, we have to take off that leg. It's your only chance."

He strapped her to the table and sterilized a hacksaw blade. My brothers and I backed away. We'd seen Grandpa gut a deer, but this animal was still alive. Will and Karl went outside. Jack and I stayed, but I looked away as Otto sawed through the bone. Finally, he cauterized the stub with a torch. The smell of burnt fur was unique and horrible.

He threw the cut-off paw in the trash can.

"If she lives, I'll bring her by in the morning," he said.

Grandma stayed to visit with Otto while we walked home, bubbling with speculation on the creature's chances. Will, the young-

Houghton - Portage Entry Lighthouse

est, didn't think an animal could live if you "sawed her in half."

Grandma named her "Inga," after a great-aunt who had two frostbitten toes amputated with only a slug of whiskey and a rag to bite on. The next morning, Otto brought Inga to the back porch in a wheelbarrow, still groggy from the drugs. She wore a sock on her stub for a bandage. We made a rat's nest from old blankets for her to lie on.

Uncle Henry said, "If she shows any signs of aggression, I'm taking her back to Emil Glare."

She lay there, curled up in her weakened state, for the rest of the day, her black tail carefully covering her paws as if guarding against further amputation.

The next day, I watched Grandma as she sponge-bathed, caressed and sweet-talked the old sock off Inga's stub. At ten years old, I was mostly afraid of carnivores that could eat me.

"Aren't you worried she'll bite you?" I asked.

"I can tell by her muscles and movement that she's relaxed. But when I was younger than you, I got too close to a lame horse. He kicked me and broke my leg. It took many years to overcome my fear."

Over the next few days, with all the excitement surrounding Inga, we neglected our chores. Jack was supposed to cut the grass; he didn't. I was supposed to weed the garden; I hadn't gotten to it. Will and Karl were having a shoving match on the back porch and broke the railing. Grandma never lost her patience. When things got out of control, she simply called Dad.

"Nick, could you come here?" She handed me the phone. When Dad was in work mode at his logging business, he was a machine. He had zero tolerance for our bullshit.

"Did you boneheads forget how to do your chores? Don't make me come out there and jar your memory." He hung up.

Knowing that a forty-mile drive from Houghton wouldn't calm his nerves, I went outside and informed the others. They knew the drill. The lawnmower whirred; I tidied the garden while Will and Karl learned basic carpentry. When I stood up from weeding, I looked around the yard for Mugsy. He was on the porch, in the rat's nest with Inga, napping.

After a week of Grandma changing Inga's sock bandage, it came off permanently. She was hobbling around the yard on three legs.

•••

An old logging railroad used to pass by the village of Nisula. All that was left, in 1984, was a path through the woods. Half a mile down that path was the culvert: a concrete tunnel that carried the creek under the railroad grade and deposited it in a small pond.

One hot July evening, after dinner, my brothers and I decided to go swimming at the culvert. The four of us, along with Mugsy and Inga, her stub fully healed, headed down the railroad grade. We were an odd group: a wiener dog, a wolf and four brothers, having different length legs and varying numbers of them. But soon, we adjusted and fell into a common pace, laughing, throwing things and practicing our swear words.

Just before we reached the culvert, on the north side of the grade, stood an abandoned farm house. The front door was swung open. We had explored it before, with Dad, but were under strict orders not to set foot there without him. "Hobos and prison escapees squat there," he said. Grandma had saved the newspaper clipping. The police had recaptured a violent felon, escaped from the Marquette prison, who had been hiding in the house.

When we reached the culvert everyone dove in, and even Inga got her paws wet. After forty-five minutes, Jack got out and started drying off.

"Come on, you guys; we've got to head back."

As we waded to shore, Karl asked, "Where's Mugsy?" We scanned the area.

*Gone.*

"When was the last time anyone saw him?" I asked, knowing that Mugsy didn't like to swim. If I set him in the water he'd immediately dog-paddle to shore.

"He was with us on the railroad path," said Will.

We began yelling, "MUGSY!" expecting to see him emerging from under the ferns. He

was a small dog at only thirteen pounds. After a few minutes of unorganized shouting, Jack commandeered the situation.

"Everyone, spread out and look for him, but meet back here in ten minutes. I'll catch hell if I lose one of you."

We waded through the ferns into the deeper woods, calling, "MUGSY." Nothing. Ten minutes later I heard Jack calling us back.

"It's going to be dark soon," he said. "We have to go back and get Uncle Henry and some flashlights."

Then Karl spoke, "Where's Inga?" We looked around. Vanished.

"Maybe they walked home," said Will.

"MUGSY! INGA!" we called, as we hurried along the path.

By the time we burst in the back door it was dark. We rousted Uncle Henry and pleaded to go back with flashlights.

"That's a half mile into the deep woods," he said. "We'll have to wait until morning."

"Can't we go back and leave some food and blankets?" I begged. "Mugsy has never slept outside."

"That'll attract predators," he responded.

I would have cried myself to sleep but I couldn't sleep. Why hadn't Mugsy come when we called him? Did he step in a trap, like Inga? He'd be dead by morning. Leg traps were in common use. Uncle Henry had warned us, "If you see a bright colored rag tied to a bush, stay away! There's a trap set nearby."

Grandpa's old traps still hung in the barn. The largest, a bear trap, required two men to step on the steel springs to set the jaws. One day, to teach us respect, he stuck a 2x4 in the bear trap. The crushing snap of the jaws almost broke it in half. Scale-wise, a coyote trap would do the same thing to Mugsy.

And what about Inga? Why did she wander off? She could survive a night in the woods. But Mugsy, accustomed to the warm blankets of my bed, was a wimp. A helpless, lost lamb. Coyote bait. A swarm of mosquitos could take him down.

Jack and I were up at 5:00 a.m. and woke Karl and Will. It was getting lighter as we hurried down the railroad path. Nearing the culvert we called out, "MUGSY! INGA!"

We paused in front of the abandoned farm house, remembering Dad's strict warning not to set foot there without him. The front door was now closed. Was someone inside? Dogs don't close doors. I clutched the flashlight in my hand expecting to flail at a mutated, wolf-man, prison escapee, dog-eater, hobo charging out the front door. Jack refocused my attention by pointing at the ground in front of his feet.

"That's fresh coyote shit," he said. Grandpa had always called it coyote scat.

Reality was settling in; there had been predators in the area. Ugly possibilities began creeping into my brain; I wondered how we'd find Mugsy's remains. I was the one who had pleaded for a dog. My parents let me get Mugsy only after I'd made a stack of promises to be responsible for him. Losing him in the woods, to wild animals, wasn't being responsible; Dad wouldn't care what the excuse was. We were all in for some schooling but the brunt of it would come down on me. At that moment, though, punishment took a back seat to losing my best friend.

All of a sudden Inga appeared from the backyard.

"Here, Inga! Here, girl!" we called, excitedly. She sat by the back corner of the house, refusing to move. Dad's stern ruling was holding us in place on the railroad grade. But then, when she wouldn't budge, Jack broke ranks and started walking toward her.

"I'll justify it to Dad," he said, as they both disappeared into the backyard.

I began to think we were in a horror movie where everyone disappears one at a time but the next moment he called out, "I found Mugsy!"

Instantly forgetting Dad's rule, we bolted around the side of the house. We found Jack kneeling by a shallow hole. Had someone killed Mugsy and attempted to bury him? I raced to the edge of the hole. It was a collapsed root cellar; used by early settlers to store food before refrigeration. Only a few feet deep, the partially caved-in hole was no threat to humans but to Mugsy, it was a dungeon. Probably on the scent of a field mouse when he fell in; he was shivering and whimpering as Jack lifted him out. There

was a circle of grass, pressed down next to the hole, where Inga had spent the night.

Will had his pockets full of dog food. Mugsy almost toppled him over trying to get it. Inga waited her turn. We stopped at the creek so they could lap up water. Karl had to help Will scrape coyote shit off his shoe.

Mugsy didn't walk much on the way home; we fought over who got to carry him. It went down the pecking order. He got handed to Will as we were walking in the back door.

We imagined how Inga faced down predators protecting Mugsy. Most of the animal kingdom was present. We'll never know for sure what dangerous animals approached them. There were definitely coyotes in the area that night and Inga's presence certainly gave Mugsy a sense of security and hope.

After that, Grandma let Inga sleep in the mudroom. We moved her rat's nest indoors. Will and Karl dismantled the fort they were building and pounded it into something barely resembling a doggie bed. They bent the nails over so Inga wouldn't get poked. I'm sure Uncle Henry broke it up for kindling after we left.

At summer's end, we moved back to town. Inga was still with Grandma the next summer; and the summer after. When we returned, she remembered us like long missing pals. I can still picture her three-legged gait as she hobbled alongside us, exploring the woods of our youth.

Grandma, Inga and Mugsy are gone now, though the lessons I learned from them are still knocking over dominos to this day. Our family still owns the house. I feel their presence when I walk the property. If any creature had spirit, Inga did. She's hobbling the grounds around Grandma's house, protecting her.

**Dave Lehto** was born and raised in the Copper Country, where he vacations every year. Though he is currently a licensed builder and artist in Traverse City, his passion is writing about adventures in the Upper Peninsula.

# U.P. Summers Are For the Bugs

## by Tamara Lauder

The winter is long, the color is white,
So summer's green is a welcome sight.
The sun shines bright, the water is blue,
Lake Superior creates a glorious view.

Winter, Spring, Summer, Fall,
Four seasons familiar to us all.
But the U.P. summers offer something more,
Each summer season has bugs galore.

I wake up early, I stay up late,
For morning coffee I don't hesitate.
But there's a mosquito in my coffee pot,
I sure don't want to drink a lot.

I go outside to get some sun,
But the deer flies have me on the run.
The mowers broke, the grass is high,
The ticks begin to multiply.

Superior View by Tamara Lauder

3/100          "Superior View"          © 2006 Lauder

Then clouds roll in, it smells like rain,
The black flies bite and cause me pain.
As I swat the black incessant pests,
A horsefly flies inside my vest.

All their sounds are like a requiem,
A procession for the noseeum.
Who bites so inconspicuously,
A bite that grows enormously.

While there are probably more I missed,
I did my best with this bug list.
An early freeze will zap the pests,
But fall colors just invite more guests.

I love the summer all in all,
But really I can't wait for fall.
While I make it sound like misery,
The U.P. is the best to me.

**Tamara Lauder** has been a frequent visitor of the Keweenaw Peninsula for over thirty years where she spends time with family and in the outdoors. Tamara works as a professional artist in the Northwoods of Wisconsin, but also has a passion for writing. She writes creative non-fiction, short stories, inspirational, and informational pieces which she often combines with her artwork. She is the author and illustrator of an inspirational pictorial book, and most recently, won the 2019 Houghton Selected Shorts Story Contest performed at the Rozsa Center at Michigan Tech University.

# Muses from a Deer Shack Morning

## by Chris Kent

Inky as a darkened cave the morning copse,
still sheltered by the towering tops.
Dawn cautiously eases through tenebrous wood,
exposing the contents of a stilly forest hood.
First, tree tops illuminated with ardent light,
leisurely erase the ebony of night.
Tacitly slipping down towering trees,
the aurora reaches its fingers through dry leaves.
Ever so gradually, unhurriedly waking,
first light just now breaking.
Mysterious shapes materialized.
Phantasm of the glade surely realized.
A wendigo, ogre, a nymph and specter,
the wraith following the fearless shape-shifter.
On the hillside trunks of sturdy trees,
their slender arms reach up with ease.
Brushy tentacles slowly emerging,
throughout the lowland ever surging.

Ghostly, sinister figures crawling,
along the moonless ground forever sprawling.
Soon exposed as mossy boulders,
when dawns light reaches earth's strong shoulders.
The snow white form of stately birch,
graceful trunk, arrow-like limbs upwardly search.
Sparse dry leaves stubbornly clinging,
in the morning zephyr, quaking.
Next the aspens, near a bend,
appear stalwart marching to the end,
as ranks of hardy warriors
without fear of battle's horrors.
And after that the shadowy maples,
barely visible, leisurely amble.
Then at last the sun's glow creeps ever so slight
cloaking all forest demons in fervid light,
ceasing their devouring might,
ending the reign of terror for the night.

**Chris Kent** and her husband moved to a remote area in the Upper Peninsula where they live with their two horses and a German shorthair after retiring from a career in marketing and public relations,. Chris belongs to a group of north woods writers and has been published in Equus Magazine, and an anthology of horse stories, "The Horse of My Dreams". She enjoys gardening, making maple syrup, raising bees, travel, riding horseback and volunteering in the community. Sharing a love of nature and animals is a highlight when children and grandchildren visit.

# Katie: Purity

## by Sharon Kennedy

Tuesday, August 11, 1959 11:55 p.m.

*Gray kittens everywhere, little open mouths covering tiny faces, crying for help that does not come. Suffocating darkness enclosing burning hot August sun. Running, flinging aside white screen doors, searching empty houses. Blue Easter eggs growing eyes, cracking, crying. Jesus hanging on a chocolate cross, blowing bubbles through a yellow straw. April water burying Blew. Blew waving just before going under. Great big teeth smiling, falling, scattering among pieces of ice. Screaming, hopping, disappearing on ice too thin to hold him.*

"Katie, wake up, wake up." I hear a gentle, sweet voice calling my name.

*A brown rubber boot. A rosary. A black-robed priest. Coffin dropping, disappearing, down, down, far from my reach. Gray closed eyes, gray sky, gray face grazed by ice. Black veils. Purple light shining through stained glass Catholic windows. Barbed wire necklace, ripping flesh. Standing, swaying on shore too far to reach. Sharp, chunky ice. Mud everywhere.*

In the distance, as if miles and miles away, as if in heaven or some other faraway place I've never heard of, I hear the whisper of Mama's voice. "Wake up," she says. "It's just a bad dream," but I can't get away from the nightmare. I want her to hold me and help me, but I can't reach her. I feel her presence, but not her touch, her warmth. Her voice surrounds me like heavy velvet, like a rich, soft fabric that's warm and inviting me to curl up in the safety and security of its folds.

*Blew surfacing, slapping wheels on church floor, cart wheeling Blew to altar. Bach's Requiem Mass. Suckers growing hands, clap-ping, cheering, opening wide mouths, receiving Blew. Red nails pulling from the hands of Christ, scratching your face, my face. Running, I outrun you running past me, heading for the thick woods behind our barn and the river behind the woods. River silently gathering strength, pulling you, leaving me alone as they lower the lid and you're gone. Gray newborns crying until silenced by the quick thrust of Papa's thumb to their throats, silencing them just like the river silenced you.*

"Mama, help me. Mama."

"Wake up, Katie. Wake up, honey. I'm right here. You're safe."

*You did it on purpose, didn't you? You wanted to go, to see what's on the other side.*

"Mama, Blew. Come back."

*To see if God is real or make-believe like we figured. Coward. 'Fraidy cat. I hate you, I hate you, I hate you, but now that you're gone...*

"Katie, wake up. You must wake up."

*What will I do without you?*

Mama's voice surrounds me, penetrating my ears, my body, wrapping around my soul like cotton candy. Now I feel the warmth of her arms as she holds me against her chest. "There, there," she says. "It was another bad dream. It wasn't real." Her voice is soft as yellow butter spreading across a piece of warm bread. Her voice is calm as the seas must have calmed when Jesus ordered them to be still. I breathe in her beauty, her strength. As she cradles me in her arms, I sink deep into her bosom.

I love her so much it hurts. She's the most beautiful person I know. She's tall and thin and strong. Her hair is the color of chestnuts, her complexion the color of a soft, pink rose.

Her eyes are the color of new leaves on a maple tree. She smells the way the earth smells after a gentle spring rain. She smells like the first winter snowflakes falling to the ground. She smells the way I imagine heaven must smell, sweet like a Cadbury Caramello candy bar.

"When I was young," Mama says as she rocks me, "I dreamed about our bull. He was chasing me until I flew into the haymow where I was safe. I used to have that dream all the time. Then one night I dreamed he sprouted wings and followed me into the mow. I awoke just before he tore me apart with his sharp horns. I was terrified, but there was no one to comfort me. I'm here for you, Katie. I'll always be here for you."

"Do you still have that dream?" I ask, snuggling closer to her.

"No, dear, that dream went away when I married your papa." Her voice is soft as a cotton ball, as gentle as a calm Lake Superior wave lapping the sandy shore at sunset.

With the tenderness of releasing a new born baby, Mama releases her hold on me, lightly touches my face, swirls her fingertips around the freckles dotting my nose and cheeks. She holds my brown braids, then lets them fall, and cups my face in her hands. My aqua eyes stare into her green ones. I want to tell her how much I need her, but I don't say anything because that's the way it is in our family. We don't tell each other anything of any importance. We talk about the weather or the price of cattle or getting the hay in before rain comes or how much it will cost for new school clothes, but we never, never talk about what's in our heart, maybe because if we ever told each other how we feel, really feel, we wouldn't be able to face each other ever again and that would be worse than keeping quiet. Maybe all families are like ours, I don't know.

"Stay with me until I fall asleep, but leave the light on," I ask. Mama pulls back the covers and crawls in next to me. She puts her arms around me, and we're like two matching spoons. I feel safe and secure, like nothing in the world can hurt me or take away the people I love most.

"I'm afraid of God," I hear my voice say in a quiet, even tone. "I'm afraid because I hate Him, and I know if I die with the sin of hate on my soul I'll go to hell." I start to cry. "I don't want to hate Him, but He let me down so bad I don't know what else to do." I choke out the words. Mama's grip tightens around me. Her voice is even softer than before, soft as a smooth stone that's been rubbed and rubbed until all its sharpness has vanished.

"I understand," she says.

"How can you?" I ask. "You're always talking to God as if He were standing right next to you."

"Do you want to know something, Katie?" Mama asks and her voice is different, stronger. It's a voice I haven't heard before. I stop whimpering and listen. "I know how you feel," she says. "Because sometimes I hate God too. Sometimes I hate Him so much I want to scream and scream until I have no voice. I hate Him because he won't answer my prayers the way I want. That's why I pray all the time. I keep hoping He will hear me."

I can't believe my ears. Mama hates God. I don't believe it. I turn around and look at her. "What do you pray for?" I ask.

"I pray to die," she says. "I ask God to take me." She says the words as simply and matter-of-factly as if she were telling me to bring in an armload of wood.

A feeling of horror comes over me. I don't know what to say. I'm twelve years old and the dearest person in my world has just told me she prays to die. "Don't say that, Mama," I plead. I touch her face and feel tears on her cheeks. She speaks and her voice is once again as soft as a new flannel blanket, soft as the down on a newly hatched chick. "Go to sleep," she says. "Forget what I said. I didn't mean it. God is good. He understands."

"Do you love me?" I ask.

"Yes, Katie, you and May Beth are my reasons for living."

"What about Papa?" Mama is silent for what seems like a long time but is probably only a few seconds. "Yes, I love your papa," she finally says. "Now go to sleep." I look at her eyes as tears blur them. "It's okay," I say. "I'll be okay."

She stays for a long time, then kisses my head and leaves the bed. Before she slips through the curtains that act as my bed-

Hancock - Quincy Street 1900

room door, I turn and watch her watching me. She smiles and pulls the string to the overhead light.

Soft moonlight replaces the bright glow from the light bulb. *Come back,* I want to call, but I don't. Instead, I put the pillow over my head and cry, not sissy tears, but great big quiet ones that make my stomach hurt and my throat ache. I cry because I couldn't save my cousin, Blew, and when I think about the future, the years stretch before me like a long rubber band that just keeps stretching and stretching with no end in sight. I see myself alone for the rest of my life. I wish I hadn't watched Blew die. I wish I had jumped in the river and went down with him. Now I'd be sleeping in the graveyard next to him instead of in my bed where nightmares come every time I close my eyes.

I take a deep breath and shudder. I see Blew. He's all around me like mist coming off the river on a foggy morning, but like va-por, I can't touch him. He surrounds my bed, and his face is the one I remember—wavy yellow hair falling over his forehead, brown eyes—a little crossed, but beautiful just the same—coaxing me into doing something I don't want to do, nostrils large enough to sail a ship through, straight white teeth grinning as he tells me a tall tale. Blew was a liar; I knew that, but it didn't matter. He had to make up a pretend life because he couldn't stand the one he was given. Cousin Sally was only fifteen when she had Blew and wouldn't tell who fathered him, so he didn't know who he was. She left when he was an infant. She didn't want him.

Aunt Rene and Uncle Johnny raised him. When Blew did or said something that was the opposite way a Greene would act, they said it was the bastard blood coming out of him, and Uncle Johnny would beat Blew. He'd take him to the barn and whip him with his belt. Blew told me his butt was harder than Star's leather harness. When he was little, he cried, but after a while he got used to the beatings. He told me sometimes he did things on purpose just to get his grandpa mad. Uncle Johnny's a religious nut—he quotes the Bible all the time—and once Blew learned the word *hypocrite,* that's what he called him. Uncle Johnny thought he could beat the devil out of Blew, but nobody could do that. You can't beat something out of someone that's not in them in the first place. People can't stop being who they are any more than a cow can stop being a cow or a bird a bird.

I feel myself nodding off again. I drift in and out of dreams—*I see purple grapes all over the ground. People are picking them from the vines Uncle Johnny planted along the barbed wire fence in the field where he used to pasture his Jerseys. I see the apple orchard behind the barn. Pink apple blossoms drift to the ground on the wings of a warm breeze. I hear crows call as they fly low to the ground, looking for supper. I see strands of scarlet and blue sky framing the setting sun. I'm in Blew's kitchen now. I see the honey stained cupboards, the cracked china pitcher that holds kitchen utensils. I see the box full of neatly chopped white birch waiting for the fire, the white farmhouse table with the stained yellow oilcloth covering its wooden plank top, the yellow granite pails that hold the drinking water, the washstand where Blew scrubs his face every morning. I see clay pots of green ivy circling the kitchen windows. I see closed windows with clean yellow curtains hanging stiffly from their rods, like soldiers in a line. I smell smoke from the woodstove.*

I feel myself shaking awake, but I'm not crying so Mama doesn't come running. I can't stop thinking about Blew and how he died. We had walked down the road to the river to fish for suckers. Everybody told us not to go because the river was too high and it was dangerous, but we didn't listen. Blew was acting silly like he always did. He said he had magical powers and had taught himself to fly by jumping off the barn roof and flapping his elbows like a Rhode Island Red rooster. He said he could fly anywhere.

I pointed to a big piece of ice floating by and told him to prove it by flying there and back again. Before I knew it, he had jumped on the ice. It drifted farther down the river. I yelled at him to come back, but he only laughed and waved. The current was swift, the chunk broke apart, and he went under.

I didn't know what to do. I screamed at him to swim to shore, but he didn't. He just kept moving away from me. I was running along the bank, but there was so much water and snow and big pieces of ice and heavy brush, I couldn't help him. He yelled at me. *"Tell Grandpa I'm getting born again and I'm on my way to heaven where there ain't no belts and there ain't no hypocrites."* I watched as the current pulled him farther from me. Then I realized he wasn't trying to get out. He was floating face up while his clothes filled with water. His Davy Crockett cap drifted upside-down ahead of him. He disappeared beneath the ice, popped up once, and then he was gone. The next time I saw him was at the funeral parlor.

*I smell fresh white bread as Aunt Rene lifts it from the oven. I see her slicing thick chunks for Blew and me. He dips his knife into the butter bowl, scoops some out, slathers it across the heel of the hot bread. We watch it melt into the crust. Then I leave the kitchen and float through the rooms, through the upstairs, touching Blew's old iron bed, his Circus Boy books, his slingshot. I see Utah, his mongrel dog, waiting on Blew's bed, waiting for his master's return.*

I feel a cool hand on my forehead, soothing, stroking, kind. My hand? Blew's? God's? Mama's? Whoever you are, you do love me, don't you? You really, truly love me. You forgive me. I feel the tension leave my body, replaced by a peaceful, loving spirit. Whoever is beside me loves me, forgives my sins real or imagined. A blanket of peace enfolds me.

From far, far away I hear a voice as sweet as honey, as soft as a kitten, as gentle as a warm summer breeze. I feel strong arms surround me. "I'm here, Katie," Mama whispers.

A picture of the Pieta drifts through my mind.

# Quiet Times

## by Sharon Kennedy

No matter how hard Sara tries, she cannot bring herself to love Mother, and although Sara will never admit it, she refers to Mother as The Corpse. *The Corpse moved today,* Sara says to the bathroom mirror, or *The Corpse needs a bath.* Sometimes Sara forgets to say things in her head and words tumble from her mouth—words not intended for Mother's ears. *The Corpse eats like a horse* is overheard by Mother one bright, cold October morning as Sara prepares breakfast.

"Who are you talking to?" Mother demands. "Me or the dog?"

"I'm talking to myself," Sara answers. She turns the bacon, butters the toast, mixes a little water with the eggs, and scrambles them in a Teflon pan, adding sea salt and cracked pepper. She's angry Mother overheard her private conversation. Sara must be more careful in her musings.

"I heard you mention something about horses. When did we get horses?" Mother leaves the comfort of her recliner and hobbles to the yellow kitchen. She takes her place at the table and begins straightening the green plastic tablecloth. She brushes imaginary crumbs to the floor.

"Never mind fixing anything for me," she says. "I have no appetite. Just tea and toast will be fine. Now, tell me about the horses."

Sara's back bristles. "I never mentioned horses. They've been dead and gone for sixty years." Sara sets a full plate before Mother, but she pushes it away. "No need for all this

fuss," she says. "Are you feeding an army or is there a man coming over?"

Mother's green eyes look quizzically over the top of her black rimmed glasses. Her tiny chin tucks into the collar of her pink pajama top. Her lips form a circle around her mouth making the lines and wrinkles appear like spokes on a wheel. She sits patiently, ignoring the food and tearing a napkin into little strips. Sara thinks she's waiting for her to react, much as a cat plays with a mouse before it eats it. Sara won't disappoint her.

"A man coming over?" she yells. "When in hell's name would I have time for a man? And who the hell wants a sixty-three year old woman whose life revolves around her mother, the cat, the dog, and this stinking house?" Sara feels the tension in her side move from her heart, down through her left arm. It's the same every day. Sometimes the tension is only relieved by putting her foot through a cabinet door or by digging her nails into her palms until they bleed or by slapping her face. Mother still has the power to break Sara with a glance or a phrase or to remind her she will be alone when Mother dies. She knows this, and her daily chant is, *Please, God, please let my heart attack come today, but only if it's fatal.* Sara does not love Mother but has no idea how to live without her, thus the prayer to a God she no longer believes in to solve all her problems by the lethal stopping of her heart.

"Now, now, Kate," Mother says, calling Sara by her dead sister's name. "I don't know why you're all riled up. You don't have to live here, you know. I can manage without you." Mother sprinkles salt and pepper over her eggs and stirs more sugar into her coffee. Sara cuts the bacon into little pieces so it's easy for Mother to push the morsels onto the spoon she always uses in place of a fork. She provides Mother with two spoons. One for her drink and one for the main meal. Three are provided when there is dessert. Sara takes her coffee and a piece of toast into the living room. The thought of eating at the table with Mother is repulsive.

*She's only a dressed up corpse waiting for the undertaker. She serves no purpose,* Sara thinks. *Will I end up like her?* As Sara drinks her coffee, she looks around the living room. Although the house is old, it's well kept. The beige carpet is new. Bookcases are filled with nicely bound books, clocks, knickknacks, and pictures of dead relatives. Lacy, cream-colored curtains peek from behind gold colored drapes. Pretty pictures of outdoor scenes and cattle drinking from a stream cover the walls. The only ugly thing in the room is Mother's twenty-year-old plaid recliner. She has not slept in her bedroom since Father died, fifteen years ago, so the recliner is her adjustable bed. That's what Mother calls it. It pleases her to recline at will or sit upright. Throughout the day, she fiddles with the electric controls as if they were a toy.

No one visits the women or knows the extent of Mother's dementia or Sara's frustration, loneliness, and fears. Nobody knows what their lives are like behind the façade of the quiet white farmhouse with the lovely summer rose garden and the congregation of winter chickadees at the birdfeeders. The morbid banality of their lives is too pathetic for Sara to share. Even if she wanted to, she has no friends, no companions or siblings to offer respite from her role as caregiver, but she has her books. Sometimes they're enough. Sometimes nothing is.

She watches Mother eat. It takes a long time for her to position the food just right on the spoon, then it takes even longer for the spoon to make the trip from her plate to her mouth. Then the chewing process begins. Sometimes Mother bites into something dis-

agreeable and places a finger in her mouth until the irritant is removed and deposited into a Kleenex. A breakfast of cereal lasts forty minutes. One of today's proportions will last at least ninety. *The Corpse has an amazing capacity for food,* Sara thinks. *Maybe she's getting ready to die. Maybe that's why the ancients put food in the tombs of the dead. Maybe there's no kitchen in the afterlife.* Sara watches Mother dunk toast into her coffee. Mother likes soft food. If something isn't soft enough, it's put on a spoon and dunked in whatever liquid is present—water, coffee, tea, milk, juice, soup—it doesn't matter. A chocolate chip cookie can just as easily get a bath in tomato soup as in a glass of milk. *The Corpse is insane,* thinks Sara. *Or maybe The Corpse is normal, and I'm the one who's losing her mind.*

"My tea's cold," Mother remarks. "And Fuzzy wants out. You know she's going to have kittens any day now. I'll have to find a box for her." Sara gulps the remainder of her coffee. The reference to the cat is her cue. Mother never directly asks for anything. Her requests are disguised as comments or questions: "Do you want out, Lard?" means, "Sara, put the dog out." "Are you hungry, Fuzzy?" means "Sara, feed the cat." "I haven't eaten all day, all week as a matter of fact," means Mother is ready for another meal. "Ma's alone at home," means Mother is going to cry over the loss of her long-dead mother. "I'm going to see my dear sweet mother this afternoon," means Mother will try to escape from the house and walk across the road to the house she was born in and in which both her parents and two little brothers died. Sara puts her dishes in the sink and opens the door for the cat.

"Why did you put Fuzzy out?" Mother yells. "She's my friend."

Sara stands on the cold back porch and grips the green railing. She looks at the naked autumn trees, at the branches of the old tamarack that reach like a thousand fingers coming at her. She looks at the plastic white chairs shrouded in a blue tarp against the snow that is yet to come. She looks at the cat stretching, snatching a bit of sunlight streaming through the bare branches of the silver maple. She looks at the gravel running north and south from one end of the road to the other, a road she's known all her life, the one she traveled to get away from home and the one that brought her back. Something snaps in Sara as it always does when she looks at her familiar surroundings.

She begins to cry. She cries because she's tired and lonely and isolated and terrified Mother will die and she will be an orphan. She cries because an orphan at her age isn't an orphan at all, just a spinster. She cries until Fuzzy runs from her and the chickadees at the feeders fly away. She cries because her life is one long endless thread unraveling from an endless spool that keeps spinning and spinning until her head whirls, somersaulting from the absurdity of her existence. From within the house, the dog barks. Mother flings open the door.

"Who the hell's yelling out here?" she asks. "Who the hell are you? Where'd you come from? What the hell are you doing on my porch?" Mother holds an orange broom handle in her right hand and strikes Sara. "Git," she yells. "Get off my porch and off my land. Git." Mother is eighty-five and looks frail, but she is strong and determined. The broom handle clips Sara's right shoulder and pain runs down her back.

*I'm going to kill The Corpse,* she thinks. *I'm going to wrap my hands around her scrawny neck and strangle the life out of her. Then I'm going to drag her to the garage, bury her underneath a pile of wood, and forget she ever existed. No one will ever know because no one ever visits. I'll get away with murder, but I won't tell the government, so Mother's monthly checks will keep rolling in. I'll spend every penny at the casino. I'll play the slots, and in return, they'll teach me how to live, how to manipulate them into submission so the icons all line up and make me a winner. People will stand behind me and beside me, cheering me on as the machine spits out money, piles and piles of money. The dismal life I'm leading will only be a hazy memory, a dream—something unreal, distant, foreign, faded and forgotten with time when I'm rich and beautiful and loved.*

"I said git," Mother repeats. "Git or I'll get the shotgun."

Sara jerks to attention. She screams at Mother. She calls her every foul name she knows. She curses her for not being the mother she needs. She tells Mother she wants her to die. "I'll gladly dance on your grave," she screams. "I hate you. Why won't you die? Why? Why won't you let me live? Why? Why?" Words flow out of her mouth like vomit. Sara puts all her anger, frustration, fear, and heartache into them.

"Oh, go to hell," Mother replies as calmly as if Sara has not spoken. "If you don't like it here, move on. I don't need you." Mother throws the broomstick down the porch steps. "I'm going to fix myself some food. I haven't eaten in three days."

Sara sits on the bottom step and muses at the unfairness of fate. First it took Father, a loving, kind man who treated Sara like a queen. She sees his face in the clouds and hears his gentle voice as he teases her about a beau. He wanted her to marry a farmer. Sara wanted a professor, but she ended up with neither. Too stubborn for the former. Too stupid for the latter. She hears Mother fiddling with the woodstove Father installed a month before he died. She goes back inside before Mother sets the house ablaze.

"Well, hello there. Where'd you come from?" Mother's voice is sweet as honey. "How about a nice cup of tea?" She pours tap water into two cracked cups and reaches for a three-day old shriveled and useless tea bag. "How about a nice piece of toast?" She puts two slices of bread into the toaster and soon they are black as tar. A blue haze hangs over the room. "I'll just scrape these a little, and they'll be fine," she says. "Good as new, don't you think? By the way, what'd you say your name is?"

"My name is Sara, Mother. I'm your daughter." The silent defeat in Sara's voice is deafening.

"Oh, no, you're mistaken. My daughter, Kate, died years ago. She didn't like the farm so she left and never came back. Spoiled brat, she was. Toast is ready."

Ironwood - loaded mine cars and miners

Sara slumps in the kitchen chair. Mother sits at the table. "Well, what do you know," she says. "Somebody left a big plate of potatoes and bacon and eggs at my place." She uses the bacon to push a piece of egg onto her spoon. "Say, that's pretty good. Cold, but good. Here, have some." With her fingers, she picks up a piece of bacon and little bits of scrambled egg and deposits them alongside the black toast on Sara's plate. "Eat up," Mother says. "You never know when you'll get another meal. By the way, who are you?"

Unable to fully grasp the intricate channels of dementia, Sara often thinks Mother plays games to see how far she can push Sara into her world. If so, it's working. Sara sees herself adjusting to Mother's way of life. What *is* the point of bathing every day? Who *cares* if you wear the same clothes for three weeks? What *difference* will it make to anyone if the day is Sunday or Wednesday or Thursday? Who *knows* if it's 5:00 a.m.? It might really be noon. Sara is beginning to think like Mother. She's beginning to understand Mother's world. It's beginning to make sense to her, and that's what scares her more than anything.

They stay at the table for a long time, but they don't talk. Sara wonders how long it will be before Mother dies and Sara loses her mind. She wonders how many years will pass before some stranger will care for her. She envisions it now. She'll be sitting in Mother's old rocker-recliner, reading the same newspaper for days on end, dipping a windmill cookie into a bowl of chili, and telling the caregiver the spayed cat's due to have kittens and she must find a box for her. She knows what the caregiver will say.

*The Corpse is at it again,* she'll say. Then she'll tell her friends about Sara and they'll all have a good laugh. *You won't believe what The Corpse did today. She put her teeth in the sink, and there they were, grinning at me as if they were privy to some joke, and the joke was on me. When The Corpse found them, she showed them to me.* "These yours?" she asked. "You look like you could use a new set. It sure would be nice to have a cup of tea and a piece of toast. 'Course, I wouldn't want to take you from your TV show or trouble you in any way." *Then The Corpse pinched me as she hobbled away. Tomorrow I'm handing in my notice. She belongs in a home with people just like her.*

Sara rouses herself and looks at Mother. She struggles to make sense of things. Corpses don't have appetites, she thinks. They don't wear colorful mismatched clothes, and they don't paint their fingernails bright red and hit people with orange broomsticks. They don't worry about dogs or cats that need a box for their kittens. They don't read newspapers or sleep on adjustable fabric chairs. They don't hobble about, talking to themselves or worrying that the old maple outside the west window might fall down with the next strong wind or the water pipes might freeze and burst on a cold winter night. They don't dust clean furniture or straighten a drape or shake a curtain. And they certainly do not cry.

"My cup's empty," Mother says. Sara ignores the coffee pot and puts water in the tea kettle. When the whistle sings, she takes a fresh Lipton tea bag from the canister and puts it in a fancy Royal Albert china cup. She pours hot water over it. Mother always did prefer china cups to ceramic coffee mugs. Sara makes a fresh piece of toast and spreads butter and strawberry jam on it.

"I'll never eat all this," Mother says. "Here, you have some." She breaks the toast in half and pushes it towards Sara. "I don't know who you are, but you're a nice girl," she says. "I'm glad you're here. I'd be lost without you." Tears cloud her eyes as she kisses Sara's hand.

Sara turns from Mother, leaves the table, and looks out the kitchen window. What meets her eyes is no Currier and Ives scene. The old barn is in various stages of neglect and decay, and the roof of the chicken coop collapsed on itself years ago. The red shed, where Father spent many hours working on his tractor and forging scrap iron into strangely shaped lawn ornaments, lists like a drunken sailor. The outhouse took its bow seven years ago. Loose tar paper flaps from the pump house roof. Sara sees rusty combines, broken hay wagons, toothless iron rakes, busted ploughs, and bits and pieces of useless farm machinery scattered around the back yard. The lush pastures of her youth are filled with weeds, scrub trees, wildflowers, red pines, spruce trees, and hundreds of tamaracks. In the spring when the snow melts, everything looks shabby and forlorn. Sara is glad Mother never goes outside. Better to remember the farm as it was when she was a young wife and kept things neat and tidy, working from sunup to sundown both inside and out. Better not to see the devastation time and widowhood have wrought. Better to stay in the house and forget all the memories outside the window.

A few snowflakes begin falling. The cat cries to come in. Chickadees fight over the last chunk of suet hanging from a tamarack branch. A squirrel dangles upside down as he steals sunflower seeds from the birdfeeder. Sara turns from the window and stares at the back of Mother's head. Tears fill her eyes as a wave of tenderness overcomes her.

*She isn't a corpse yet*, she thinks. *She's my mother.*

**Sharon Kennedy** writes a newspaper column that runs twice a week in the *Sault News*. She's a monthly contributor to the *Mackinac Journal* where she recalls memories from her childhood in "View from the Sideroad." She also writes feature pieces about interesting people. *Senior Wire* based in Denver continues to carry her work. Sharon can be reached at sharonkennedy1947@gmail.com.

# Discover Hidden Campgrounds, Natural Wonders, and Waterways of the Upper Peninsula

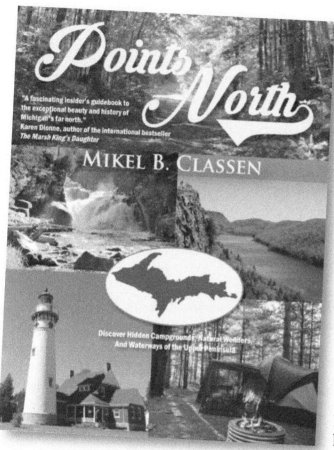

This book has been a labor of love that spans many years. The love is for Michigan's Upper Peninsula (U.P.), its places and people. I've spent many years exploring the wilderness of the U.P., and one thing has become apparent. No matter what part you find yourself in, fascinating sights are around every corner. There are parks, wilderness areas, and museums. There are ghost towns and places named after legends. There are trails to be walked and waterways to be paddled. In the U.P., life is meant to be lived to the fullest.

In this book, I've listed 40 destinations from every corner of the U.P. that have places of interest. Some reflect rich history, while others highlight natural wonders that abound across the peninsula. So many sights exist, in fact, that after a lifetime of exploration, I'm still discovering new and fascinating places that I've never seen or heard of. So, join in the adventures. The Upper Peninsula is an open book--the one that's in your hand.

"Without a doubt, Mikel B. Classen's book, *Points North*, needs to be in every library, gift shop and quality bookstore throughout the country—particularly those located in Michigan's Lower Peninsula. Not only does Classen bring alive the 'Hidden Campgrounds, Natural Wonders and Waterways of the Upper Peninsula' through his polished words, his masterful use of color photography make this book absolutely beautiful. *Points North* will long stand as a tremendous tribute to one of the most remarkable parts of our country."

—MICHAEL CARRIER author *Murder on Sugar Island*

"Mikel Classen's love for Michigan's Upper Peninsula shines from every page in *Points North*, a fascinating insider's guidebook to the exceptional beauty and history of Michigan's far north. Whether you're still in the planning stages of your trip, or you're looking back fondly on the memories you created—even if you wish merely to enjoy a virtual tour of the Upper Peninsula's natural wonders from the comfort of your armchair, you need this book."

—KAREN DIONNE, author of the international bestseller, *The Marsh King's Daughter*

paperback • hardcover • eBook
Learn more at **www.PointsNorthBooks.com**
From Modern History Press
www.ModernHistoryPress.com

# Join us for epic adventures in the U.P. on land and lakes!

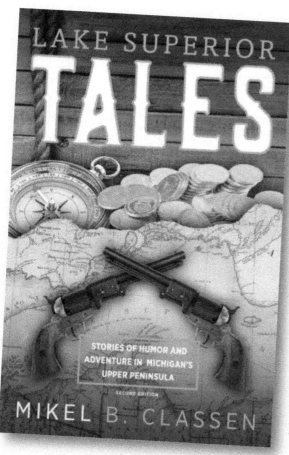

Pirates, thieves, shipwrecks, sexy women, lost gol and adventures on the Lake Superior frontier awa you! In this book, you'll sail on a ship full of gold, ou wit deadly shapeshifters, battle frontier outlaws ar even meet the mysterious agent that Andrew Jacksc called "the meanest man" he ever knew. Packed wi action, adventure, humor, and suspense, this book h something for every reader. Journey to the wilds of th Lake Superior shoreline through ten stories that spa the 19th century through present day including "Th Wreck of the Marie Jenny," "The Bigg Man," "Wo Killer," and "Bullets Shine Silver in the Moonlight."

**Mikel B. Classen** is a longtime resident of Sault Sain Marie in Michigan's Upper Peninsula. His intimacy the region, the history and its culture gives this book feel of authenticity that is rarely seen. As a writer, jou nalist, columnist, photographer, and editor with mo than 30 years experience, his breadth of knowledge is un paralleled.

"It's clear that Mikel B. Classen knows and loves the Lake Superior area of Michigan and brings it to life in a delightful way. If you want frequent laughs, unusual characters who jump off the page and the fruit of a highly creative mind, you've got to read this little book."
—BOB RICH, author, *Looking Through Wate*

"Michigan's Upper Peninsula is a unique place in this world, and Mikel's lovely little book, Lak *Superior Tales* makes that clear. Classen has long been recognized as a leading proponent of all th wonderful attributes of the Upper Peninsula, and currently he serves as the Managing Editor of th *U.P. Reader.* So, seeing him tackle this project does not surprise me. But what I did find exciting is th electricity he captures on every page, and the energy he uses to express it.

My father was a lumberjack, moonshiner and 'gunslinger' in the U.P. a century ago, and every nigl he told me stories about his adventures (he was on his own from age thirteen!). Classen's *Lake Superic Tales* brings back those wonderful memories. If you like to let your imagination wander uninhibitec Mikel is the perfect tour guide. I hope this becomes a series."
—MICHAEL CARRIER author *Murder on Sugar Islan*

paperback • hardcover • eBook
From Modern History Press
www.ModernHistoryPress.com

# Addiction

## by Jan Stafford Kellis

My addiction—I'll call him Pierre—is responsible for my low checking account balance, my lack of focus on a given task, and my constant yearning for the next hit, the next bump, the next delicious swig of...literature.

Pierre lives in the shadows. He lurks, seemingly casual, highly attuned to my every mood, waiting for the first sign of weakness, of distraction, of ennui. When he notices my inattentiveness, he pounces. Silent as a Ninja warrior, he leaps into my head and assumes control.

This year started with the shine of a positive light. My sister Jen and I went shopping at a secondhand store in early January where I purchased eight used books for the grand total price of $19.78. She drove while I shuffled my treasures. I put them in the bag, took them back out, re-read the back covers, replaced them in the bag, repeat, repeat, repeat. I arranged them by color, then size, then alphabetical order.

"I can't imagine why people buy brand new books," I said.

"Oh, because you never buy brand new books?" She raised an eyebrow.

"Not this year. This is the Year of the Used Book," I said.

She looked up from the road to see if I'd grown two heads or morphed into a cyborg.

"*You're* not going to buy new books?" Her sarcasm filled the cab of the truck. "Okay."

"Look at this stack." I held up the literary totem pole. "I have three hardbacks and five paperbacks. That's about $150 worth of brand new books, and I bought them all for $19.78. Which was a good year, by the way. I was eight years old—I had no regrets yet."

"Okay, so you're not buying any new books. Let me know how it goes." Her tone dismissed my nascent resolution.

I shrugged.

"You'll see."

Weeks passed. Used books were my new drug. Searching for them was like a scavenger hunt, and I bought used books at every opportunity. I bought two at the library auction ($8 each, a bit high for used books, but it was for a good cause). I bought four more at the dollar store (technically, they were new, but they were $1 each, so I qualified them as used). Eventually, I had to remind myself not to purchase books simply because they were used—they had to be books I would actually read, such as literary fiction or nonfiction. Or something recommended by a friend, or something I'd seen in passing at a bookstore or online, or a new book by an author I'd previously enjoyed.

Come to think of it, not many books were disqualified.

To make matters worse, I kept receiving enticing email invitations from the Book of the Month Club (BOTMC), which has updated its entire business model since my great-grandmother joined it in her 87th year. Granted, a couple of decades have passed (okay, three decades and change) but I didn't know the BOTMC was still in business, let alone that it had embraced technology with such enthusiasm.

Was Pierre somehow behind these alluring emails? Had he commandeered the BOTMC email system?

I sighed a virtuous sigh and deleted the emails without reading them. Stronger than Pierre, I celebrated my freedom from addiction with a victory cheer. Oh, it felt good to be in control of my life!

I announced my determination to purchase only used books for the entire year at our monthly Bookworms Anonymous meeting. The Worms seemed skeptical. They made vaguely supportive noises, but they'd witnessed my struggles before and had little faith in my full recovery.

Meanwhile, the BOTMC kept emailing, using ever more interesting, more intriguing subject lines. I once caught sight of a beautiful book cover, but I deleted the email. I clicked with authority. I'd already decided—there was no reason to waffle—this was not the year to purchase brand new books.

I unsubscribed from all BOTMC communications.

I added up the money I'd saved so far by not purchasing new books. Nearly three hundred dollars. I envisioned this money in stacks, crumpled balls, folded into origami birds, crammed into a jar. Tangible green proof of my self-control.

The BOTMC emailed me yet again. Had Pierre given them my email address? Had he whispered my name to their marketing department?

One day, I checked my email while waiting on hold with my insurance company, and I opened a message from BOTMC. Before I realized what it was, I (or Pierre) clicked on the link. Oh, what a great plan they had! The books were only $13 each, or $11.50 each if you took advantage of the annual rate and bought twelve book credits to be used throughout the year.

Any sensible reader would pay for all twelve books at once.

Not only that, each member could choose from five books every month, or skip the month entirely! No more forced mailing, just a simple click here and there, and voila. New book(s) would arrive in the mail.

I clicked out. I closed the window and jumped to my feet, all the better to pace about the room until my insurance agent picked up her extension.

The emails did not cease. I unsubscribed again but they kept rolling in, relentless pleas to offer these fabulous books a place on my shelf.

It wasn't the books' fault they were homeless. Every book just wants to be loved, a shelf of its own, a reader to flutter its pages.

You can imagine what happened next. Pierre sensed my hesitation during my third salvo into the BOTMC den. He sensed my hesitation, and he pounced. He pounced and he forced my finger to click the "Join Now" button and WHAM.

I now belong to the Book of the Month Club.

And let me tell you, it's wonderful, tremendous, dizzying. I'm not sorry. And yet, I miss those few virtuous weeks when I successfully combatted my insidious addiction.

I now have twenty books on my To-Be-Read shelf. Twenty-one if you count the nonfiction book about writing. Two of the books are from BOTMC and the rest are from a used bookstore. You know what that means: I have ten more pre-paid books whispering, *Pick me.* Their pre-paid status lends them an even greater cachet—I can acquire ten more books without any additional cash outlay. A click here, a click there, and I'll receive a lovely box of books delivered to my house.

I promise I'll draw this out, carefully selecting only one book each month. Yes, I will! I'll partake of one scrumptious literary morsel each month, savoring my pre-paid tomes. I won't squander even one book credit on a questionable book. I'll research every offering before I choose. I won't be click-happy; I won't be star struck by the books themselves, posing in their fancy covers on my screen, stuffed with so much potential I want to reach out and buy them all, but I won't!

No, I won't do that.

I'll control myself. Really, I will.

# The Ratbag Family

## by Jan Stafford Kellis

Dad referred to the family five doors down as Ratbags. Whenever we drove past their house—a grimy blemish at the edge of our picture-perfect neighborhood decorated with forlorn statues of broken toys and bikes with bent frames—Dad would shake his head and mutter.

"What are the Ratbags up to?" or, "The Ratbags are performing today," or, my favorite, "The Ratbags think we can't see them."

I felt smart, easily spying them despite their natural dirt camouflage.

The Ratbags ran barefoot, dried sludge crusted beneath their noses like mustaches, matching non-haircuts and clothes so grubby they appeared mud-colored. But they always seemed busy, those kids. They never sat still unless they were working on a broken skateboard or Sit-N-Spin.

I coveted that Sit-N-Spin. My parents didn't appreciate the value of sitting pretzel-legged on a plastic disc and spinning around, but to me, it looked like a carnival ride without the fuss and bother of yelling carnies and puking children.

One day, I ventured to the end of our cul-de-sac, all the way to the place where you had to choose left or right. The Ratbags on the corner were playing Tag, their Sit-N-Spin abandoned on the sidewalk. One of them, a girl I'd mentally dubbed Sister Ratbag, tiptoed across the yard to perch at the edge of the dirt, as if to avoid contact with the concrete sidewalk and the civilized society it represented.

"You can use it if you want." Her voice rode out on a high-pitched, melodic breath.

I shrugged. "Okay."

My pants were clean, and for one full second I experienced intense discomfort as I sat down on the dirty toy. *I bet this used to be red*, I thought. I arranged my legs so none of me would drag on the ground and cranked the steering wheel hard.

The world spun and all of the colors ran together, just as I'd imagined. I closed my eyes and gave in to the feeling of pure movement. A thrill ran through my stomach and I cranked faster and faster, finally letting go and raising my hands to the sky to allow the air to flow between my fingers. I felt like a ballerina, graceful and light.

The disc lurched to a stop.

I looked down at a foot with three toes pressed on the Sit-N-Spin right where my ankles crossed. The thrill in my stomach took a drastic turn and the grilled cheese I'd eaten for lunch threatened to reappear. I followed the leg up to the frown and furrowed brows of Brother Ratbag. His arms were folded tightly and when my eyes met his he spat on the ground, barely missing my knee. He looked much bigger than when we drove by, safe inside the car. Nearly twice my size.

"Get off my proppity."

My stomach clenched and I tasted the half-regurgitated sandwich at the back of my throat. I cocked my head to move the sun behind Brother Ratbag's inglorious mop of hair.

"You deaf?" He moved his hands to his hips, elbows jutting out like bird wings. "Get. Off. My. Proppity."

I cleared my throat and pointed at Sister Ratbag. "She said I could."

"Does she look like she's in charge around here?" He was shouting now, and I feared I'd leave a trail of urine all the way home if I chanced running.

I closed my eyes to concentrate on controlling my bodily functions.

"You don't even know us."

"I know you're Ratbags."

That's when I noticed a bald man wearing a formerly white T-shirt standing on the porch.

"The hell'd you call us?" His voice was high and whiny.

"Uh, Ratbags." I swallowed. "Sir." I stood carefully, brushing off my pants, now stained where I'd touched the Sit-N-Spin.

I don't recall how much time passed between Mr. Ratbag ordering me to, "Run fer home before I pepper your ass with BBs," and me reaching my front porch. It wasn't long.

I was tucked into my favorite spot in the living room, on the floor between the end table and the wall, when Dad slammed the phone down and ended Mr. Ratbag's call.

"Take Jan's plate off the table," Dad said to Mom. "She's not eating dinner tonight." Dad's punishments usually involved the paddle, quick and painful. I'd never been denied dinner.

Mom murmured something in response, and Dad said, "She called that family on the corner ratbags! She knows better than that."

*What was I supposed to call them?* I thought.

Something slammed, and footsteps stomped around the kitchen. I tucked myself tighter against the wall and rested my chin on my knees.

Mom found me a few minutes later and walked me to my room. She closed the door and sat on my bed so we were closer in height.

I stared at her bare feet. Mom worked as a chemist in a laboratory, and she wore dress shoes and pantyhose every day. They were the first to go when she returned home. She had perfect feet, shaped like the ones on the poster in the doctor's office. Dad and I had bony feet with high arches and crooked toes.

Mom touched my arm and I looked into her blue-gray eyes. "Why did you call those poor souls ratbags?"

I shrugged. "Dad always says, 'there are those Ratbags,' when we drive by. I thought that was their name." My cheeks burned.

"An honest mistake. And a hard lesson." She gripped my upper arms and studied my face. "We don't know everyone's story."

The next day, she marched me down the street and stood by as I apologized to Mr. Ratbag and his kids. His name was Bill Beaumont, and his children were Brock and Melody. Their mother had died in an accident, a calamity I couldn't imagine.

How does one go on without a mother? Though I didn't realize it at the time, my mom was my only nonjudgmental witness; she was my steadiest guide and my most stable influence. The possibility that she could perish rendered me mute.

I held Mom's hand on the walk home, where she served me ice cream and told me I was growing into a fine young lady.

**Jan Kellis** joined the UPPAA Board in 2019. She holds a bachelor's degree in Business Management and works as a field engineer for an electric utility company. Jan's been writing since she's been able to hold a crayon and she has published seven books. *Bookworms Anonymous*, Volumes I and II, are a true account of the non-traditional book club she helped found in 2000. The group meets monthly and provides Jan with great material. She's also written a travel memoir about her 2010 trip to Italy with her reluctant teenaged daughter, and three novels, all based in the UP. She loves to visit reading groups and libraries to talk about her books. When Jan isn't reading or writing, she's traveling, knitting, quilting, camping, or making soap. For the latest news, or to book an appearance, please visit http://jankellis.com/

# U.P. Reader is Accepting Submissions for Volume 5

The *U.P. Reader* is an annual publication that represents the cross-section of writers that are the membership of the Upper Peninsula Publishers and Authors Association. This annual anthology will be used as a vehicle to showcase and promote the writers of the Upper Peninsula. Each issue is released in paperback, hardcover, and eBook editions in early Spring following the deadline. Copies of the *U.P. Reader* will be made available to booksellers, UPPAA members, libraries, and news services. The *U.P. Reader* has received more media coverage each year since the inclusion of the Dandelion Cottage Award. We hope the *U.P. Reader* will be a great place for you to showcase original short works, too.

## Submission Guidelines

- Must be a **current member of the UPPAA** to submit.

- Submissions **must be original** with no prior appearance in web or print. Submissions will be accepted for **up to 5,000 words**. Writers who submit work which has previously appeared in blog posts, web pages, eBooks, or in print will be disqualified.

- Submissions **can be any type of genre**, Fiction, Nonfiction (memoirs, history, essays, feature articles, interviews, opinion) and Poetry. These also can include photography or artwork, but author must show permission for use.

- All submissions will be **reviewed through a jury** and the submissions will be chosen through this process.

- We prefer **Microsoft Word Document** (.DOC) files only or plain text files (.TXT).   Do not submit PDF files.  If you have some other type of text file, please inquire.

- **Authors may include photos,** with the understanding that they will be converted to black-and-white.  We reserve the right to limit the number of photos per story. Photos should be at least 300 DPI and no smaller than 2 inches on a side (i.e., 600px minimum). If the Author is not the photographer, we may ask for a simple one-page "Photo Release" form to be sent in.

The U.P. Reader will require FIRST time rights in print and digital. After one year, rights will revert to the author. The UPPAA retains the right to use submitted works in perpetuity.  For example, we look forward to the "Best of U.P. Reader" edition to be issued for the 10th anniversary.

## Publication Schedule for U.P. Reader Volume 5

- Submission deadline: Nov. 15th, 2020

- Dec 21, 2020   Jury / peer-review process beginss

- Jan 15th, 2021 announcement of selected submissions

- April 1, 2021, official publication date

Send submissions to submissions@upreader.org.  Be sure to put "U.P. Reader Submission" in the subject line.

# The Bait Pile

## by Rich Hill

When the war in Europe finally ended, and Hitler was defeated, Ethan Powell returned to the States and built a rustic cabin in the deep U.P. woods of Michigan. He wanted a simple place to hunt in the fall, a place to get away and forget all he had seen and felt the past two years. A humble hunting camp would be his refuge when he needed an escape from the frustrating demands of the world. Ethan was tired of taking orders, tired of foxholes and trenches, tired of the endless explosions ringing in his ears. His dream was to return to the peaceful woods of the U.P. after the war and make a fresh start.

Returning home, Ethan found a job working at the Soo Lumber Mill and, before too long, saved enough money to buy a forty-acre parcel just north of Hessel. He soon married a pretty waitress named Norma, who had waited patiently for him while he served in the war, and together they raised two sons, Jake and Jeremy. Every season, Ethan took great pride teaching his boys the art of hunting and fishing. They both loved the outdoors as much as their father and especially looked forward to deer season in mid-November each year. A month before opening day, they had spent many carefree hours hiking through the crisp autumn foliage and building a deer blind near a clearing.

The hunting camp that Ethan had built was near the southeast corner of his forty acres. A two-track road wound through the small spruce forest about a half mile leading up to the cabin. The land was hilly in places, with a narrow creek flowing through the middle of the parcel. A horseshoe-shaped ridge stretched around the perimeter and enclosed a swampy area full of dense cedar growth where the deer liked to bed down. One of only a few cabins in the area, the Powell camp was adjacent to hundreds of acres of heavily-forested state land. After many pleasurable hunting seasons, Ethan died and left the cabin to his sons. Together, the boys would carry on the Powell camp traditions that their father had taught them over the years.

Every fall, Jake and Jeremy had posted signs around the boundaries of their property that read: "Private Property, No Hunting," in an attempt to ward off trespassers. There were occasional hunters who wandered onto their property, supposedly tracking a deer that had been shot. But, for the most part, hunters respected the boundaries and restricted their hunting activities to state land.

November 15, opening day of firearms deer season in Michigan, fell on a Saturday one particular year. Jake and Jeremy took it upon themselves to arrange the annual get-together at the camp, stocking the cupboards with potatoes, pancake mix and beans and filling the cooler with ice, beer, bacon, and eggs. Their cousins came from far and wide– Iron River, Escanaba, Drummond Island, Texas, and Tennessee– to spend a week or so in the autumn woods. They came not only to hunt trophy bucks, but also for the camaraderie, the late-night poker games, and the far-fetched tall tales that tended to boil over around the fire every evening.

Early on Saturday morning, after a good breakfast, the eight hunters at the Powell camp broke into three groups. Two of the hunters took their places in the deer blind near the swamp. The other groups hiked through the woods toward state land where they had seen fresh tracks the day before.

Several inches of snow had fallen that week, and the hunters were hopeful of seeing some action in the woods. All week long, Jake had stocked the bait pile near his deer blind with carrots, discarded pumpkins, and corn cobs. He'd broken them up and scattered them loosely under a large red pine a week earlier, and the deer had been feasting on them regularly.

On the far side of the ridge, just past the swamp, Jake and Jeremy were hiking down a two-track. Wearing their hunter-orange winter jackets and tukes and carrying their deer rifles, they walked quietly as they moved through the woods. It looked like a perfect morning for opening day. The sky was a soft blue, the sun filtering through the yellow birches onto dried leaves that had stubbornly refused to fall.

Around the bend of the trail, they heard the loud crunch of human footsteps on the frozen path. They stopped to listen. Into the clearing came four individuals clad in hunter-orange. They carried no rifles, but pots and pans instead, with heavy metal spoons. When the group saw Jake and Jeremy with their deer rifles, they instantly started beating vigorously on the pans, piercing the quiet stillness of the woods.

"Hey!" Jake shouted. "What the hell are you doing? You'll scare the deer away."

"Good. That's what we mean to do," said the tall, hollow-cheeked one, stepping forward. "You people have no need to kill deer or any other animals."

"Oh yeah?" said Jeremy. "Who put you in charge?"

The leader of the group looked Jeremy in the eye soberly and spat a wad of tobacco juice on the ground. "Listen up, boys. We represent the local animal-rights group and the anti-hunting faction. This here is state land you're on, and we have every right to come here and do as we please."

They beat their pots and pans again to make their point. Jake waved his arms at them to stop.

"Why are you bothering us here?" asked Jeremy. "We all paid for our hunting licenses, and we're not disturbing you or anybody."

One of the protesters, with a bushy beard and long black hair, pushed forward. "We own these woods and streams and animal habitat just as much as you. And we want to protect them along with the animals that happen to live here. I'm sure you don't need a deer to survive, and you can probably do without another trophy head on the wall of your den."

Jake and Jeremy both shook their heads in disbelief. They wanted to get away from the pot bangers and get back to hunting. "Just leave us alone!" shouted Jake. The hunters turned away and headed down the narrow trail through the trees. The animal-rights group let them get about twenty yards ahead but followed them, beating the pans without mercy, creating as much noise and chaos as possible. This went on for half an hour, and soon Jake and Jeremy relented and returned to their camp.

In over ten years of deer camp, the boys had never encountered anything like this. The camp was meant to be a special place for sport and relaxation, not a political theater.

The rustic camp had no electricity and utilized a large propane tank for heat and cooking. It had a fieldstone fireplace and a simple outhouse and used kerosene lamps for light in the evening. As the family grew in number over the years, the small camp was expanded to include a couple of additional bedrooms with double bunk beds. The camp had established many deep-rooted traditions over the years but was mainly meant to be a refuge for relaxation. The boys weren't looking for trouble with these protestors, but trouble had surely found them.

Later that afternoon, the cousins returned to the camp, having seen plenty of tracks but no bucks. Jake relayed stories of the animal-rights people who had followed them throughout the woods all morning, creating chaos and scaring away any possible deer.

"What business is it of theirs to come out here and raise hell?"

Jeremy stood up and cracked a can of Pabst. "Our family has been coming to camp here every November for over thirty years. It's a tradition."

He sipped his beer while Jake cleaned and polished his rifle. "If I see those assholes here again tomorrow, I'll give them something to think about. You watch."

When the hunters arose the next morning, they found two inches of fresh-fallen snow on the ground, perfect for tracking. After a quick breakfast of coffee, eggs, and toast, the hunters headed down the trail to check the bait pile. When they arrived, the pot bangers were there waiting for them.

"You boys are awful late gettin' started this morning," said one of the orange-clad protesters. He stuffed a plug of tobacco in his cheek and spat on the leaves.

"Why don't you just leave us be?" Jake said. "We're not bothering any of you."

They beat their pots and pans non-stop for half a minute. "Why don't you boys just put your firearms down, go back to your cabin, and play cards or whatever you do?"

Just then, not fifty yards away, two shots were heard. The pot bangers, thinking the hunters had sighted a deer, raced off in the direction of the shots, beating their pans along the way. When they reached the road, they found their Ford Bronco with both tires on the driver's side shot out. There was no trace of anyone in the vicinity.

"They'll pay for this," one of them warned, "somehow."

As they surveyed the damage to their vehicle, a DNR officer drove up the gravel road and stopped near them. "Hello, gentlemen," the officer said. "Having some trouble?"

"Look what someone did to our tires. I'll bet it was those hunters at that camp over there. "

The officer noted the vandalized tires and sensed trouble brewing. "I heard about the problems between you and some hunting group. You best be careful. I don't want any trouble out here."

"It's state land we're on. We have every right to protest if we don't like what these hunters are up to."

Clearing his throat, the officer spoke to them calmly. "Sure you do, but hunter harassment is a misdemeanor in Michigan. So, just take it easy, that's all. I'll go over to that camp and have a talk with them, too."

The officer got back in his car and drove away. He stopped by the Powell camp and found two of the hunters sipping coffee. "Morning, boys. Having any luck so far?"

"Not much yet, but plenty of fresh tracks."

"I just stopped by to ask you about an encounter you had yesterday in the woods with an animal-rights group. What did they say to you?" the officer asked.

"They want us to stop hunting deer," said Jeremy incredulously. "They've been beating their pots and pans like maniacs and scaring the bejesus out of every deer within two miles of here. This harassment shouldn't be legal."

"Well, gentlemen, maybe it's not the smartest thing I've ever heard of, but they have a legal right to be on state land. No, harassment's not legal, but you would have to file charges against them. Why don't you just hunt on your own land for a few days? They can't set foot on it."

"I just wish they'd stay away from us."

"By the way," the officer asked, "do you boys know anything about the tires that were shot off that Bronco out on the road?"

"Haven't heard a thing, officer, but we'll keep our eyes open."

That afternoon, Jake and Jeremy decided to hunt as far away from the pot bangers as possible. They hiked over the ridge on the north side of their property to the adjacent state land. With only a couple hours of daylight remaining, the boys took their positions beneath a tall spruce tree that was within sight of a deer run.

Their patience paid off finally, and Jake shot a twelve-point buck just before dusk. It was his first buck in five years and would make a fine trophy mounted above his fireplace at home. He would take the buck to a meat processor in the Soo, who would package all the venison for his freezer. After Jake

Ishpeming Lake - Angeline Mine

and Jeremy gutted the animal and dragged the deer carcass through the woods and back to camp, they strung it up on the buck pole outside and took pictures posing with it.

Around the dinner table that evening, the cousins all toasted Jake with their beer and laughed at the hapless animal-rights crazies who had harassed them for several days. After all their efforts, they hadn't prevented a successful hunt. They played cards and told stories until midnight before blowing out the kerosene lamp and crawling into their bunks.

It was a long, peaceful sleep in the Powell camp that night, under a starry sky and a moonless night. A northwest wind swirled in the pines overhead and gusted until early morning.

Just after sunrise the next morning, Jake was the first one up and started a pot of coffee on the stove. On his way to the outhouse for his morning ritual, he suddenly spied a horrible sight. His twelve-point trophy buck hanging from the pole had been sprayed with some kind of black dye. It looked like a mutilated corpse from another world. Someone had crept quietly into camp overnight and disfigured his trophy buck. The head was so damaged that it could never be mounted.

"What the hell!" he shouted. "Sonofabitch! Who did this to me?"

The other hunters heard the commotion and scrambled out of the cabin and stared up at the dismembered carcass. "You know damn well who did this. Those bastard tree-huggers, those lousy animal lovers," one of the cousins said.

"Why don't we report this to the DNR, take'm to court and charge'm with harassment like the officer said?"

"No, that would be too good for them," said Jake. "They'll mention their tires being shot out, and we'll be in hot water. Let's just take care of this ourselves."

"OK," a cousin vowed, "it's payback time. We've got to chase those pricks out of these woods for good."

By the time they had cooled down, it was nearly 10 a.m. They spruced up the cabin and climbed into their long johns, wool coats, and hunter-orange jackets. It wouldn't take long, they knew, for the pot bangers to locate the hunters in their preferred spots. Jake, Jeremy, and two of their cousins grabbed their rifles and marched down the trail towards the bait pile. They had barely crossed the ridge onto state land when the racket of banging pots and pans assaulted them. A group of five protesters approached the hunters nonchalantly.

"You guys sure don't give up easily, do you?" said Jeremy.

"So why don't you big, strong men just lay down your arms and surrender peacefully?" said a red-faced man at the front. "We don't plan to quit anytime soon."

Jake bristled and took the safety off his rifle.

"We have the god-given right," said Jeremy, "to put food on our table. We've paid for our hunting permits, and you're not going to stop us."

The protesters beat their pans again, and two of them blasted air-horns, like you might hear at a hockey game. The hunters stared grimly at them and were not amused.

"And we have the right to free speech," said the apparent leader of the gang. "But you don't have any right to kill poor, defenseless animals. Look at you big, macho guys stomping around the woods with your high-powered artillery and high-tech scopes. The deer don't stand a chance. You call this a sport? Give me a break."

Jeremy tried one more time to be reasonable. "Believe it or not, deer hunters do serve a worthwhile purpose. They help to thin out the herd and make it stronger. Many of these deer would starve over the winter otherwise."

"Oh, yeah? We've heard that line before, and we don't buy it."

Finally, Jake snapped. He couldn't take their arrogance and smugness anymore. "Just get the hell out of here right now!" he shouted.

Jake fired three shots directly over the protesters' heads. They were so startled, they turned around and raced back down the trail toward their vehicle.

"And don't ever come back, you hear me?" Jake yelled. He fired another round over their heads for good measure. Payback, he thought, was sometimes a cruel business, but oh so sweet. He may have scared the protesters off for a while, but he had unwittingly stirred up their outrage and calls for revenge. Jake had crossed a line he would later regret.

Late Monday afternoon, it was time to return home. The hunters packed up their gear, gathered their empties, and headed for the main road in their pickups. Jake and Jeremy were planning to return to camp the following weekend. They hoped that, by that time, the protesters would be long gone.

Two days later, the anti-hunting group showed up after dark. They wanted to make sure the Powell camp had been vacated. An empty long-necked beer bottle had been filled with gasoline and stuffed with a rag. As one of them lit the fuse with a match, he said, "This will teach those bastards not to mess with us again." And he whipped the lit bottle through a window glass. The cabin exploded in flames that soon engulfed the entire structure. By morning, there was nothing left but the foundation and the stone fireplace. The protesters had disappeared without a trace.

It didn't take long for the DNR officer to figure things out. He knew the volatile situation had escalated out of control and that he should have stepped in sooner. The five protesters were arrested and charged with arson and hunter harassment. Jake was the only hunter arrested and was charged with reckless endangerment with a firearm.

Several weeks after the cabin had burned down, Jake returned to the camp to comb through the ashes and charred remains for anything of value. In one corner where a bedroom dresser would have been, he bent over and picked up a blackened pocket watch. He rubbed the soot off on his canvas jacket and read the inscription on the silvery back: *Please come home safely. Love, Norma.* It was the pocket watch his then girlfriend had given Ethan before he'd gone off to war. As Jake held the watch in his hand, he thought of all the sacrifices his father had made and all the hard work he must have put into building the Powell camp. At that point, there was no longer any question in his mind. Jake vowed that, one way or another, he and Jeremy would rebuild the camp just the way it had been earlier. They would go back to hunting on their own land and taking care of the bait pile. It would need renewal with fresh carrots, corn cobs, and apples for the deer. It would always be part of a long-standing family tradition.

# Whiteout

## by Rich Hill

It's a damned shame. My friend Allen shouldn't have suffered such a horrible death. It was preventable, in my opinion, if only he hadn't panicked and taken matters into his own hands.

About three years ago, Allen and I had both retired from working for Chippewa County. I worked in the Treasurer's office, and he was in the Register of Deeds. We both liked to hunt and fish, especially in the winter. Al had built his own shack to ice-fish on the upper St. Mary's River. By early February every year, he hauled it out on the ice and set it in about six feet of water so he could spear or line-fish. Usually, he caught his limit of whitefish or perch and often shared them with me.

The two of us were good buddies when we'd fought together in Vietnam, where we each served our year of duty back in the 60s. He was always stubborn and independent-minded back then, hard to persuade once he'd made up his mind. So, after the Army, he went one way, and I went the other, but we both wound up working together years later. Just luck, I guess.

Allen never married or had a family; it just wasn't particularly important to him. He liked his freedom too much and never wanted to feel tied down. He stayed in good shape, too, much better than me. I've put on probably forty pounds more than I should— too many cheeseburgers and beer. But Allen got his exercise walking and biking wherever he went. No need for him to belong to a gym; he took good care of himself. That's why I don't understand how he got himself in such a bind. He was always so methodical and self-disciplined, so well-prepared in everything he did.

It was a frosty Saturday morning in early March when Al headed out to his fish shack on the upper river. The ice had been melting and freezing for several days so that sometimes you could see open water way out in the river. In a few weeks, everyone would have to remove their shacks from the bay to make way for the shipping season. The ore freighters, the size of several football fields, would be opening the season in late March after the Coast Guard icebreakers had busted up the frozen channel.

Allen usually hauled his equipment on a toboggan—his wood for the stove, his lunch, bait—and hiked the hundred yards or so from shore for the exercise. Most of the other fishermen rode their snowmobiles out to their shacks, but Al thought they were just lazy, spoiled by high technology and too much retirement money. They probably all had electric snow blowers and riding lawn mowers, he often said, and would never get a decent day's worth of exercise.

But Al was wise enough to carry a simple cell phone on him to call friends, if the fish weren't biting, or for an emergency. This particular morning, he had asked me to come out and fish with him, but I was busy with a few other household jobs and couldn't make it. I wish to hell now that I would have. He might still be here.

When Al called me about mid-afternoon, he seemed to be in good spirits. He'd caught several whitefish by jigging wax worms. The fish were attracted by the canned corn that was spread on the sandy bottom for feed. He planned to fish until early evening, about six o'clock. A lot of fishermen believe the fish bite better in early twilight. Meanwhile, he said he had finished his lunch of ham-and-cheese sandwiches, washed down with a couple shots of Jack Daniels. Al usually brought his *Detroit Free Press* to read during slow times, to catch up on the Red Wings and the Pistons and all the hoopla back in Washington, D.C.

He didn't mind being all by himself out there on the ice. He never felt lonely or bored and said it was a relaxing way to spend his retirement. From a health standpoint, I worried about him a little if there was to be an emergency, but he was always in good health.

About 7 p.m., my phone rang, and Al was not quite himself. He tried to sound calm, but I could hear the alarm and fear in his voice. An unexpected winter storm had moved into the area.

"Ray, this is Al. Can you hear me?" he shouted. I could hear the wind howling in the phone and Al's labored breathing.

"Yes, Al, I hear you. Are you on your way back to shore?"

"I don't know for sure," Al said, nearly out of breath. "I left my shack twenty minutes ago, and I'm a little turned around. This squall came in out of nowhere, and I can't see a damned thing."

Apparently, the temporary squall he had expected turned into a full-blown winter blizzard with high winds and falling temperatures. The lights on shore, which he normally used as a guide, were no longer visible.

"Have you checked your compass yet?" I asked.

"I left it in my other jacket pocket when I changed this morning."

The wind kept howling in my ear, and I had a hard time hearing him.

"I should've stayed in my shack until the storm blew over," Al shouted, "but I ran out of wood and started getting cold. Can't seem to find my way back now... my tracks disappeared."

"Hang in there, Al. I'm calling for help right now."

"OK, Ray, I'll get back to you in a little while."

I knew he was scared out of his wits but trying to remain calm. This situation could not be easy for someone who was normally so

well-prepared. I called the Coast Guard and the Sheriff's department. They agreed to dispatch a search-and-rescue team immediately.

Usually, the hike from Al's shack to the mainland is no more than fifteen or twenty minutes, even if you're pulling a toboggan full of gear. In the dark, with the snow blowing sideways, Al had been walking long enough to make shore but must have gotten off course.

After so much time, hypothermia and disorientation could set in, and there was no place to take shelter out there. He was at the mercy of the elements, and these spring storms can be vicious on Lake Superior.

I pulled my boots on, threw on my winter parka, and raced in the truck to meet the sheriff's people. I drove a few miles west of the Soo to the upper river where Al's car was parked. The storm was blowing so hard I could barely see the road. I thought of Al wandering around on the ice, half-frozen and delirious, and felt sick. As long as I've known Al, he was never the kind of guy to take chances out on the ice, always safety first with him. I know he was cold, but he should've stayed put in his shack, out of the wind. Too late now. What am I saying? I should've been there with him.

A couple winters ago, Al lost a good friend over on Lake George, to the east of Sugar Island. It was in the springtime, late March, when this guy had driven his pickup out on the ice to fish and had fallen through and drowned. He got trapped under the ice in his vehicle. Al would never have taken that sort of chance, but people still do it.

I remember hearing about a few snowmobilers a couple years ago who were riding out on the ice late one night, following the Canadian shoreline about a hundred yards out. They were bar-hopping that night and on their way back home, and for a little excitement, decided to jump some ice floes over open water. To me, that's practically suicide. One of them jumped just short of the next ice floe and crashed into the icy water and drowned. They say that a person has less than two minutes to crawl out of ice water before his muscles become limp and useless. I doubt if Al would have ever done such a reckless thing.

Keweenaw - Calumet Red Jacket Mine

I tried calling Al's cell phone over and over again, but he wouldn't answer. The poor fellow must be frozen stiff by now, I thought. By the time the sheriff's people arrived, the storm was letting up somewhat. The rescue team fanned out near the shore and shone their powerful flashlights out into the darkness on the river. They called out for Al, but there was no answer. As the wind diminished, the searchers made their way out to his shack, but there was no one there.

As we called out for Al and searched the area with our lights, I vaguely recalled an old Jack London story, "To Build a Fire." A man freezing in the Alaskan wilderness had finally kindled a small fire under a fir tree when a clump of melting snow from a branch above fell on the fire and doused it. The helpless man could do no more physically as hypothermia set in. It was a gradual, almost peaceful, feeling as his body shut down and drowsiness slowly overcame him. I feared for Allen's life at that moment, but still held out hope.

After searching for hours, including the aid of a Coast Guard helicopter, the sheriff's people finally had to quit for the night. At that point, the search-and-rescue had, by necessity, turned into a body recovery. We would have to wait until morning to continue.

By daylight, the searchers had returned to comb the area thoroughly. They dis-

patched divers into the icy waters of the upper river and within a few hours discovered the body under the ice. Apparently, poor Al must have gotten totally turned around and thought he was walking towards shore, only to walk right out to the open river. They found his toboggan near the edge of the ice field.

If hypothermia can lull you into a sleepy delirium, I hope Al went peacefully. The guy loved ice-fishing and died doing what he loved most. I miss him dearly.

**Richard Hill** has lived in Michigan's Upper Peninsula for more than fifty years. He has published three books previously: *Lake Effect: A Deckhand's Journey on the Great Lakes Freighters*, *Hitchhiking After Dark: Offbeat Stories from a Small Town* (first-place winner in humor at Midwest Book Awards), and *Lost in the Woods: Building A Life Up North*. Richard attended the University of Michigan, Northern Michigan University, and the Great Lakes Maritime Academy. He currently lives near Sault Ste. Marie with his wife and cocker spaniel. His new collection of short stories, *When the Rooster Crows and Other Stories*, will be published in October 2020.

# Paper Tracks

## by Elizabeth Fust

One day a dream, which quickly faded, roused me from sleep just before a dawn lost behind mumbling storm clouds. I had a longing for old family pictures, the same way one wants a glass of water when they first wake up. While searching for Nana's album, I found a trunk full of family odds and ends. It was tucked in her old craft room under a length of cut fabric remnant acting as a tablecloth for the chest that held her hat boxes brimming with artisanal supplies. I spread every paper and photo across the living room carpet, constructing a timeline paper rug.

The bits were hard to piece together — some of the pages were thin and torn or thick and brittled by age. They were also hard to piece together because I could not read the chicken scratch of faded writing in a hodgepodge Italian/English. Also because the family stories Nana and Papa told, as well as all the aunts and uncles who retold what their aunts and uncles had told them, did not all match — with each other or the primary sources I found.

Not that the sources always said anything important. They were penmanship practice and receipts or noted dates of ordinary things and such. There were notes of friends leaving to fight in the Spanish American war, letters from friends who survived forest fires, clippings about closed mines, all ranging from my earliest emigrant relative to my grandparents. In all the bits of paper and the photos there exists a sort of duality. The lens of history can only show so much. I began to wonder about the thoughts and feelings of the people who had taken these notes and photos and about what the words and pictures could not fully capture and convey. These were thoughts that can only be mused at, that can never be known.

My exploration came with a heady sense of knowledge, as if such a brief glimpse into an intimate past made me an expert and qualified to make suppositions on the thoughts of a life lived long ago. The only indication of that thought is a brief newspaper clipping of a railroad accident tucked next to a journal entry that says, "there has been yet another accident on the iron," and the next word is erased by time. But sometimes there was something reflective and prosaic written that captured more thought that history, like one journal entry I found, *"We live our life on iron. Iron rails and iron ore. One proliferates the other. The ore forms the rails which expand to where the mines can go which provides iron for the rails which then expand farther for more mines which then provide iron for more rails. We live and die by the iron. The men in the mines that die of accidents, cave ins and machinery malfunctions and sickness contracted from the dark, sodden depths. Men and children on the rails who die at work or in accidents. And those who do not die are scarred for life, the loss of limb and work a festering wound that can't be healed in their families. The ore bleeds red dust and covers the workers, the buildings, the families. It fills our lungs and chokes our throats. That which kills us gives us livelihood."*

Why the focus on the tracks and trains? Because in the dream that woke me, and that had vanished now like a blast of smoke, I was lulled by the chugging of a train and awoke to the hiss of steam, a family story now forgotten riding the rails of my subconscious. I wanted to find it, and my great-grandmother's family papers held the secret. I don't remember my great-grandmother well, only that as a little girl I played at her feet with the Victorian style paper dolls she gave me while she listened to Italian operas, "like my father used to sing, though he never saw an opera," she told me every single time. She also told me how her father had saved a child from a terrible death, a death of dismemberment at the wheels of a train that rode the rails of the Menominee Track. After that dream that prompted these memories of her short tale, I wanted to know the names, the dates, and the locations.

Perhaps it was subliminal, in my own raucous state of feeling torn from family, and that personal identity, and how it all fit into a life today. Like many, I was born in the U.P., left for many years, came back, and imagined this would be where I died and be buried in some hilly cemetery in the woods with a plot in between somebody who died in a mine accident and somebody from a shipwreck, identity unknown. It still felt like there was a disconnect after what I had missed during my years away from the homestead. I felt at risk of being dismembered like that little child and I wanted to find the story of my great-great-grandfather saving the child so he could save me, too. Along the way, like just as many stops along a route, I found station in other memories unknown to me.

My great-great-great grandparents had followed my great-great-great uncle from Capistrano, Italy, to Iron Mountain, Michigan. My family was only one of the many Italians to emigrate to this part of the forest-clad and water-bound Upper Peninsula; they moved from a boot to a mitten, as went the family saying. These six generations of Italians were writers and artists and all their creations, or scraps of them, had been saved by my grandmother in that one cedar chest.

"Momma fears mining strikes," one snippet of a dismantled journal reads. "Papa says they will not strike. Mamma has heard from Mrs...," the Italian and Finnish names in the scratched pencil lead are often too hard for a modern English eye to make out, the vowels curling into each other and blending into consonants. I blinked away the eye strain and picked it up again, "who has lived in many company towns here, that in some strikes the men bring clubs and guns and even if no one is killed there have been men disfigured, missing parts of ears or having permanent furrows from bullets." It is undated. I think they mean the Menominee Iron Range, but without a date or an author to attribute, I do not know and set it aside in a pile of "interesting" documents. It is not a delicate filing system. And still I want to know, what was the writer thinking and feeling that their neophyte English writing journal cannot convey?

Spencerian — I believe that's the name for the type of cursive they used. It was like hieroglyphics before my eyes. I had to assume much of the content as I read the nice writing too delicate for my eye to trace with the rare Italian word, a test to what was left of my knowledge of the language from my grandma's Italian lessons in her kitchen as we made spiced sausages. The faded papers were a test of imagination. There are bits which I supposed might be poetry, but were so faded that they read as lists of aspects of nature with an adjective interspersed, and perhaps, a line about a lover.

I had an aunt once tell me that she'd met Babe Ruth. That he had come on tour to her little corner of Dickinson County. She was the only sibling in the family who had the honor as she was the oldest and the other children were too young to go out. Her siblings say she is lying and she always protested that no, Babe Ruth really came to Dickinson County. She was right. And so were they. I found an Iron Mountain newspaper clipping and a picture of the Bambino — dated a good many years before my aunt was born. Time, memory, and people's stories are tricky, fluid things.

After some time, I discovered I was not the only one who sought to verify this recollection. I came upon a bundle of newspaper clippings from *The Menominee Range*, one of those newspapers that started out only to serve the men of the company town. The compilation featured articles from over a hundred years past and must have been an ongoing project: a sort of macabre loose-leaf scrapbook of life by the tracks.

Life by the tracks. My grandma had said that all the time. Wrong side of the track. That kind of thing. It has to do with the direction the wind blows. She said that the shops built up along the tracks would shake, their wooden frames slowly coming loose and plaster cracking. She said that's what the railway did; it shook you from the inside out, you, your family, your community. It runs everywhere like veins, she'd say, carrying livelihood. If it stopped, that was death. But as it ran, that could bring death just as surely. Shaking you apart, inside out.

I began to wonder if this bundle of clippings was what inspired her to make these comments. Or perhaps my great-grandmother or her mother had compiled them and passed on the sentiment. The articles were all about accidents on the line. Little boys who lost limbs, young fathers who died hours after they fell from a train, horrendous gruesome ends to lives in a community just starting to grow.

Tucked amidst this bundle was a yellowed envelope with a longish article preserved inside, a greater care than had been taken for the other bits of newspaper. Sensing this extra caution taken by whoever had compiled these notes, I gently pulled it out with the least bits of my fingertips touching it. Then I slowly read the page.

UNDER THE WHEELS

*A sad fatality occurred at the Ludington street crossing of the M. & N. railroad last Saturday evening, by which Peter Judge, a well-to-do farmer of Oconomowoc, who was here visiting his daughter, Mrs. Peter Collins, was instantly killed. Mrs. Collins and her father were crossing the track just as a long train of empty ore cars were being backed up, and their attention was attracted by the Swedish company of the Salvation Army, which was marching to their barracks in Laing's building with their usual base [sic] drum and tambourine accompaniment. The religious enthusiasts were making so much noise that the repeated shouts of the train-men and bystanders, the rumble of the cars, and ringing of the bell failed to apprise them of their danger, and when the accident was seen to be inevitable, Night Yard Master McBride and Mr. Baker, who were on the end car, at the risk of their own lives, jumped off, one grabbing Mrs. Collins and dragging her off the track and the other rescuing two little girls. There was no time to save Mr. Judge, and he was knocked down and terribly mangled by the cars. Mrs. Collins had to be restrained by force to prevent her rushing between the cars in a wild attempt to rescue her father and her agonized cries were pitiful to hear. The mangled remains of Mr. Judge were sent to Oconomowoc Monday for burial.*

Excerpted from*: The Iron Range, Volume XIV, Number 13* [Thursday, June 16, 1892], page 1, column 5. Iron Mountain, Dickinson County, Michigan.

It was too depressing any more to go on, the screams of the now fatherless daughter echoing in my head, mingling with the blare of the train horn, hiss of steam, and squeal of too late brakes. Whether they came from reading the article or the dream of the night before, I'm not sure. I set the bundle of papers back down, the article back in its envelope on top, and did not retreat again to the chest for any more family papers to sort through.

It had all been over one stormy late summer day that I worked at this from early morning to late afternoon. I had only stopped for a midday supper of buttered noodles like grandma used to make me, and a stiff mug of black coffee like grandpa used to drink. By the end of the afternoon, there was much more than the excerpts I noted laid out. Only a small space was left for me to kneel without crushing any of the documents I had set out. The moment was imbued with a subtle magic. The storm clouds had broken to allow a few of the strong golden hour sunbeams through that highlighted the family history I had found for myself. Thunder in the distance predicted a future storm and a harbinger gust of wind rushed through the open window. My carefully handled history was swept across the floor and tumbled into another mess, one more tangle of history to sort through.

# The Great Divide

## by Elizabeth Fust

On either side the great divide stand Past and Future, the wardens of time.

No one knows what Future holds; he keeps his hands in a tightly clasped fold.

It is Past who willingly offers the trepidations and blisses from yesterday's coffers.

Sometimes Future likes to tempt and taunt; what he has to offer he humbly flaunts.

Sometimes Past likes to hoard her treasures and withholds them against the most drastic of measures.

Though they face, Future and Past shall never meet, the great divide between them is your present heartbeat.

**Elizabeth Fust** is a self-published and freelance writer. In addition to the pieces published in this issue, she has short stories in Issues 1 and 2 of the *U.P. Reader*. Elizabeth graduated with a Bachelor of Arts degree in English Writing from Northern Michigan University. Now she lives and works in Marquette and is a contributor to *Marquette Monthly*. She recently self-published her first children's book, *The Hungry Kitten's Tale*.

# A Stone's Story

## by Deborah K. Frontiera

Our stone began over a billion years ago as sand eroded from an even earlier rock, part of a chain of ancient mountains. The sand flowed with the rain and rivers down and down until it settled on the shore of an ancient lake bed. Waves rippled the sand. More sand washed over that, and over that, and over that. The only life existing on earth then was colonies of Stromatolites, or blue green algae, which through photosynthesis would raise the level of oxygen in the air to a point where other life would evolve in time. Cyanobaceria also grew and sometimes blocked the flow of water through the sand so iron particles did not oxidize. This left white spots in some of the red sands around what would become our stone. It had taken nearly half the planet's history to get to this point. Dinosaurs, still in the far distant future, would never leave a trace in this rock.

Layers and layers of sand washed upon each other, compacting, pressing down and down, over 9000 feet thick. Our rock felt the pressure of those layers squeezing individual particles of sand together until they fused into rock, a special type of sandstone that humans, eons later, would call Jacobsville Sandstone. Our stone was patient through all this, having gone from rock to sand, to a new kind of rock, enduring through it all. What else did he have to do? So he remained in darkness, deep below Earth's surface, dimly aware of the flows of lava cooling into basalt, cracking with fissures which would fill with copper and other metals in subsequent eruptions not so far from this stone.

The land above our rock changed over millions of years; oxygen levels rose, the planet warmed and teamed with life, and death, and new life. Millions and millions of years

more our stone waited. Time marched on. At four different intervals, glaciers hundreds of feet thick gouged and carved the rock on the surface, souring out life in their advances, renewing life in their retreats, sculpting the land to their way of thinking, dragging some pieces of rock and metal hundreds of miles from where they originated, then leaving them behind on the surface. But our stone knew none of that which occurred way above where he waited. Waited for what?

Earth circled the sun millions of times; species of life came and went. Very late in geologic time, human beings evolved, spread over Earth, and during the last Ice Age reached the area where our rock waited far below the surface. Our stone didn't know they were there, hunting, gathering, finding some of the red metal near the surface not all that far from him. They hammered the red metal into bowls and jewelry, traded it until bits of it reached far south on the continent. Centuries went by.

In the modern year of 1883, the stone began to hear strange noises—pounding, grinding, scraping. He pondered what these noises were as he lay in the dark, some many feet in from a cliff edge and below the noises. Later he would see that human beings had removed some 50 feet of overburden glacial drift and shale, had cut channels into the face of the sandstone cliff, drilled a series of holes, cracked out blocks eight feet, by four feet, by two feet, and with steam-powered machines, lifted the blocks onto tram cars, hauled them to a dock on the shore of Lake Superior and loaded the blocks onto ships. The quarry was a beehive of human activity.

Closer and closer, louder and louder the noise came to our stone. One day, the light reached him. Wedges separated him from surrounding rock. What a different world it was from his last view of it as sand, water and sky—no green or moving, living things. Now, life was everywhere: creatures on two legs, birds, trees, grass .... As men and machines removed our stone from the cliff, he heard voices.

"Where are these blocks headed?"

"Calumet—for the building of a church. They'll be pleased with these blocks for the front—not a speck of those strange white spots."

As our stone was loaded onto a tram car, he heard he would travel some eighteen miles, first by ship and then by rail, to a town called Red Jacket. He continued to listen to the voices around him and learned that other blocks of stone like himself had been shipped as far away as Chicago and New York for handsome buildings in those great cities. Hundreds of buildings and a few of the most expensive homes in what he heard called "The Copper Country" had been built and would continue to be built from blocks cut from the cliff from which he came.

Once at the building site, he was again admired for his pure red color. "Hey, Cap," he heard one man say, "This one would be great for the name stone above the door!"

Cap agreed. "Get the sculptor over here."

A man with a special chisel admired our stone and carved into his surface: St. Anne's Church 1900.

Some of the side walls of the church contained sandstone that was striated with white and red, pieces with white spots in them and other features considered less perfect by the builders. But the entire front of the edifice was as our stone, solid red. All around him, blocks were cut, shaped, fitted together with mortar, formed into Gothic arches, stairs, and a towering spire. People passed by, admired the progress, awaited the day the church would be complete. The stone was proud to be part of it, especially the part that declared the building's name.

From the people walking by, admiring this grand addition to their community, he learned that this new church stood where an older building had been. Called St. Louis de

France, it had grown too small for the 375 families worshiping there. The priest had inspired his congregation to raise $45,000 (a huge sum in those days) for their new church. At its height, the parish would have over 900 members. Inside were not just one main altar, but two side altars, finely crafted panels and walls, stained glass windows that would be the envy of other churches. Architects would copy some of the ideas for another church a few blocks away, and others in nearby towns.

On Sunday, June 18, 1901, a solemn and impressive parade with several bands and thousands of people walked the entire length of Fifth Street in Red Jacket before coming to a stop in front of the church. The Bishop of Marquette was there, many priests of other parishes, people from all over. The church, in song and ceremony, was consecrated for its sacred purpose. If our stone could have, he would have radiated gold light from himself, so happy was he to be part of all this. After all the eons in the dark, he was part of something filled with light and spirit. And it happened in a mere blink of time in his existence.

For sixty-five golden years, the stone rejoiced as people entered every Sunday—so many there was more than one service held—to sing, pray and receive Holy Communion. On weekdays, there were fewer people, but they still came. Our stone watched brides and grooms enter to be married, and over the years baptize their babies, lay their parents to rest, watch their children marry, the cycle of faith and life going on and on. He loved to hear the grand music of the organ, hear the choir singing and chanting in the loft behind the wall he adorned. He enjoyed the echo of the French language being taught in the basement of the church.

But nothing ever stays the same. For nearly a year between July 1913 and April 1914, the copper miners and the mine owners quarreled violently over working conditions. Other area churches had several more than the usual number of funerals. The spire of St. Anne's spread the word that men marched in the street, fought with each other just a few blocks away. The following Easter brought calm, but no one seemed truly satisfied. For a few years, things were "normal" again, but our stone noticed that the numbers of people living in the area gradually declined. Fewer worshipers on Sundays, then only one Mass held, and even fewer people. The spire reported that many people and families boarded the train and never came back. Some mines closed, and businesses, too. The train stopped coming to the depot. Automobiles became the main mode of travel.

In half a blink of his life, the glow was gone. The organ fell silent. In 1966, St. Anne's was deconsecrated, no longer a sacred place. Our stone would hear from the people that St. Anne's was one of three churches closed that year. Remaining parishioners left and attended one of the other two Catholic Churches in the Calumet area. People wept. If he could have, our stone would have cried, too.

For five years, the church sat empty. No one entered the great door below our stone. He sat patiently, as he had for a billion years, wondering what would come next. What came was disappointment.

"Did you hear?" a person said, "Some guy bought St. Anne's from the diocese for only $4,000! Plans to open an antique store." The person to whom she spoke shook her head. It was 1971 when the sign went up: Olde St. Anne's Antiques and Collectables.

Perhaps the stone might have said, *Well, at least I'll be used again.* But only $4,000? The stone had listened to the words of the priests all those years—Jesus, betrayed for a paltry 30 pieces of silver. The stone felt betrayed, too. The shop was basically a junk shop, an on-going garage sale, and a mess. Few people came in and even fewer bought things. The owner cared nothing for the building itself, performing not a speck of upkeep.

The stone probably cringed when in 1991, a second-rate movie company used the "sanctuary" to film a scene of the horror movie *Children of the Night*. The stone could not see inside, but he heard that the movie featured shots of the stained glass windows reflected on a flooded interior. A beautiful place of reverence had been reduced to a place of horror. But the worst was yet to come.

The junk shop owner died, leaving the mess for his estate to clean up, with no elec-tricity or water connected. Plaster sagged in the choir loft, missing stair treads stood to trip any who entered, having to skirt broken boards and holes in main floor. One woman who entered had to catch herself on her elbows when the floor gave way beneath her. Pigeons flew through the former sanctuary entering through holes in the eaves. The steeple swayed, sandstone blocks loosened. Feathers, bird waste, and dead pigeons, junk from the "antique store" lay everywhere. The hardwood floors were gone from the basement meeting room, the dirt floor beneath torn up. An eight-inch-thick tree with knobs of branches held up held up the floor of the chancel area. Some of the glass bricks in the basement windows broke and animals entered. Mold covered the walls. Small trees took root in the cracks of the front steps. Mortar holding the stones together deteriorated.

Two people passed by the front. One of them said, "The estate people want to get rid of the mess. I heard they want to sell to someone who only wants to take out stained glass windows."

"I heard that, too," said the other. "Removal of glass would create a wind tunnel. With the leaking roof, cracked glass blocks in basement, and that porous sandstone expanding and contracting summer to winter... Look at all the cracks! The whole thing will just fall in."

If stones could weep, our stone did. Perhaps I shall be worn down to sand again. *Be Patient*, he reminded himself. *Perhaps in another billion or so years...*

But the pride of the community would not let that happen. In 1994, the Calumet Downtown Development Authority appealed to area churches for help. Our stone heard that Rev. Bob Langseth alerted people to the situation, and began a fundraising campaign to buy the building. A committee formed a board to raise the purchase price of $38,000. The Township would own the church and provide insurance, but some other organization would have to do all the restoration and future maintenance. The Village of Calumet and the Township had barely enough tax money to maintain basic services. Volunteers entered the old church for first time in many years, beholding the reality of the building's ruin.

St. Anne's Church - Calumet

"I can't believe you didn't just walk away from it," our stone heard someone say as they surveyed the disaster. But this community did not give up. They raised the purchase price and took the first steps to stabilize the structure. Our stone began to have hope.

Mask-waring volunteers scraped away old plaster from walls and deteriorated ceilings. The roof could not be replaced as yet, but they patched the leaks. The flea market junk had been thrown down through a hole in the main floor and piled up. Five, two-ton dump trucks carted away that junk, rotting lumber, dead animals and pigeons and their accumulated waste.

Three years later, a loose block of sandstone from the steeple crashed onto Fifth Street. This new crisis diverted funds from full repair to the roof. A grant from State of Michigan allowed improved heating pipes to basement, restoration of tuck-pointing of mortar between the blocks of sandstone. But lead in the stained glass windows had deteriorated and the windows were in danger of collapse. Michigan granted another $75,000, and people of the surrounding communities raised another $87,000 in donations to save the windows. Some were repaired onsite, others carefully removed and shipped to Philadelphia to Willett Studios where specialists worked on them through the year 2000.

That was a turning point, 100 years after completion of the original construction. Seven years after the resurrection work began, the roof was finally completed. One of the board members said, "Well, old girl, you're going to stand."

Our stone wanted to shout for joy.

The following June, the board, eager to have people see their efforts, raise more needed funds, and promote the use of the building for local events, celebrated 100 years with a banquet in the basement meeting hall. They served elegant d'oeuvres. There was one working toilet there. The church was a mere shadow of its former self, but hints of its beauty were everywhere. The event's main speaker quoted Emerson. "'If eyes were made for seeing, then beauty is its own excuse for being.' People ask why we want to continue. My answer is, 'It's a beautiful building. It deserves to live.'"

A new sign went up on the front: **Keweenaw Heritage Center**

Where the altar once stood, lies a stage with a line of flags along the back wall. On the far left, Quebec's flag stands to honor the French-Canadian congregation who'd built St. Anne's. The United States flag stands on the far right. Between them in alphabetical order are the flags of the countries from which people immigrated to the area in the early 20th century. These are also symbolic of their descendants who rolled up their sleeves to resurrect the building and preserve their history.

Every summer, a new historical exhibit lines the walls of the former sanctuary. Chairs in rows welcome people to listen to concerts by local musicians. A basket passed at each concert collects donations for ongoing restoration.

In 2007, the first wedding took place with a reception following downstairs. The building also hosted a traveling exhibit from the Smithsonian, and ethnic group meetings in fall and spring. The board began finding funds to restore an antique Barckhoff Organ to be placed in the choir loft. It was not the original organ, but it was built around the same time. Volunteers dismantled it, and carried it piece by piece from the main floor to choir loft. They accomplished this through an "Adopt-a-Pipe" fundraiser. The following year, the wood floor was refinished, sanded and varnished. Organ music once again echoed through the building.

A caring community continued to pour money and time into the Keweenaw Heritage Center. In 2008, a "Lift the Lift" campaign to make the building accessible for all became a reality because of donated funds and a grant from the Keweenaw National Historical Park. People with disabilities could now enter the building from a back door on Temple Street and go up to the main floor or down to the banquet room area.

Lightning struck the steeple in 2013 (the second time such a thing had occurred). Heavy rain put out the resulting fire, but there was still damage. People poured out into the streets, cleaning up shingles and wood that fell, putting plastic tarps over the damaged area to keep out the rain, donating money for the repairs.

The Keweenaw Heritage Center Board reported to the community that over the years, people donated over 80,000 hours of work and in excess of $1.5 million with day to day maintenance and utilities, and more projects to come. Of that money, 53% came from private donations of mostly local residents in an economically depressed area. The other 47% came from grants. All these things our stone heard people discuss as he looked down over the main door.

Was it only someone's imagination when she thought she saw tears of joy dripping slowly from our stone on a recent sunny summer day?

Note: Anyone may see this beautiful building located at the head of Fifth Street in Calumet MI 49913. For more information visit: **www.keweenawheritagecenter. org** This story will become a chapter in the author's upcoming book, *Superior Tapestry: Threads in Upper Michigan History*, to be released in the spring of 2021 by Modern History Press.

**Deborah K. Frontiera** grew up in Michigan's Upper Peninsula. From 1985 through 2008, she taught in Houston public schools, followed by several years in Houston's Writers In The Schools program. A "migratory creature," she spends spring, summer, and fall in her beloved U.P. and the dead of winter in Houston, Texas. Four of her books have been honor or award winners. She has published fiction, nonfiction, poetry, and children's books. She edits the newsletter for the Upper Peninsula Publishers and Authors Association. For details about her many books and accomplishments, visit her web site: www. authorsden.com/deborahkfrontiera

# Awareness

## by Ann Dallman

Pain lifts from his surgery-scarred body
as reality starts to intrude on his survival.

No longer occupied with mundane worries
He starts to realize the damage
he caused racing through the corridors of
his life
like an escaped animal.

The choices he made then are now
haunting entities taunting him
with promises made.

Promises of sexual vitality and vigor
Promises of strength and leadership
Promises of personal fame and prominence.

Empty promises.
Once important but now hollowed out and
worthless in the stillness of his soul.

Ann Dallman is the content editor of _Tri-City Neighbors_ magazine focusing on the residents of Marinette and Peshtigo (WI) and Menominee (MI). A former English teacher, she edited, wrote, and did the graphic design for _Sam English: The Life, Work and Times of An Artist_ (2009 Coffee Table Book of the Year/PEAK Award). A former newspaper editor, she has also published in national trade magazines. The Society of Children's Book Writers and Illustrators/ Michigan Chapter named her as Runner Up in its 2016 Multicultural Mentorship Competition. Her first book _Cady and the Bear Necklace_ was just published by Three Towers Press

# The Light Keeper Hero of Passage Island Lighthouse and the Wreck of the Monarch

## by Mikel B. Classen

In the early days of settling the Lake Superior frontier, life was a constant battle with danger. A life and death situation could arise in the flash of a moment. This was particularly true when sailing the moody water of Lake Superior. Late season travel was the most dangerous of all. From October through November, shipwrecks were common, loss of life, not unusual. It is during these situations that heroes show themselves.

In December of 1906, a passenger steamer named the *Monarch* left Port Arthur, Canada, during what was beginning to be a blinding snowstorm. The ship carried 41 passengers bound for Sarnia, Ontario, which was on the southern tip of Lake Huron. The snow was thick and blinding. Visibility was only a few feet. The captain of the ship, Edward Robertson, a thirty-five-year veteran of the lakes, had been sailing on a compass heading as the surf began to build and the winds turned to a gale. Unsure of his position, the captain ordered a check on what was known as the "log," a cylinder that trailed behind the ship to record mileage.

Visibility was near zero, but a break in the blizzard showed a light in the distance. The mate on watch reported to the captain that he had spotted the Passage Island Light. That simply couldn't be. In the captain's estimation, there was no conceivable way that they had traveled that far. It was simply too soon. What was the light then?

The *Monarch* kept churning its way through the darkness and blinding snow. The propellers were turning hard, because the captain had hoped to outrun the storm front or at least break out of the blizzard. The *Monarch* was sailing at full speed when it hit the rocks. Water poured into the stern as seams broke from the impact.

Captain Robertson immediately assessed the desperate situation of his ship. He had to keep it afloat. If not and she slipped off the rocks, there was a good chance everyone would drown. He ordered the engines to be kept running at all costs. Water was pouring into the engine room, but the boilers were still fired and the crew did their best. With the propeller turning, the force kept the bow against the rocks.

It was now early morning and in the dim light, the captain and crew could make out Blake's Point on Isle Royale. They now knew their location and they could see the treacherous rock shoreline. The only way off the ship would be to run a line from the ship to the rocks on the shore. One of the crew, Watchman J. Jacques, volunteered to take one of the small lifeboats ashore to string a line. They lowered the boat and the surf was rough. It swelled and tossed the boat but Jacques valiantly rowed to the rock shore. The waves rose and tossed, slamming the little boat down on the rocks, breaking it to splinters. Watchman Jacques was thrown into the water. Struggling was futile. He was Lake Superior's now.

The crew and passengers watched as their companion drowned. But there was no time to dwell on the loss. Time was running out and they still had to get off. A new plan was formed. Using a long rope and another volunteer, a deckhand, different sources give different names for who exactly it was, the volunteer would be tied to the rope, lowered to just above the surf and then swung to shore, hopefully close enough to grab onto one of the rocks and pull himself to shore.

Like a giant pendulum he was swung back and forth, and when they thought he was close enough, he was released and they missed. He fell into the surf, only to be pulled back to the ship and out of the water. Again the swinging and again the release. Another miss.

He was hauled up for a third attempt and they started swinging again. Out the rope stretched, and it broke! The momentum carried the man towards the shore and by his fingertips, he was able to catch onto a rock. He pulled himself up, wet and cold. At least he was on the shore.

The crew on the ship, using a long ladder, ran a new line across and the deckhand had to then climb to the top of the rocky cliff that made up the shore. When he reached the top, he tied the rope to a tree and it was pulled tight. Now the passengers and crew had a way to safety as long as the ship stayed afloat.

The stern had submerged, but the bow clung to the rocks. The crew and passengers now had to go one at a time, hand over hand, above the rolling, churning surf to the rocks on the shore. Each one made the dramatic crossing, including one elderly woman.

Chippewa hut

One man, a watchman, grabbed the wrong line and went into the water. Quickly, Lake Superior claimed his life.

The rest made it successfully with the captain waiting to be the last off his ship. The cold wet group huddled around each other at the top of the rocks. The group watched as the bow of the *Monarch* rose to a 50 degree angle and the unmanned engines finally quit. The stern broke and sank into the lake. The bow stayed where it was, the waves battering it mercilessly.

Now there was a more pressing matter: staying alive. They began collecting driftwood for a fire. One of the passengers was carrying matches that were still usable. It wasn't long and they had one started. The captain hoped that the fire would signal any passing ships, though he knew that every day that passed, that hope would get slimmer. Theirs had been the last run of the season for the *Monarch*; few other ships would be passing this late in the year. Their situation was desperate.

A few miles away stood the Passage Island Lighthouse. The head light keeper, Mr. Shaw, could see the smoke of the fire from the light tower. He called his Assistant Light keeper, Klass Hamringa to help take bearings and to keep a watch on the smoke column to determine if it was stationary or moving. They came to the conclusion that it was stationary and probably a fire of some stranded fishermen.

They decided to keep watch on it. Lake Superior was rough and the winds were still blowing a gale. The pair decided that when the lake calmed, one of them would go take a look.

The survivors of the *Monarch* were actively working to keep themselves alive. They gathered brush and branches and made a makeshift windbreak. Some flour and frozen salmon washed ashore from the wreck and they managed to grab it. The little food helped. They were in a dire situation. It was cold enough that a few feet away from the fire, fingers and ears could freeze. Forty-one people huddled around a fire trying to keep from freezing.

Four of the men knew of a hunting camp that was at Tobin Harbor, some twelve miles away. The four decided to strike out, hoping to recover some food from the camp and maybe, if they were lucky, someone might be there to help. It was a long hard trek and when they got there, they found it deserted and by all appearances, it had been for a while. They did find some left-behind provisions, but not many. They hiked back to the survivor camp and added the food to the community stores.

After two days, Lake Superior began to calm. The gale winds had abated some. The light keepers at Passage Island were still watching the smoke from the fire of the survivors. The pair decided that Lake Superior was calm enough that one of them could go to investigate, thinking that some fishermen had gotten in trouble. It was against the rules of the Lighthouse Service to abandon the lighthouse completely, so only one could go. Assistant Keeper Hamringa was the logical choice.

He readied the lighthouse's rowboat and set out toward the smoke. Lake Superior was still rough and there was the sharp, icy cold of winter still in the wind. He had packed himself some lunch and had the foresight to pack some wool blankets. He also assured himself that he had dry matches along. Hamringa knew in the back of his mind that there was the possibility that he himself could become shipwrecked.

Hamringa had been shipwrecked twice before: once off the banks of Newfoundland and once while rounding the Cape of Good Hope. Now, he was always prepared for the worst and hoped for the best. He continued to row hard against the rolling waves. Snow squalls still passed over, obscuring his view and forcing him to keep the shore in sight. It was a four mile row that took several hours to complete, but finally as he rowed around the rocks of Blake's Point, he saw what was left of the *Monarch*.

The bow was still wedged between the rocks, covered with a layer of snow. Hamringa rowed the boat over where the stern should have been. The drop was so deep, he could see nothing of it. He moved his rowboat toward the shore. There was nowhere he could land due to the steep cliffs, so he kept the boat offshore. He shouted. There was no response, but he knew someone had kept a fire going for several days. He shouted again. There was movement on the rock bluff above.

The stranded passengers and crew of the *Monarch* weren't expecting help. They were huddled together around a smoky fire. They had constructed a crude shelter out of spruce and balsam branches and they were beginning to suffer frostbite. Though the weather had subsided, it didn't help their situation. Then they heard the shouts from light keeper Hamringa.

They ran to the top of the ridge yelling and waving handkerchiefs and hats. Hamringa responded, yelling and waving back. He didn't have room to take everyone. He shouted up to them, "Is there one of you than can row a boat? We'll go back to the lighthouse and bring back help!"

The group talked amongst themselves and the purser of the *Monarch*, Mr. Beaumont, volunteered. There are two differing stories about how the purser got to Hamringa. The first was that Beaumont was lowered down the ice-covered face of the rock by the survivors above. He waited until he was within jumping distance of the rowboat and was able to land inside.

The other version has Beaumont jumping into the water and swimming to the side of the rowboat while Hamringa pulled him in.

However he got there, light keeper Hamringa was able to get him wrapped in blankets and they began the long row back to the Passage Island Light. Beaumont was given the lunch that Hamringa had packed. Several hours later, they made it back.

Mr. Shaw, the head light keeper, spotted a steamer named the *Edmonton* which had just left Port Arthur and was able to signal it with the fog signal. The *Edmonton* hove to and Shaw and Hamringa took Beaumont out to it. The captain listened to Beaumont's tale of the shipwreck and explained how many people were still left out there.

Realizing that a ship of that size wouldn't be able to get anywhere near the wreck site, the captain turned his ship back towards Port Arthur to get help. Shaw and Hamringa went back to their lighthouse, Beaumont went with the *Edmonton.*

Arriving back in Port Arthur, the captain of a tug, named the *James Whalen*, was roused from his bed. He was sick, but when he heard of the predicament of the *Monarch* survivors, he jumped to the emergency. Loading extra coal—twenty tons; blankets, food, medical supplies, and two doctors, the tug was loaded for rescue.

The sail to Isle Royale was long and rough, but as the day passed, the weather was favorable.

The *James Whalen* was a large, stable tug that was frequently used as an ice breaker. As they pulled into the rocky site of the *Monarch* wreck, the tossing surf forced the captain to hold the tug offshore. Seeing no one, the *Whalen* sounded its whistle four times.

At the top of the ridge, figures could be seen floundering in the snow above as the passengers and crew of the *Monarch* ran towards the sound of the whistle. As the survivors watched, the tug moved around to the lee side of Blake's Point and lowered its lifeboats, landing a party on the shore. They hiked from there to the survivors, who were rapidly making their way to them, slipping through the snow and tumbling over the deadfalls.

They were taken on board and fed hot food and were covered with blankets. The doctors went around treating frostbite in several of the survivors' feet and hands. They had all survived, including the elderly lady who had been a passenger. She was complimented as the "best man of the party." Several passengers expressed regret that they hadn't saved their one and only axe that had kept the forty-one people alive through the harsh weather. It would have made an interesting souvenir. They had been stranded on Isle Royale for four brutally long days. If they hadn't been rescued when they were, there would have been much more loss of life and certainly the frostbite would have led to loss of limbs.

Klaus Hamringa, the light keeper who rowed to the party, was given a commendation for valor from the Lighthouse Service. His heroism did not go unnoticed. He would again be instrumental in saving survivors of another shipwreck several years later when he was transferred to Au Sable Point Lighthouse.

When the need arises, heroes show themselves. They rise up unknowing to themselves and do what has to be done, regardless of their own safety and wellbeing. Heroes, they surround us today as they have in our past, and every day, another is revealed.

**Mikel B. Classen** has been writing about northern Michigan in newspapers and magazines for over thirty-five years, creating feature articles about the life and culture of Michigan's north country. He's written about Upper Peninsula history, travel, outdoors, the environment and many other subjects. A journalist, historian, photographer and author with a fascination for the world around him, he enjoys researching and writing about lost stories from the past. Currently he is managing editor of the *U.P. Reader* and is a member of the Board of Directors for the Upper Peninsula Publishers and Authors Association.

His book include *Au Sable Point Lighthouse, Beacon on Lake Superior's Shipwreck Coast;*, *Teddy Roosevelt and the Marquette Libel Trial, Lake Superior Tales, Journeys into the Macabre,* and *Points North* To learn more about Mikel B. Classen and to see more of his work, go to his website at www.mikelclassen.com.

# The Kalamazoo

## by T. Marie Bertineau

was eight years old when I rebelled against the Kalamazoo.

Or at least I think I was. That's what I recall about the old wood stove with the chipped porcelain, which was parked like a Sherman tank in Gramma's Keweenaw kitchen. It was our winter warrior. Our commander-in-chief. And as a frequent guest at Gram's house, I was, by default, born into its battalion. The roar of that stove taught me winter was the enemy, the season for combat. It was the time for stockpiled ammunition crafted of hardwoods, for donning wooly uniforms, for plopping bread-bagged feet into marching boots and trudging off to the attack armed with scoops or shovels or rusted coal scuttles. Yes, some might say winter was a battle in the Copper Country. But if you asked the Kalamazoo, winter was full-out war.

It all began one early fall. I remember a nickel sky, gold-plated leaves, a pinch in the air. My two older sisters and I stared at a mountain of scrap wood looming before us in the yard behind Gramma's house—offcuts of raw flooring which would be sacrificed as firewood in the coming months. Earlier in the week, in preparation for winter, a truck from Hoikstra's Hardwoods had dumped a load of maple—the first sign of things to come. The six- to eight-inch pieces of tongue and groove had tumbled from the truck's scarred metal box in a frenzy of *clacks* and *thwops* and were now heaped high in a dome, like a fortified beaver dam. It was our duty to "throw the wood"—to spend the next week or

so tossing it into the cellar through a small window in the home's poor rock foundation. The scraps, in turn, would be hauled upstairs throughout the winter and burned in the Kalamazoo to heat Gram's old saltbox, or *headquarters* as the case may be.

"This'll be worth pasties," Janie said as she climbed to the top of the pile and began chucking handfuls of blonde blocks through the opening. We had worked on it a few days already, but there was still much to be done.

Anne, the more experienced of the squad, turned to me from her perch on the wood pile. "Reka," she said using my childhood nickname. "You're gonna help, eh?"

"Yah, I will!" I smiled up at her from where I stood along the path to the outhouse, which had been worn to a narrow strip of dirt throughout the years. For me, *anything* was worth pasties, a dish rooted in Cornish history and handed down through generations. Since Gramma was a second-generation Cornish immigrant, pasties were common fare in our diet. They were also a favorite reward for a job well done. *Work hard*, Gram would say, *and there'll be pasties for supper.* That always took the sting out of chores.

I say that "we" threw the wood, but truth be told, it was mostly Anne and Janie. They were the enlisted—I was still a cadet. I busied myself in the shadow of the overgrown burdock—"sticker bush" we called it. I built pretend roads with the maple blocks and searched the clover for yummy buttonweed seed pods, or mallow. *Look at all the belly buttons!* I would say, popping the pods in my mouth one after the other, forgetting what it was we had come to do. No, I wasn't much help when it came to reducing the size of the woodpile in the yard, but I was good at spreading it out once it was inside the cellar.

"Hey," Anne called to me after they'd been at it awhile. "We need you. Come kick the wood down."

The scraps they had tossed were at peak and needed to be leveled out. This is where I came in handy—Special Forces. I was still wiry enough to fit through the cellar window, so I scurried to the top of the pile and straddled the opening. Janie pressed her hand to the crown of my head to keep me from bumping it on the window frame. "Watch for spiders," she said.

"Keep talking," I said as I slid through, a scout on reconnaissance, "so I won't be scared." Inside, I eyed the dim space. It was murky and desolate, lit only by four small windows, the panes laden with dust and grime. Only a faint light filterd through. It played tricks on my eyes and cast eerie shadows in far corners where I dared not venture. The air was thick and stale as a trench, and an earthy odor clung to my nostrils. Fear squeezed. "There's a lot of wood in here already!" I called out in an effort to self-soothe. "We're doing good!"

"Well, *we* are anyway," one of them mumbled.

I went right to work crab-crawling back and forth across the growing heap, heeling loose wood down the slope, widening the base and lowering the peak. After a bit, I stood up to kick the wood. As a rookie I tended to revert to haste, which often ended poorly for me.

"You know what happens when you stand up too soon," Anne said, always the voice of reason.

"I know. I'll be careful." No sooner had I spoken when the pile slipped out from under me and down I went on my backside, bruising my tailbone on the sharp cuts of wood. I grimaced and rubbed my rump. "Cripes!" Wood kicking was hazardous duty—darn that Kalamazoo.

Mission complete, I squeezed back through the opening, which was more fun than using

the cellar steps, and doubled back indoors to check on the pasty making. The aroma of fresh-baked crust and tender root vegetables had seeped out into the porch shed. Inside, baking trays lined the stovetop, each covered with thin flour sack towels. I could make out the familiar D-shaped impressions of the pasties beneath. I had to hand it to that wood stove—at least it knew how to redeem itself.

"It smells soo good!" I said. "I'm starving!"

"You worked up an appetite, eh?" Gram said. "Did you help your sisters?"

"Mm hmm." I wasn't sure my sisters would agree, but I thought I'd been helpful.

•••

Seasons passed, and winter had come to the Copper Country again—it never seemed to stray very far. I was dropped off alone at Gram's on a Friday after school to find the old Kalamazoo barking orders. It had been back in commission for a couple of months now, an integral part of winter in that home. The white, enameled appliance—divided into two parts—occupied the north wall of the kitchen. One side was comprised of a propane cooktop and oven, but the other side was the wood stove with its black, cast-iron top, which we learned early in life to be off-limits. A big stovepipe extended out the back of the unit and bent at a ninety degree angle through the chimney wall. A small coil on the pipe controlled the damper. One winter evening when Gramma fired up the stove, she forgot about the damper.

"My eyes sting," I said as smoke backed up and a haze filled the rooms.

"Cripes! I forgot the damn flue!" She scampered to the kitchen to remedy the problem, batting the air as she went. Afterward, to clear the house, we opened the door to the porch shed along with a couple of windows. Her storm windows were in place by then, but at their base were three holes which provided ventilation once we poked out the packed snow. The draft rushed in. Wood smoke and cold collided. "One of these days," she said in mock frustration, wielding a clenched fist in the direction of the wood stove. "Pow! Right in the kisser." That was the only time I ever saw Gram disrespect the Kalamazoo.

Now, Friday's snow was accumulating in the drive. I heard Mom gun the accelerator as she pulled out onto the highway. Gram was sitting in the living room watching the weather. "Oo," she said. "We're s'posed to get a big one next week. You'll have to stack the shed good for Gramma tomorrow."

I rolled my eyes hearing tomorrow's playtime would be sidelined by the Kalamazoo. During the school year, every Saturday after morning cartoons, we kids hauled wood from the cellar. First, we had to fill the big box behind the stove, but when the temperatures plummeted and snow mounted, the porch shed had to be stacked too, clear to the ceiling. The stove burned round the clock in the winter, and it seemed we could never keep enough wood upstairs to satisfy demand. "I wish Anne and Janie was here," I said. The work went faster with three.

"You're getting old enough," Gram said. "You can do it. There'll still be plenty o' time to play."

Somehow, I doubted that.

That weekend, hauling wood became my nemesis and the Kalamazoo nothing short of a tyrant. I descended into that cellar so many times I quit counting. I scaled steep steps with boxfuls of maple, heaped wood in the kitchen, stacked blocks for hours in the shed. Even the window disappeared behind the store of artillery. Resentment grew— I considered going AWOL. Who made that stove *boss* anyway? I should have been out playing. I should have been having fun. I decided right then and there: no matter how many pasties it baked, I was done with that wood stove.

After that grueling weekend, the relationship between me and the Kalamazoo cooled. Everyone else may have been enamored with that old rust bucket, but I'd had enough of its dictatorship. Respect went by the wayside, and I thumbed my nose up at it each time I passed by—until one snowy afternoon, when Gram stepped in to reconcile things.

"There's something for you in the parlor," she said when I was dropped off on a Fri-

day after school. I had come alone again that weekend. That was happening more and more. My sisters were teenagers now. I had regretfully moved up in rank.

Around the corner, on the seat of the upholstered rocker, I found a baggie of marbles: purees, cat's eyes, bumblebees, and even a boulder. I dropped to my knees and dumped them all into the chair. They rolled toward the seat back, enchanting me with their delicate *clickity click* as they puddled in the crevice of the seat cushion. I smoothed my fingertips over them, entranced by their swirl of color. "Where'd you get these?" I asked. All the kids had been shooting marbles at recess, but marbles cost money, and money didn't grow on trees as I'd heard said.

"LeMaire's," she said. LeMaire's owned the local IGA. They must have come with that week's grocery order.

"They're for me?" It wasn't even my birthday.

"Yah. You haul a lot of wood."

I went to her where she stood in the doorway, wrapped my arms around her waist. I burrowed my cheek in her pillowy chest, warm and cottony, like Mrs. Rabbit from the Beatrix Potter books. "Thanks, Gram. I never had marbles." In the next room I heard the pop and crackle of the Kalamazoo, warming my limbs, toasting my toes. *Well done, Soldier,* it seemed to say.

Perhaps I had been too hard on that old stove.

**T. Marie Bertineau** was born amidst the copper mining ruins of Michigan's Keweenaw and is of Anishinaabe-Ojibwe and French Canadian/Cornish descent. She is a member of the Keweenaw Bay Indian Community on the L'Anse Reservation. Her work has appeared with the Carver County Arts Consortium in Minnesota; in *Mino Miikana*, a publication of the Native Justice Coalition and Waub Ajijaak Press; and will appear in the upcoming anthology of the Chanhassen Writers Group of Minnesota. Her memoir, *The Mason House*, will be released in the fall of 2020 by Lanternfish Press.

# *Party Animals*

## by Larry Buege

◆❖◆

Over the weekend, Marquette city police received a breaking-and-entering complaint from a prominent Marquette resident. Central Dispatch sent Officers Koski and Beaudry with appropriate back-up to investigate. Finding nothing amiss upon arrival at the house in question, Officer Koski punched the doorbell. Wally Higgenbottom opened the door moments later.

"You called 911?" Officer Beaudry asked?

"They won't leave," Wally replied.

"Who won't leave?" Officer Koski asked.

"Amorous Spotted Slugs. The attic is infested with them."

"Who's at the door?" Ethyl Higgenbottom pulled aside the drapes on the front window. Members of Marquette's elite S.W.A.T. Team consisting of the police chief's hunting buddies were hunkering down behind trees and squatting behind parked squad cars. Weaponry varied from hunting bows to muzzle loaders, although deer rifles with high-powered scopes predominated. All weapons were pointing menacingly toward Ethyl's front door.

"Wally, there's a S.W.A.T. Team out there. You told me you paid your library fine!" Wally skillfully ignored his wife's accusation.

"Why are you guys dressed like that?" Ethyl asked when she joined Wally at the door. Large curlers cluttered Ethyl's hair leading Officer Koski to wonder whose appearance was more inappropriate.

"Someone called 911 and said you had intruders infected with Ebola."

Everyone looked at Wally. Wally shrugged his shoulders. "Didn't think you guys would come otherwise."

"Got any idea how difficult it is to maneuver a squad car in hazmat gear?" Officers Koski and Beaudry removed their hoods and goggles. They did not look happy.

Wally stared at the floor. "Does that mean you won't evict the intruders?"

"What makes you think they're Amorous Spotted Slugs?" Officer Beaudry asked.

"That A.S.S. who stole my pasty last year followed me home—must have liked my pasty. Now he's invited all his friends. They hold wild hoedowns every weekend."

"They're so cute," Ethyl offered.

"Can't get any sleep," Wally countered. "Their dance music is too loud."

"And you say they're in the attic?" Officer Beaudry examined the stairs leading to the attic and considered calling in back up. He could handle one A.S.S. but if the attic was truly infested with Amorous Spotted Slugs, he would need the S.W.A.T. Team.

Beaudry drew his nine millimeter and cautiously headed up the stairs, followed by Koski with a can of Pepper Spray in hand. When Beaudry reached the top of the stairs, he gingerly pushed open the trap door and climbed into the attic. Beaudry's posse, consisting of Officer Koski armed with Pepper Spray and Ethyl armed with hair curlers, followed closely behind him. Feeling prudence more appropriate than valor, Wally brought up the rear.

Beaudry scanned the attic with his Maglite. Except for a pile of boxes and some old lamps in the far corner, the attic was empty. "No evidence of Amorous Spotted Slugs," Beaudry proclaimed with some relief. Even the friendliest animals can become vicious when cornered. He had no desire to confront an A.S.S. in a dark attic no matter how amorous their reputation.

"They're hiding," Ethyl said. "They knew you were coming."

"They knew we were coming?" Officer Beaudry waited for an explanation.

"Ethyl thinks the A.S.S. are clairvoyant and can predict the future," Wally explained. "She spends too much time on the Internet."

"According to S.L.I.M.E.'s web site at AmorousSpottedSlug.com, Amorous Spotted Slugs became clairvoyant when lightning struck the coconut they were sailing on," Ethyl replied.

"Slime?" Koski wasn't sure he wanted to hear more. Central dispatch should have dispatched a psych team—with large nets!

"It stands for *Slug Lovers In Michigan Empowered*. S.L.I.M.E. nominated the Amorous Spotted Slug for State Slug. They're so cute."

"They steal pasties," Wally countered.

"Well, I don't see any slugs, spotted or otherwise." Officer Beaudry again scanned the attic with his flashlight. The light came to rest on a square piece of wood the size of a cutting board. "What is that?" Beaudry asked.

"That's Ethyl's cutting board. They use it for a dance floor." Feeling it was now safe, Wally rejoined the others in the attic.

"They are such graceful dancers," Ethyl offered. "The choreography of their dance routines is delightful."

"Perhaps they're hiding under the cutting board," Wally suggested.

Officer Beaudry gave Wally's suggestion some thought. "Koski, I'll cover you while you flip over the cutting board." Beaudry leveled his pistol at the cutting board with his right hand while his quivering left hand maintained a beam of light on the board.

Koski considered voicing a complaint; he had a wife and child to consider. But he did not wish to display fear in front of civilians. He had his pride. "Here, hold my pepper spray, but don't press the top or it'll release the gas." Koski passed the canister to Wally and then cautiously approached the cutting board. Grasping the cutting board with trembling hands, he gingerly raised the board. Slimy yellow creatures scampered in all directions.

"Whoa!" Beaudry reflexively stepped backward into a pool of slime as a hoard of Amorous Spotted Slugs stampeded toward him. His hand impulsively tightened around his pistol as he fell, and a healthy dose of smokeless gunpowder propelled a nine-millimeter projectile into the cutting board Koski was holding. Wooden splinters were sent flying through the air.

"Don't let them get me!" Beaudry pleaded as he hit the ground.

"I got you covered!" Wally extended the pepper spray canister toward the approaching Amorous Spotted Slugs and pressed the top. Unfortunately, the nozzle was pointing toward Beaudry.

Wally's arraignment is scheduled for July 2nd.

**Larry Buege's** short stories have received regional and international (English speaking) awards. He has also authored nine novels including the ever-popular Chogan Native American series. More information about his novels can be found at www.Gastropod-publishing.com or by contacting the author directly at LSBuege@aol.com. For a tongue in cheek look at the campaign to make the Amorous Spotted Slug our state slug, please visit www.AmorousSpottedSlug.com/

# I Watched Someone Drown

## by Craig Brockman

watched someone drown, and did nothing. It's one of my most vivid memories of living near Lake Superior.

There are not many perfect beach days along the shores of the U.P. You may get a handful of these summer days—if you're lucky. That's when the sun is just as warm, the beach as wide, and the waters as sea green as any tiki-hutted, palm-studded paradise around the world. There is one marvelous difference: there is no one else around.

The water temperature is cool but tolerable, if you know where to go. The stable flies could flay the flesh off your ankles if the winds are from the south on an August day. But there are no sharks, stinging jellyfish or red tide.

Yet, don't be fooled. This lake is a soul magnet, with rip currents and hazards that pull you into numbing depths and kill you quicker than anywhere in the world. It's swallowed people ever since the mile high glaciers crawled back north, and will continue until soon, geologically speaking, those walls of ice return.

We were out there on one of those perfect days. A dozen swimmers along two or three miles of beach made it uncommonly crowded. We watched as a horror unfurled that has haunted us ever since, even though, at the time, it scarcely disturbed our delightful day.

It was probably a guy on one of those day boats that look like a plastic snow sled with a mast, we thought. It was a mile out in the bay, too far away to see anything but the sail. We later learned it was a man and a woman.

With a stiff westerly breeze, the whitecaps gamboled like lambs while waves crashed like rams. We frolicked in big surf for most of the day, beers all 'round. I'm embarrassed to admit that this episode is part of the reason I quit drinking nearly twenty years ago.

We thought we were watching a comedy unfurl way out there. The boat launched on the west side of the bay and immediately the sail flattened against the water. It's not uncommon to see sail boats in the bay, especially on a nice day, but we all thought it was way too windy to try to navigate Lake Superior unless you were expert. It was quickly obvious this was no expert. Why the hell would anybody be foolish enough to learn to sail on a day like this?

The sail went up, then flattened again. We laughed: They'll figure it out. This routine continued; sail up, sail down. Sure, we became a little concerned. Cell phones were rare and clunky, reception impossible in the U.P., and why would you carry one to the beach? We had a big old satellite phone in the truck, but that was a half mile away. A fish hatchery, about the same distance away, could've called the Coast Guard for us. But why bother? That would ruin our day and we'd look like slightly-drunken fools.

Sail boats don't sink. They can just ride it out. The sail went up. It probably went down again but we had already moved on. They'd be okay. Have a beer.

They weren't okay. "Woman Survives, Man Dies in Sail Boat Incident." He died of hypothermia and they were found near Canada the next day. It was them. We read about where and when they had launched and we read about the type of vessel they had. It was them. We had done nothing.

The feeling was a hollow, needling shame. It still is. If we had only said something, the coast guard may have been able to rescue them. Our rationalizing was ridiculous: Foundering sail boats were seen on the big lake all the time. Just right your boat and sail away. The coast guard or police may have thought we were nuts. They may have rationalized it away just like we did. But probably not. Someone would have done something. Someone other than us. We weren't the only people on the beach.

"See something, say something" is a worn out cliché. We could have invented it that day. Since then, reminded of that day, there have been many times that we have stepped up. That doesn't justify what happened that day. We failed— badly. There is no lovely parable. It's painful to admit that we learn from events where others have been hurt. But now I'm more likely to say something or do something if things don't seem right, despite the risk of inconvenience or embarrassment. That's worth something... I guess.

We did better another time.

House hunting can be fun—it's not all a pain in the butt. At this point there wasn't much to see online, but we scoured the real estate sites. We came up with a simple scheme. We made a circle on a map and determined to drive every road looking for our dream farm. It was fun—fruitless—but fun.

One warm, windy early spring Sunday afternoon we were tooling around. We came to an area of open fields, and about half a mile away a ribbon of smoke was blowing horizontally in the stiff breeze. It seemed a little close to the outbuildings of a farm, but not too alarming; lots of people were carelessly burning brush and grass as we drove through the countryside.

We slowed and watched. Everything was probably fine. Besides, we had things to do,

and wanted to get home. Then we remembered what happened on Lake Superior and reluctantly turned around and headed down the dirt road to the farm. As we got closer, it looked ominous. Flames were licking the branches of pine trees standing behind a long metal building. We still couldn't tell if any buildings were affected, but the fire was obviously out of control. We called 911. We had to drive back to figure out the name of the road and then find the house number.

This was a landscaping business that had transformed a farm into their warehouse and garages. It was packed with trucks, tractors and other shiny, high-end equipment. Much of it was crammed into that long building backed by burning trees. We drove ahead into the yard near the building. A big pile of smoldering stumps lay at the end of the yard with a scorched trail that lead to the back of the building and a mound of pallets and other trash that was ablaze. Looking up we saw flames already licking through the roof.

I ran up to the door of the big farm house and pounded and shouted, but no one answered. The flames were growing, whipped by the wind. Moving some of the equipment would be no problem if keys were in the ignitions. Back at the shed, I was just sliding the door open to start driving trucks, tractors and other machinery away from the building, when a kid, nineteen years old or so, came dashing out of the house buckling his belt and pulling on his shirt. He didn't seem to understand for a while until I pointed toward flames towering behind the building.

The long shed with all the equipment was a metal building, but it was insulated and lined with paneling that the fire was consuming. Flames were crawling across the ceiling and scorching the rafters. The young man was frantic and wanted to dash in. I stopped him. Nonetheless, we were able to move a lot of equipment including a tractor and truck that were inside the building near the entrance. Flames were blasting across the ceiling in sheets over tractors and mowers far on the other end of the structure.

The scream of sirens—a lot of sirens— came quickly, considering how far out in the country we were. First responders and emergency vehicles poured into the yard, eager men and women in bulky pants and big boots dropped from moving trucks, some still pulling on thick coats over suspenders.

It turned out the young man was an employee who lived in the house. The owner lived about a quarter mile away; heard the sirens, saw the smoke, and soon arrived in tears.

We hung around the periphery, did little else, never talked with any one, and only listened. The emergency professionals spoke with that nervous humor they like to use when performing their duties.

The building was badly damaged and they lost some equipment. Unfortunately the owner didn't have insurance. But it could have been so much worse. They could have lost everything, even the house with the young man inside; a life and a business gone.

We slipped away, everything under control. We were far from ecstatic. We thought about how close we'd come to just driving past. It was sobering. It had been especially hard to see the owner's pain and all the devastation.

There have been other times when we saw something happening, stepped in, but everything was fine. That's always a relief even though it can be embarrassing. We have no regrets when that happens.

Since that fateful day on Lake Superior, when I saw someone drown and did nothing, I have to live with my conscience. And now I live with a sense of duty.

# Shirley's Cabins

## by Craig Brockman

"We moved here in nineteen seventy-six. I was only twenty-two, I think, and Bill was twenty-three. We already had Jon and Becky. They would've been only three and one. I thought this place was the end of the world, but it was all we could do at the time." Shirley stretched out her thin hand and flicked ashes mostly into the tray as her oxygen tank hissed.

The agency had a contract to make home visits for a behavioral health evaluation based on referrals from visiting nurses. It worked well for Adam. He could take care of some of those time-consuming home visits while therapists who had regular clients could continue to see their clients at the clinic. Along the highways, dirt roads and two-tracks of Chippewa County, he was able to cover a lot of territory––on the road and in his mind. He went looking for the lost and lonely amid a population of less than forty thousand who were folded into forests and rivers, swamps and valleys knit together by twisting trails and scenic highways covering an area larger than Delaware.

Shirley was homebound with Chronic Obstructive Pulmonary Disease and a bone disorder. Nurses monitored her health, checked her blood pressure and oxygen levels and faithfully chanted their quit-smoking invocation. They became concerned that she was becoming demented. If she could not take care of herself safely, *apart from smoking while using oxygen,* she would lose her ability to stay in her home.

Adam agreed that the interview would be easier in the home, but now he had second thoughts as he kept a wary eye on her cigarette and the hissing tank. The house was small and neat, filled with the smell of cigarette smoke and fried breakfast.

She paced her words to stay ahead of her shortness of breath. "It was all that we could do 'cause Bill was still messed up from the war in Viet Nam and he couldn't hold a job." She took a breath. "We figured the place was cheap enough and the cabins would give us some income while we got on our feet. It actually worked out pretty sweet. Billy took care of the cabins, avoiding any contact with people as much as he could, of course," she looked at her cigarette and smiled, "and I took care of the booking and I did all the face to face stuff. We both did the cleaning but we hired help when we needed it. We were proud of our place, still are, and we raised four kids here ta boot." She took a slow drag and set her hand near the ash tray again. "Danny, our youngest, teaches in Newberry and he still helps out a lot. I hired Sheila from Hulbert to take care of the day to day, but I still do all the booking."

She looked out the kitchen window across Whitefish Bay. The sash was open a few inches despite the cool day: a smoker's courtesy, but also relief from the claustrophobia of COPD. The bay was hung with gray sky and waves were restless ahead of a moderate breeze. Shirley's thin frame sat slumped in her wheelchair pulled up to the kitchen table. Dressed in sweat pants and an orange sweatshirt, her gray, scraggly hair was held back on the right by a purple barrette with a bunny on it that was probably found in a cabin. She reached for her cup.

"Would you like more tea, Dr. Knowles?"

"You can call me Adam. No, no, I'm fine." He looked again at the proximity of the cigarette to the oxygen tubing and hoped that the oxygen was set low enough so he didn't have to deal with a flame thrower.

After a while she began again. "So, you didn't drive all the way up here to learn about the history of Shirley's Cabins, I'm sure. The nurse told me that you'd be coming here to decide if I was crazy or not because she thought that I started ha-*loo*-cinatin'." She cleared her throat gruffly.

"Yeah, I guess I have a few questions. I want to help, if I can. The nurse was concerned about you. Since you mention hallucinations, I just have to ask; *are* you seeing things and what sort of things are you seeing?"

"Okay, good. Looks like you're not one to beat around the bush and neither am I. I'll be straight with you 'cause you seem like a nice guy. I think the nurse thought I was a little screwy and I even think Sheila, my helper, thought I was going off the deep end." She snuffed out the cigarette and sat back with her elbows resting on the arms of the wheelchair.

"What I came here for was..." Adam began.

"Let me finish," she held up her hand, "I want to lay it all out the way I see it, 'cause I think you're going to get me off course by asking too many questions. I'll save ya some time and you'll be back in the Soo by supper time." She smiled and took a breath. "You are here to find out if I'm nuts and I can give you the answer you're here to find out: I'm not nuts and I don't have that Oldtimer's disease, either. I really think something is going on. I tell ya, I went through hell with Bill and all his war crap and I sure as hell know crazy when I see it." She looked Adam in the eye, then out the window to where two of six cabins sat near the shore. She pointed with a long, thin finger.

"It was right out there about two weeks ago toward evening. It wasn't dark yet, more like late in the afternoon about four-thirty or five. The sun hadn't even set, yet. This guy, I swear to God, walked out of the water, like he'd swum right up to the beach, but he wasn't swimming, he was walking: straight up. And he came right out of the water. It looked scary as hell 'cause he was fully dressed and he didn't look left or right, he just walked on down to cabin 3. That's what made me just about shit-- 'scuse my French––I recognized that guy!"

"Was he staying here?"

"Ha! Yeah, he was staying here. About twenty years ago!" Her right hand clasped her left tightly. She nodded, "He was the guy that left in one of our motor boats and never came back. I mean *never* came back. We thought he stole it and went back to Toledo, where he was from, but he never showed up there either. So they figured he'd drowned. I always

CANAL ENTRY TO LAC LA BELLE AND GOVERNMENT LIGHTHOUSE.

NEAR KEEWENAW POINT, COPPER COUNTRY, MICH.                          107108

Keweenaw - Lac la Belle Mendota Lighthouse

thought maybe he just took off somewhere—ran away—because it was weird that they never found the boat or anything else, like even a paddle or cushion." She waved her outstretched finger around, pointing at the dock. "I had everything marked with our name and phone number 'cause someone was losing something all the time and it would float in somewhere a couple days or months later. I actually got a cushion back from a guy up by Wawa one time!" She covered her mouth with a balled-up tissue and coughed.

She grabbed her cigarette pack and stared at it while she flipped it end to end on the table. "Anyways, this guy had been staying here for a few days and then he disappeared with our boat. He'd been here a few times before. Always alone."

"What did you do?"

"You mean when he left or when he came back?" She laughed hoarsely, coughed, then laid her hand on the table, leaned toward Adam and grinned.

"Well, uh, when he came back, I guess." Adam smiled thinly, brows raised in anticipation.

"After I seen him, I got my walker and trudged down the walkway here and toward the cabin. Just then Sheila was coming out of cabin 4. No, no, it was cabin 5 and I yelled at her and she came across and met me. When I asked her, she said she hadn't seen anything 'cause she was in the cabin, but I asked her to come with me into 3." She took a breath. "When we went around to the front, she pulled out her key and helped me up the step onto the porch. The door was locked so she opened it."

"And nothing, right?" Adam said as he opened his brief case to take out his tablet, and based on his experience, felt that he knew where this story was probably going. He clicked on his tablet and looked up at her; she was staring at him with eyes narrowed.

"NO! Dammit! There he stood in cabin 3: Peter Lane, the guy who went missing twenty years ago! Sheila saw him. He was the same guy, the same age. He looked at Sheila, he looked at me and he looked around the cabin as if he realized where he was, and what was happening and he was, I don't know, kinda sad, confused, anxious." She looked blankly at the table a moment. "He turned around all of the sudden, and just headed south, right through the door at the back of the cabin and back home. He just walked right into the woods over there and was gone."

"So, Sheila saw him?"

"Sure, she did, but Sheila is a bit, how would you say––simple. She would never put it together. She probably didn't see him walk through the back door. But the guy walked right into that brush and not even a leaf stirred as he slipped in. You could see it out of the back window of the cabin. How'd some guy end up in a locked cabin in the middle of the day with all of us around? Nobody would be in there. I saw him walk out of the lake and up to that cabin. I remember the guy! How could I forget?"

"I honestly don't mean to doubt you, but you're *sure* this was the guy?"

"Sure's hell! Same guy, same cabin, same age, even." She drew her hand across her mouth. "An' Sheila saw him, too." She clutched her cigarette pack. "Do you think I'm nuts?"

"Shirley, I don't think you're nuts. You've probably heard what's going on all over, too, and I..."

"Come on, take a little walk with me. I keep a nice place and I like to show it off."

Before Adam could offer to help, she swept the walker near and stood in one, smooth maneuver. The tank and tubing were already attached to the walker, so before Adam could gather his things, she was headed for the door.

"Let me get that for you."

"Got it," she called over her shoulder as the walker was rowed out the door and toward the boardwalk that led to the dock.

The dock was built over a narrow crescent of beach. Choppy waves gurgled under the gray-green wooden deck and slapped clear and cold against the sand. A rock barrier cut down some of the force but a steady breeze kept the waters in constant agitation. All the swimming gear and boats were long ago put up for the season except for one decrepit row boat that bobbed in the waves on the south side of the dock. She slowed and scraped her walker the last couple steps to the boat and paused to catch her breath. Adam resolved that there would be no way that he would consent to an offshore tour of the property. He was about to speak up when she broke in.

"The last few days the water is low. It seems like something is sucking all the water out of the lake. I don't know what the hell that's all about," she looked down. "Well, there she is."

"What is it?"

He stepped beside her, and looked down at the boat; flaking paint and worm-eaten wood. He felt the small hairs at the back of his head stand up when he noticed the waterlogged cushions and rusty motor sagging from the stern. Even the chipped, red gas can sloshed in the back under a broken seat.

"Holy shit! I mean..."

She smiled around an unlit cigarette and looked sideways at Adam, "That's exactly what I said when I saw 'er tied up here."

**Craig A. Brockman** lived in the eastern U.P. for nearly twenty years while employed by the Indian Health Service, Lake Superior State University and at other facilities. In 2017, an article in the *Ontonagon Herald* chronicled the final 140-mile leg of his circuitous 450-mile hike across the entire U.P. from the Drummond Island Ferry Dock in DeTour Village to a sandbar at the mouth of the Montreal River on the Wisconsin border. Craig currently lives with his wife in Tecumseh, Michigan. In 2007, he published *Marty and the Far Woodchuck*, a middle-grade novel. *Dead of November: A Novel of Lake Superior* is his first novel for adults and "Shirley's Cabin" was excerpted from that book, which had not been published at the time the story was submitted. You can visit craigabrockman.com for more information or contact craig@craigabrockman.com.

# U.P. Notable Books List

◆❖◆

The editors of *U.P. Reader* have compiled our list of recommended U.P. books that we've discovered over the past year in consultation with reviewers and booksellers. We call this list, the *U.P. Notable Books List*—or "the Yoopie" for short. These ten books have been deemed essential reading for every U.P. lover and we highly recommend you ask your local librarian or booksellers for them today!

1. *Camera Hunter: George Shiras III and the Birth of Wildlife Photography* by James H. McCommons (University of New Mexico Press, 2019)

2. *Out* by John Smolens (Michigan State University Press, 2019)

3. *Cady and the Bear Necklace* by Ann Dallman (Three Towers Press, 2019)

4. *Go Find! My Journey to Find the Lost -- and Myself* by Susan Purvis (Blackstone Press, 2019)

5. *Hunter's Moon: A Novel in Stories* by Philip Caputo (Henry Holt and Co., 2019)

6. *The Marsh King's Daughter* by Karen Dionne (G.P. Putnam's Sons, 2018)

7. *Yoopernatural Haunts Upper Peninsula Paranormal Research Society Case Files* by Tim Ellis (Visionary Living, 2019)

8. *Murder on Sugar Island (Getting to Know Jack Book 2)* – Michael Carrier (Greenwich Village Ink, 2013)

9. *Lake Superior Tales: Stories of Humor and Adventure in Michigan's Upper Peninsula, 2nd Edition* by Mikel B. Classen (Modern History Press, 2018)

10. *Three Fires Unity: The Anishnaabeg of the Lake Huron Borderlands by* Phil Bellfy (University of Nebraska Press, 2019).

# What I Learned from Writing my Breakout Book

## by Karen Dionne

*The following article is a transcript of the plenary address given by Karen Dionne at the Upper Peninsula Publishers and Authors Association (UPPAA) Annual Spring Conference held at the Peter White Library in Marquette, Michigan on June 8th, 2019. Although space prevents us from reproducing the Q&A following this talk, you can find that transcript on www.UPPAA.org.*

Thank you, Tyler, for the nice intro and for inviting me here, and thank you everyone for coming. *The Marsh King's Daughter* has been kind of a door opener for me, and it's brought me to a lot of places, but the Upper Peninsula is my home; I say that. I lived here for thirty years, and while I'm in the Detroit area now, and writers are my people so yay for writers, right? I'm going to talk less about what *The Marsh King's Daughter* is about and more about how it's changed my life, the lessons that I've learned from what's happened with this book, and then hopefully there's something in that that you can take away. I've summarized the six points on the handout.

As Tyler was starting to say, I've been writing seriously for twenty years. My first novels, *Freezing Point* (2008) and *Boiling Point* (2011) were environmental thrillers, science based thrillers similar to what Michael Crichton writes [Ed. Note: *Jurassic Park*, *The Andromeda Strain*, *Congo*, et al.]. I started writing those because that's the kind of book I like to read. Isn't that what we all do? We write what we like. They had modest success, but they didn't really take off or do anything huge, although I was published with a major publisher. They came out in mass market paperback size. They were available in grocery stores and drug stores and book stores, so of course it was very exciting. The sales were such that my publisher dropped me after *Boiling Point,* and that was the end of that.

## Lessons Learned Handout

### 1. Begin with character

Character is less likely to be a stereotype

Character shapes the story at the developmental stage, instead of reacting to events.

### 2. Explore writing techniques you haven't used before

Get the basics down, but don't be afraid to try something new. No writing is ever wasted. In the process, you might discover you're a better writer than you thought.

### 3. Listen to your gut

Is the book you're working on going to knock people's socks off? If not, why not? Can this be fixed? Or would your career be better served by setting it aside in favor of one that will?

### 4. It's all about emotion

In order to resonate with readers, a book has to touch them on an emotional level, and not just an intellectual one. Particularly in a psychological thriller, it's less about **what happens** in the story, and more about **who it happens to.**

### 5. Universal themes

You want your novel to do more than intrigue or fascinate: you want to touch them deeply. One of the best ways to achieve that is to give them a commonality with the character that they can relate to.

### 6. Novels should be novel

You want your novel to feel fresh, surprising, and unexpected.

---

*The Killing: Uncommon Denominator* was a television tie-in novel published in 2014, based on the television detective show, *The Killing*. I was hired by Fox, through a publisher, to write an original story using the characters from the show. It sounds glamorous, but, some of you at least probably know that was what's called work-for-hire. I was paid a flat rate (as opposed to royalties) and I don't own the copyright to that book.

At the same time I was doing that, I got really involved with writers, first online. I started an online writer's organization called Backspace. We had discussion forums, we had articles; the whole theme was writers helping writers. Again, now that Backspace is no more, sadly, I'm really happy to be able to talk to you guys today.

I got involved organizing conferences in New York, did a dozen or so of those. Toward the end, my business partner and I were asked to organize and run a weeklong conference for a retreat for writers on a private island in the Bahamas. Yeah, I was like, "Well, I don't know, okay." My writing career wasn't doing anything much. The conferences were very successful and it was really satisfying to have other writers reach their publishing goals. There were a lot of times that I thought, *Oh, maybe I should just never mind the writing and concentrate on the conferences and do that instead.*

And so it happened in the lead-up to my 2013 conference in New York, I noticed that an author who had gotten her literary agent at one of my previous conferences was coming out with her subsequent book, and it just hit me because I hadn't written anything. I thought, *All right, I've been helping other people reach their publishing goals but I haven't reached my goals yet.* My business partner and I decided that would be the last conference. I was on the board of directors of the International Thriller Writers, and so I went off a year early. Basically I had gotten really involved in doing things around the edges of writing, but I wasn't writing.

It wasn't too much longer after that that I got the idea for *The Marsh King's Daughter*. I'm sure everyone knows the rough outlines of the story. It's a family, a story of a girl who grows up off the grid in the Upper Peninsula wilderness. I'm not going to go into detail about that because I want to talk more about the lessons that I've learned from it, but my husband and I homesteaded in the Upper Peninsula for thirty years. We moved to the UP as a young married couple with our six week old baby and we lived in a tent, and we built a little cabin and we carried water from a stream. That's how come I was able to write the novel with some degree of authority. We lived right on M-28, so we went to the grocery store for our food. It was nothing as nearly off the grid but writers have imaginations, correct? Yeah.

The reception for this book was just astonishing and I'm going to go through it quickly because otherwise you guys are going to really hate me for everything that's happened for this book. It was my first novel that came out in hardcover and paperback. My agent sent the manuscript to thirty-six editors on a Monday, by Tuesday morning he had heard back from twenty-nine of them. Wednesday we had our first offer. It was a preempt, and we turned it down. My agent sent me the email with the amount. It was for world rights and we knew we weren't selling world because my agency has a good foreign rights department. My agent sends me the email and he says, let me know when you're ready to say no, and I'm like, no. Send.

That went on pretty crazy. It ended up being, like I say, a twelve-way option in the US, and I'm with Putnam, which is really cool. Immediately after that, the book sold in a seven-way option in the UK and a five-way option in Germany, and a three-way option in Korea. I didn't know there were three publishers in Korea who would want to buy the book. Then it sold for a record amount in Poland. When it published in Germany, it made their paperback best seller list for eighteen weeks. Altogether, translation rates for the book have been sold in twenty-five countries, twenty-five languages, yeah.

*The Marsh King's Daughter* was published in June of 2017. This means a lot to me as a writer--it started getting some recognition for the quality of the book, iBooks chose it as one of their "10 Best Fiction Novels of the Year." Others did too. It was chosen by the Library of Michigan as a Michigan Notable Book last year, and the Macavity Award, and others.

*The Marsh King's Daughter* was also reviewed in *The New York Times*. It was a rave review. *The Marsh King's Daughter* is under development as a major motion picture for a theatrical release. The production company that optioned the book is responsible for the movies *Spotlight* and *The Revenant* (2015). The screenwriter for *The Revenant* adapted my book to write the script. We do currently have a new star attached to perform as Helena, that would be Blake Lively, and so, I know by now you probably all hate me.

I have a lot of writer friends and to be honest, we look at the success, we're happy for their success, but at the same time I used to think, *Why not me? What are they doing that I'm not doing? Why is it working so well for them and not for me?* So this is what I hope to share with you. First, my first takeaway—don't quit—which seems obvious, but at the same time remember when I was organizing the conferences? I thought many times of stopping writing because what I was doing was satisfying, and the writing wasn't taking me where I wanted to go. If I had, that'd be my whole oeuvre and all the things I just showed you, none of that would've happened.

It's really quite staggering when you think about it, and so likewise, if we haven't quite attained what we hope for, what's to say it's not right around the corner? What's to say the next book won't bring you there? Don't quit. And now I want to get into the meat a little bit and leave room to ask questions. You know what? If you want to ask questions about the specific points as we go along that would be fine, but we'll just kind of run through them.

So, yeah, I ask myself, why? Why did all this crazy stuff happen? I isolated these six reasons, which I've also highlighted on the handout. My previous novels, I've started with the plot, *this and this and this is going to happen*, and then I created characters to serve the plot, hopefully interesting and engaging characters but still, I started with the plot. But *The Marsh King's Daughter*, I actually woke up with the opening sentences fully formed in my head. The sentences are, "If I told you my mother's name you'd recognize it right away. My mother was famous though she never wanted to be. Hers wasn't the kind of fame anyone would wish for. Jaycee Dugard, Amanda Berry, Elizabeth Smart, that kind of thing though my mother was none of them." Inspiration, it's pretty nice.

So anyway, this one, it was just like *boom*. This character, my brain, my subconscious dropped this character on me. She was intriguing, I thought this was the daughter of a kidnapped girl and the man who took her, this could be an interesting story, and so forth. The reason why I think it's important to start with character over plot is because, as I say here, the character is less likely to be a stereotype. If we think to ourselves, *I'm going to write a detective story*, your mind immediately goes to certain tropes, right? And I'm sorry, I know you write in all genres but everything is kind of thriller and mystery-ish because that's my knowledge base.

If you start with the character, I have a person who is like this and wants that and this is her background or his background, and then find the story that fits the character instead of the other way around, I think in the end you end up with a stronger book. That's my point about how then the character shapes the story instead of the story shaping the character. The last point there, this may be a little enigmatic, but, you know how often a new writer will load up the front of their book with back story? We all do it because partly it's us getting to know the character too, and it isn't necessarily things that the reader needs to know but the author is sorting it all out. But if your character is the focus of the book and not the plot, then their back story is important.

In the case of my novel, it's told in two timelines. One is the character's past and then the other is what's happening in the present. Her back story, how she grew up in the marsh with her family is half the book, and it's essential. The other thing that I think was one of the keys is, I ended up trying new writing techniques, things that I had never done before. My previous novels were just told strictly chronologically, they were basically action adventure thrillers, and so they just went start to finish. This was the first time that I told a book using dual timelines, I had never done that before. There are tense shifts.

In the present day story, it's told in first person present with flashbacks in first person past. In the past story, it's told in first person past bracketed by chunks of first person present in the beginning and end. It is a little complicated and it intimidated me because I had not done that before. There are also multiple flashbacks. Before the novel published and sold, my agent asked me to see if I could get endorsements from some of the bestselling authors I know from my

conference organizing and I did, but one in particular, David Morrell. He's the creator of the character *Rambo* and also, he's written a lot of books and he taught at Iowa University in the English department.

He loved the book, but he called me and he had some suggestions for improving the ending, which was lovely, but he said I broke so many rules with the tense shifts and he said God knows how many flashbacks, and it was just funny. But for a thriller, normally flashbacks would be a no, because it stops the action and it takes it backward. For instance, there is the fact that, in the story in the present, Helena's hunting down her father. She goes into a cabin where she thinks her bad man father is and I say like, I open the door and go inside, and then there's a scene break, "I was fifteen, the first time I broke into a cabin," and it goes on to this long memory, that was something new. Directly addressing the reader, those opening sentences, "If I told you my mother's name you'd recognize it right away," I'd not done that.

The book has a fairy tale element, it's called *The Marsh King's Daughter* after the fairy tale. How was I going to work that into the book? And then the book also introduces imaginary characters three-quarters of the way through, which, I mean you're not supposed to introduce a character at all, right, three-quarters of the way through. The fact that these are imaginary characters besides, I really thought I was going out on a limb with it. I do think it's interesting because it's the story that made me do this, right? And so, my urge to you, my exhortation is, don't play it safe. Push yourself a bit.

This is the point. We're told not to break the rules and I think that that really applies only for a very beginning writer who's still learning the rules, but once you know the rules, by all means break them, because how are you ever going to write something that is exciting and fresh and new if you just play it safe? Like I say here, push yourself. Make yourself uncomfortable. When I sent the first chapter of the book to my agent, I had no idea if it was working because it was so far outside my comfort zone, and he told me very much later, it was so good, he didn't think I had written it. It's okay, he's been my agent for a long time. We're like an old married couple, right?

Yeah, that's why to me, these are the two main points: start with the character and then push yourself. Try things that you haven't tried before, because here's the thing, I basically discovered that I was a better writer than I realized because I could do all these things, and the book did get such recognition. If I had just continued to write those science based thrillers, I would've been telling one kind of story never knowing that I could tell a different kind of story in a bigger way. And so, that kind of leads into point number three, which is listen to your gut, because when I got the idea for *The Marsh King's Daughter* I was working on another novel.

I was actually looking for a back story for a character in that novel. She goes to great lengths to solve a mystery. She goes to France; she goes to China, why? Everything I suggested to my agent as what motivates her to go to these lengths, he's like, "No, that's dumb, that's stupid." He says, "dig deep." And so that apparently is what I was doing when I woke up in the night with those sentences. I did send him the opening paragraphs, which is now the first page of the novel, the next morning asking: would this work as a back story for this character? I was still thinking of that book, and he said, it was cool and it was creepy and it would absolutely work, in another book.

It was too much back story to shoehorn into the existing story. As soon as the pieces to the book fell together, including incorporating the fairy tale element, I knew that this book had commercial potential. I'm sure you have had ideas for books that just immediately resonated, right? I mean your gut just said, "This is the good idea—this is the one that's going to work." And so as a conference organizer, over the years I met a lot of different writers, and because I was the organizer, many times the same writer would come with the same book year after year after year. Your heart kind of breaks for them. I mean it's good to stick with it, right? But comes a point where you have to say, is this project getting me where I want to be?

It takes a year or more to write a novel, whether it has the potential to be a good one, or a great one, or a fantastic one, so hold out for that idea, or, really look honestly at your project. It's not to say that writing something that has regional appeal was wrong. No, no, if you aspire to international sales you really have to step it up and push yourselves. That's one point. This point, when I was writing *The Marsh King's Daughter*, I'm a very practical person, very down to Earth. I don't cry at weddings and stuff like this, I write thrillers. There were a lot of times as I was telling Helena's story, the level of emotion in the book almost felt silly.

I don't know if you've ever felt that, like you're writing over-the-top a little bit because your character was so upset about something. I myself naturally wouldn't have been quite that upset. But David Morrell, whom I mentioned earlier, advised me at one of my conferences to *make it real*. I think that's a really nice catch phrase to keep in mind, because we're selling a fiction to people, right? When we're writing fiction, we're taking something that isn't true at all, doesn't exist, but we want them, the readers to become so invested in it that they care, right?

As I mentioned here, a lot of the Amazon and Goodreads reviewers said that they had to go back and see if they were reading a memoir, if this story really happened. Of course, part of the deception is that it's told in first person present tense so it looks like it could be. But so, these are the points. If your reader is going to feel what the character is feeling, we have to make the characters real and to do that we have to go deep into emotion. It's like, if the author won't go there, then the reader can't go there either, right?

I will say this too, and this is kind of a side point, in *The Marsh King's Daughter* the story went a little darker than I personally am comfortable with, but the story required me to go in that darker place, a place that made me uncomfortable and readers accept it, but I wouldn't have been true to the story if I didn't do that. Another is universal themes, because I asked my editor once, why did *The Marsh King's Daughter* settle in all these countries? Why do people in Turkey and Israel and Iceland, and whatever, China, Japan, want to read this story? Because obviously its publishers buy the rights to publish it in that language and they think their readers will enjoy it.

As I say here, his answer was that the book is at heart a father-daughter story, and the way the progression works in the novel, for those first twelve years that Helena lives in isolation with her mother and father in that cabin, she never sees another person, so she loves her father, because there is no one else to share it with. And then when she and her mother leave the marsh, things don't go well for her because she has no knowledge of technology and pop culture and social norms. I gave her a stack of *National Geographic* magazines so that she could learn to read as a little girl, and because every cabin has a stock of old Nat Geo, right? Yeah. And so from those, she knows what a ball is but she doesn't know how to play because she's never had a ball.

So anyway, at that point she goes from loving her father with this pure unique love to hating him, and not so much for what the father did to her mother but for all the things about the outside world that she didn't know. And then, when she turns eighteen, she reinvents herself, takes a new name, moves away, in effect denying her father, and then by the end of the story she has to come to terms with who and what she is. That's the story. That's the reason that readers in other parts of the world are enjoying this story too. Even though I homesteaded, I did not live as Helena did and I didn't have a murderous psychopath for a father, but there's elements still of that story that I think everyone can relate to. So, like at the end there, it's not so much the situation that resonates with readers but the characters.

And I will digress just for a minute here. After one of my recent conferences, I was talking to a gentleman and he had his novels with him—because we're all hungry for help, right? We aren't born knowing this stuff and that's why you came to the conference today. He spent a lot of time telling me about his book and he never mentioned the characters, it was all just what happened, the plot, and then a group of guys and then

they do this, and whatever, and I was like... And I pointed it out to him after however long that you haven't told me anything about the characters, *who is this story about?* I think that's something to remember, too, as far as the story as a whole.

The last point is really brief. I went to a conference once and a prominent editor had this little saying, "Novels should be novel." You can probably tell, I like these little pithy things that you can remember, make it real, novels should be novel... And the keywords that he used in his talk were surprise, fresh, unexpected. Don't just tell the same story, not if you want to get noticed, you have to have something just a little different. In *The Marsh King's Daughter,* the unexpected part of it is that the story is told from the point of view of the daughter instead of the kidnapped victim. You guys are probably better readers than I am.

I'm sure you can think of other books where that's the case, where something is just a little skewed. Sometimes people do that deliberately: they'll take a famous story that's in the public domain and they'll take a side character and elevate the character to a major one, but those are fun, so that's one way anyway to make something fresh. That's takeaway number two. Number one was don't give up; number two is stretch, reach, and grow. In addition to this quote that I love which I put on the bookmark for you guys to take home with you. I pulled a quote from an article about James Holzhauer—he's the *Jeopardy* game show guy who's blowing it out of the water right now. He comes from a sports betting background and so he has the temperament to take risks. And so this quote I thought really applies to us too. He said, "There are times in a football game where a team goes for a big touchdown pass. If you don't take a risk like that you're not going to win. Really, the big risk is never trying anything that looks like a big gamble." I thought that was really kind of an interesting point. Don't play it safe or you might be like me, organizing conferences and writing environmental thrillers that publishers don't want. Or you can take a few risks and, yeah, some really cool things will happen.

# Young U.P. Authors Section

✦❖✦

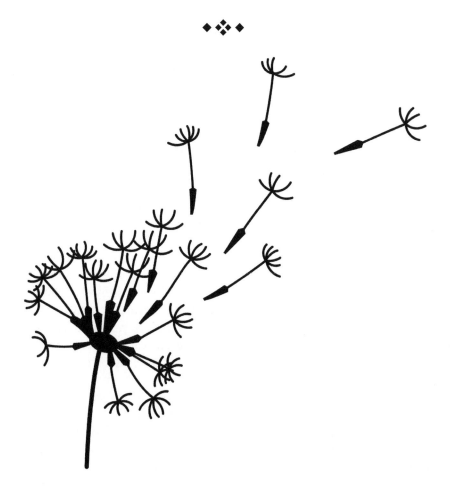

Once again, the *U.P. Reader* is proud to present the winners of the Dandelion Cottage Writing Contest. This is a competition open to all students in U.P. Schools, and is presented annually by the Upper Peninsula Publishers and Authors Association. Last year's winner was nominated for a "Best of the Small Press" award after it appeared in the *U.P. Reader*. Who knows what this year's winners will bring, but once again they are exceptional. Starting in 2019, we have inaugurated two divisions for the contest: Senior (grades 9-12) and Junior (grades 5-8) So without further ado, here are our winners and stories:

Junior Division recognizes only one writer each year:
1st Place went to **Megan Sutherland** of Lake Linden-Hubbell Schools

Senior Division recognizes the top three writers:
1st Place went to **May Amelia Shapton** at Lake Linden-Hubbell High School
2nd Place went to **Cora Mueller** at Houghton High School
3rd Place went to **Fenwood Tolonen** at Lake Linden-Hubbell High School

# About the Real Dandelion Cottage

Carroll Watson Rankin is the pen name of American author Caroline Clement Watson Rankin (1864–1945). Rankin was born May 11, 1864 in Marquette, Michigan, in the Upper Peninsula, and raised her four children there. Her first writing assignment came at the age of 16, when she was hired as a reporter for the *Daily Mining Journal*. She kept the job until her marriage to Ernest Rankin in 1886. Her freelance stories were published by *Century*, *Harper's Monthly*, *Youth's Companion*, *St. Nicholas*, *Leslie's*, *Lippincott's*, *Metropolitan* and other widely circulated periodicals.

Her best known novel is *Dandelion Cottage*, published in 1904 by Henry Holt and Company. She first wrote the story serially for her own children. Considered a regional classic in the Midwest, it tells of four young girls who negotiate the use of a derelict cottage belonging to a church as a playhouse by pulling dandelions for the senior warden of the church, prosperous Mr. Black. The real life model for Mr. Black is generally acknowledged to be Marquette businessman and philanthropist, Peter White. The original Dandelion Cottage is located at 440 East Arch and is privately owned. Now that the book is in public domain, it is available from Project Gutenberg and a print edition is available from the Marquette Regional History Center, published by the Marquette County Historical Society.

Rankin allowed her characters much latitude in emotion and behavior at a time when writing for children was often tepid and tutelary. Other of her novels for youth include:

The Girls of Gardenville (1906)
The Adopting of Rosa Marie (1908)
The Cinder Pond (1915)
Gipsy Nan (1926)
Wolf Rock (1933)

The Anti Foster Pet Association (1907)
Castaways of Pete's Patch (1911)
Girls of Highland Hall (1921)
Finders Keepers (1930)
Stump Village (1935)

Source: *Wikipedia*

# Confliction

## by Megan Sutherland (1st Place Jr. Div.)

◆❖◆

"Sarah? Wake up."

I had fallen asleep to the horses' hooves on the dirt road, the sun on my pale face. We were passing the old wooden markets in downtown Torch Lake, a mining village in the Upper Peninsula of Michigan. We moved here from Texas years after Michigan became a state—1837. The year was now 1877.

"We're almost home," Mama said, turning a page in her book. "Are you excited to start school in a few days?"

"Yes, Mama," I replied, tucking a lock of my curly auburn hair behind my ear. "When will Papa and Peter be home?"

"I don't know, dear," Mama murmured, straightening my blue and white bow. "I expect soon. And oh, I forgot to tell you, my boss is coming over, so wash up when we get home."

"Yes, Mama."

Mama seemed to sense that I was thinking, so she didn't press matters after that. I was thinking about her new job as a seamstress. She'd be making a lot more money now than in Texas, which would be nice, but not enough to get Papa here. He told us he would get money, but it would take two hundred dollars for him and Peter. We needed all the money we could get.

The wagon stopped in front of our cabin, just outside Torch Lake. It had a long porch with a swing and a big backyard, as well as a tall, triangular roof that was dark brown in contrast the rest of the house. We had a barn out back with two horses, three goats, four pigs, five cows, and six chickens. Mama picked up her purse, thanked the driver, and ushered me into the house.

I took off my brown cowgirl boots Papa got me and started up the stairs to my bedroom. From my window you could see our two acres with the barn. You could see Lake Superior shine at dawn in the sunrise and hear the birdsong in the trees.

I changed into a white, lacy tank top and a blue and white plaid skirt to match my bow before rushing down the steps and out the back door to the stables. Who cared if Mama had a co-worker coming over? I would be on

Daisy's back, enjoying the last few bites of summer.

Daisy was a tall, white horse with chocolate brown patches all over her body. She had a soft brown mane and tail, as well as honey-colored eyes. Mama's black horse, Midnight, came forward to the gate so I could touch both of their noses. I chuckled a bit as he tried to step in front of Daisy, and she neighed loudly so he would back up.

"Nice horses you got there."

I whipped around. There was a girl leaning against the doorway, wearing blue jeans, a T-shirt, and a cowboy hat. She was about twelve years old, like me. She smiled at me as she brushed her long brown hair over one shoulder, and I noticed a gap between her two front teeth. "Do you talk?" she asked, her big brown eyes wide.

"Um, yeah," I replied, blushing.

"I'm Ellie. My mama's inside, talking with your mama about sewing. I don't want to be a seamstress. I want to farm like my papa. No girl does that, but I want to be the first one."

"I'm Sarah," I mumbled. "Sarah Lynn."

"Nice to meet you. Can I ride your horse?"

I opened the horse gate, and she swaggered in before squaring up and jumping onto Midnight. I glanced at her, then took a saddle off a shelf that was attached to the wall. "Would you like one?" I asked Ellie.

"Nah."

"You don't talk very formally for a lady." I raised my eyebrows as I set up the saddle on Daisy.

"I don't wanna be treated like a lady. I want to be treated equally with the men. Who says I can't mine or vote or hunt? I can't even talk like this in front of my own mama, because she's so obsessed with etiquette." Ellie ran her hand down Midnight's mane.

I shrugged. "My mama says that it's the men's job to be loud and improper. We make them look good."

"That's what my mama says," Ellie chuckled.

As we opened the gate and set out along the road that led out of town, I decided I liked Ellie. We talked and talked the whole time we walked. She explained how her papa took her fishing and hunting. She told me she had four siblings and sighed when I said I only had one.

"You may not like 'em, but they're amazing," she told me.

We turned around and started heading back to town. After putting Daisy and Midnight away, it was dusk. The warm smell of stew wafted from the house, and as soon as the pot was set on the table we were in our chairs.

"Ah, Miss Lynn," a woman greeted me. She had short brown hair, green eyes, and formal dress-wear. "Sophia has told me so much about you."

"Thank you, ma'am," I replied, laying my napkin out on my knees as Mama set a loaf of bread on the table.

"I see you are as much of a lady as anyone, Miss Lynn. You could give Eleanor lessons."

"Ellie," Ellie muttered.

"No daughter of *mine* will eat at a table with no manners," Mrs. Norfit commanded. "Put a napkin on your knees."

Mama and I exchanged a glance before she cleared her throat.

"Oh, my apologies, Sophia," Mrs. Norfit said kindly to Mama.

"Not at all, not at all," Mama replied, smiling. "Allow me to serve dinner."

Mama took the serving spoon and Mrs. Norfit's bowl. The stew wasn't much, just gravy, beef chunks, carrots, and potatoes, all grown ourselves. Mrs. Norfit scolded Ellie for 'poor posture' before daintily dipping a piece of bread in the stew and biting it.

After Ellie, stew was poured into my bowl. I neatly spooned the warmth into my mouth while Ellie gulped quickly and hungrily. I didn't say anything as a gravy mustache formed on her lip.

"Eleanor Maye!" Mrs. Norfit scolded. "You are a *lady*, need I say it anymore? It is time you started acting it!"

"I eat like Papa," Ellie replied smugly.

Suddenly, I stood up. Mama, Ellie, and Mrs. Norfit stared at me as I rushed away, up the stairs and into my bedroom. They didn't know why I left. My papa ate like that.

•••

At dawn the next day, I put on an apron and tied my hair back without saying 'good morning' to Mama. I went out to the barn, took my basket off a hook on the wall, and went out to the chicken coop. I had loved mornings like this back in Texas. After the rooster crowed, I would be out at the coop collecting eggs. Then the cows needed to be milked, the goats needed to be fed, and the pigpen needed to be cleaned. Normally, this would be Peter's job, but I enjoyed it. Mama counted on me to take care of the chores.

"Sarah, I'm leaving. The wagon's here!" Mama called from the back door. "I left a list on the table!"

"Bye, Mama," I shouted back.

The door slammed as a chicken nipped my finger, looking for grain. I tossed the seeds, snatched the eggs, and trotted inside to put them away. The house was silent. Suddenly-
*DING a ling! DING a ling! DING a ling!*

I rushed to the phone, picked up the speaker and earpiece, and listened.

"Hello?" said the voice, thick with a country accent. "Sarah?"

"Papa?" I whispered hoarsely.

"Sarah!" the voice exclaimed. "Oh, darlin', it's so good to hear your voice. I got good news."

"What?" I gasped, my voice still hoarse.

"Peter and I are makin' our way. Only a day or so trip."

Confused, I replied, "But Mama and I moved here three months ago, and we were broke! How did you get money?"

"Never you mind," Papa replied sharply. His voice softened, and he added, "I miss you, Sarah, but I'll be there soon."

"I love you, Papa," I murmured.

"Love you too, darlin'. G'bye now."

There was a click and a silence. I set the phone down and collapsed into a chair. There was no way Papa got all that money on his own. It would have taken the richest man six months to get two hundred dollars, and Papa got it in three. Something suspicious was going on.

"Paper!" a voice yelled, and there was a light *thwack* as the *Daily Yooper Gazette*

hit the front porch. The paperboy's horse clopped away as I opened the door and picked up the day's newspaper. The headline blared:

### LOCAL BANK GONE BANKRUPT PORTAGE
**Officials reported that local Portage bank was robbed two nights ago. The bank was emptied completely except for a single penny, and police are still searching for suspects.**

I gasped.

No.

There was no way Papa got his money from that bank.

*But,* a voice in my head said, *he said he was only a day away.* Sand Dollar Bay was twelve miles from Torch Lake, which was a day's journey. Papa was extremely defensive when I asked him where he got the money. Obviously, the police would not suspect an innocent tourist and his son from Texas coming up to get with their family. Even if I did fully and one hundred percent think it was Papa, which I didn't, the police wouldn't believe a twelve-year-old girl. *Okay,* I told myself. *Okay. I'm going to call someone, and they will help.*

I walked into the kitchen and looked over a list of phone numbers tacked to the wall. As I walked back to the phone and dialed a number, I felt more confident. It rang for a few seconds, then I breathed a sigh of relief.

"Ellie Norfit speaking."

"Ellie, it's me, Sarah."

"Sarah? Hello! Can I come over?"

"Yes, please," I replied shakily. "I need to talk to you. Can I trust you with something important?"

"Yes!" Ellie shouted through the speaker. "I'll be there right away. I live a few blocks away from you, but my horse is fast. See you in a few minutes."

"Goodbye," I whispered.

Ellie hung up, and I set the phone down again. *Do the chores,* I told myself, and went out to milk the cows.

•••

I finished all the chores just as Ellie rode up to my house. She situated her horse with Daisy and Midnight, then we sat down in the kitchen. I got out a bowl of Tootsie Rolls and a kettle of tea, and we sat across from each other at the kitchen table.

"So. What did your papa say?" Ellie demanded.

"Nothing, really," I replied, shrugging. "I asked him where he got the money from, and he just told me it was none of my business."

"That's a signal," Ellie agreed, taking a sip of tea.

"And then the paper came," I pointed to it where it sat between us, "and I just connected two and two."

"Do we have proof?" Ellie asked. "Were there any pictures with the article?"

"No."

Ellie made a noise. "Okay. When did your papa say he'd be home?"

"A day, so most likely today or tomorrow."

"Here's the plan. When your papa comes home, we send him a letter—"

"No, Ellie. I'm not doing anything ignorant."

Ellie rolled her eyes. "Fine. Every other day, ask your papa for five cents."

"For what?"

"For chores. Would he ever do that otherwise?"

"No," I mumbled. "He'd tell me he didn't have money."

"If he says no again, we'll forget it. If he agrees, we move to stage two."

"What's stage two?"

Ellie shrugged. "Let's see if stage one works before we worry about stage two."

I raised my eyebrows.

"Just trust me, okay, Sarah?"

I nodded. "I trust you."

Ellie grinned. "Let's go for a ride into town."

"Why?" I asked dubiously.

"I have some money. Let's go get some candy from the general store."

"Again, why?" I repeated. "What's the point?"

Ellie sighed. "Look. My mama cares about where I am and what I'm doing when she's at home, but during the day, I can do what I like. Let's go, and you can meet my friend Belle."

"Who's Belle?" I asked as we went out the back door.

"My first best friend, next to you. She's really nice. Her dad owns the store." Ellie pushed the door to the barn and it swung open.

I touched the unfamiliar caramel colored horse on the nose. "What's her name?"

"Butterscotch. It's frustrating that I have to ride her with a saddle, but at least I have her." Ellie took a saddle off the shelf and started setting it up on Butterscotch.

I saddled up on Daisy, and after giving Midnight a sweet we set off. It was warm out, and the sun peeked out from the clouds. We set out, Ellie leading the way, and I was thankful that it was a silent journey. Papa had worried me, and a tornado raged inside my brain with questions. *How did he get the money? Did he steal from the bank? Would he ever lie to me?*

"Sarah?" Ellie's voice, for the first time, was tentative. "Are you okay?"

"Yes," I replied, shaking my head. "I just feel so ignorant. I have so many questions."

"We'll figure it out," Ellie promised. "Let's think about something else."

"I can't," I murmured. "Papa got me all shook up. I don't know what to think."

"When he comes home, we'll set up our plan," Ellie soothed. "It'll be fine. Like my papa says, 'when the going gets tough, the tough get going.'"

"At least you know for sure your papa isn't a criminal," I said mournfully.

Ellie groaned.

It was noon now, and there were people scattered throughout the market down Main Street. It was warm and sunny, too, with a light breeze and barely any clouds. A perfect day for everyone. Everyone except me.

"We're here," Ellie said cheerfully, hopping off Butterscotch. She took a rope tied to a metal pole and attached it to Butterscotch's headset, and I mimicked her. Ellie pulled a five dollar bill out of her jeans pocket and led the way inside.

It smelled musty and sweet. The bell above the door gave a little *ding-a-ling* as we stepped onto an old green carpet set on steps above a wooden floor. There were shelves of candy everywhere, packed to the brim. At the very front of the store, a girl our age with long, dark brown hair was wiping the counter. In front of it was a row of stools. Rows of glasses were hung on the wall above her, and on the back wall there were two signs, one on the left and one on the right. The left said **LIQ-UOR,** and the right **COCA-COLA.**

"Hey, Belle," Ellie called, strolling up to the counter with me at her heels. The girl glanced up, grinned, and set down the rag. I noticed she had big blue eyes that were almost clear.

"Who's this?" Belle asked, nodding at me. She wore play wear like me: a cotton T-shirt and a skirt.

"I'm Sarah," I replied, offering my hand.

Belle took it, and we shook twice. Ellie slapped the five dollar bill on the counter and sat on the swiveling stool. "One Coca-Cola, please, in the bottle. We'll be here a while."

Belle turned around and opened a large fridge door, took a Coca-Cola off the rack, popped it open, and slid it to Ellie. She shut the fridge and turned to me. "What would you like, Sarah?"

"Um…" I stared into the clear fridge door. Mama never let me have soda. I didn't know what I liked.

"She'll take a Squirt." Ellie sipped her Coke and smiled.

Belle pulled a glass bottle with the yellow and green logo on it from the rack, popped off the lid, and gave it to me. I sat down and gingerly took a sip.

"You like?" Belle asked, smiling and sitting on a stool behind the counter.

"Yes!" I exclaimed. It was bubbly, sweet, and stung my throat as it went down, leaving an aftertaste of lemon lime. I took a larger sip, still being as ladylike as I could. "Knew it," Ellie laughed.

Belle gave us three dollars and fifty cents back as change and sat down again. "Did you just move here, Sarah?" she asked.

"Indeed," I replied, sipping the Squirt again. "I'm from Texas."

"Anything interesting going on in your life?" Belle continued.

Ellie and I exchanged a glance, then burst out laughing.

Belle stared Ellie down, grinning. "Fill me in."

"I will," I told Ellie. She shrugged. Belle turned to me with wide eyes.

"Did you hear about the bank robbery?" I asked her.

"Sure. It was in the paper this morning. Gave my papa quite a scare. He hid all of our money, and it took Mama two hours to coax him to tell us where he hid it."

"My papa had to stay in Texas because he didn't have enough money to get our whole family here. Then yesterday, he called me and told me he was only a day away from here."

Belle looked thoughtful. "I don't know. Do you have a plan?"

"Yeah."

"Then follow out the plan and forget about it until he gets home. In the meantime, go get some candy. We have our usual Sunday sale on—"

"Penny Candy! Yes!" Ellie shouted. She swiped a dollar and seventy-five cents off the counter and vanished into the piles of sweets.

I took my half and gasped as I walked into an aisle. There was everything I loved! Peppermint drops, lemon drops, sour drops, gum drops, rock candy, butterscotch, jelly beans, all in big clear bins with tongs to get the exact number. There were little brown paper bags next to each display, stacked on a shelf. I took a pair of tongs in the peppermint drop bin and counted out ten. Then ten of lemon drops, ten of sour drops, so on and so forth, until I had exactly seventy pieces of candy. Stacked in a glassy storage container were mini cookies of all types. Chocolate chip, peanut butter, macaroons, snickerdoodles, shortbread. After neatly placing two of each in each bag, I left the aisle. When I rounded the corner to go back to the counter and pay, I saw Ellie. She had a bag and a half of sweets and was chomping on a string of red licorice. Belle raised her eyebrows.

"One dollar and seventy-five exactly," Ellie mumbled, slapping the money on the counter. Belle rolled her eyes.

Manistique German band

I neatly placed my half-full bag on the counter and gave Belle the one dollar and seventy cents. She handed me a nickel. "Thanks for that. It contributes to my paycheck."

I smiled. "Anytime."

Children were starting to crowd the shop, so after waving goodbye to Belle, Ellie and I walked out of the shop. I placed my bag in a pouch on the side of Daisy's saddle, and we were off. A man stopped us, spoke to Ellie, and she groaned before turning to face me. "I gotta go. Mama needs some help with the shop, but I'll come to your house for dinner."

I laughed. "Okay. Goodbye, Ellie."

"Bye." Ellie rode her horse away, behind a shop.

I started home, occasionally reaching into the bag and grabbing a lemon or peppermint drop. When we got to the house, there was an unfamiliar wagon outside. When I put Daisy away, there was a new handle on the barn door. Could this mean...

"Baby!" a man shouted as I closed the barn.

Him. All in his glory, with the sun shining on his overalls, boots, old shirt, cleanly shaved face, brown hair, and green eyes. He picked me up and spun me in a circle above his head while I laughed and sobbed. For so long I'd waited, and now I was in Papa's arms. He smelled like sweat and dust and cheap cologne, the smell I missed for three months.

Papa set me down on the ground, kneeled down, and pulled me into his strong arms. I wrapped my arms around his broad back and felt his muscles shift under my hands. I felt the stubble on the back of his head and his breath on my shoulder. I watched his spine rise and fall with each breath he took, and didn't let go until be pried my hands from him.

"Sarah Rose Lynn, I missed you so much." Papa put his big paws on my shoulders and grinned, showing me the gap in his front two teeth that looked just like Ellie's.

"Papa," I forced out, because I was too shocked for words.

"We're gonna have a better life here, you hear me? I got some money. We're gonna fix up this house with my money and Mama's, and it's gonna shine like new. I got a job as a blacksmith, and it makes almost as much as Mama."

I giggled. "Papa, I don't care about the house. I'm glad you're home."

"School starts in a week, baby girl. Are you excited? I'm going to be there to walk you in, tell all those little trouble-makin' boys to back off on my girl."

I snorted. "Whatever you want."

"Mama's makin' a feast tonight," Papa beamed. "In celebration of Peter and I comin' home. We're havin' pork, beans, corn, and I bought some fruit along the way."

"Apples?" I gasped, hope rising. I had loved granny smith apples since I was a little girl, especially in pie.

"Apples in a pie for my little girl." Papa pulled me into a hug again. "And Mama's havin' the Norfits come over. Good impression on 'em, you know."

I smiled. "You'll like Ellie, Papa. She's just like you."

Papa smiled back. "Let's go inside. Peter's probably whining, wonderin' where I am." He took my hand, stood up, and led the way into the house. Papa pushed the door open and let me go inside in front of him.

Mama was at the kitchen table, cutting up apples. She wore a big smile and her finest clothes under her apron.

"I cannot believe Mrs. Norfit let you go early," I said to her, beaming, as she set down her knife and hugged me.

"I got a call," Mama replied, releasing me. "It was Papa, and he said he was home, and when I told her she practically pushed me out of the place and told me she'd be round at six p.m. sharp with Eleanor and her husband."

Just then, Peter came rushing into the noisy kitchen. His short brown hair was askew, his pants were dirty, and his white T-shirt had mud on the sleeves. He saw me, and his face lit up with joy.

"Sarah!" he shouted, running over and hugging my hips. He was short for a seven year old, so I had to bend to hug him back.

"Papa got money from—" Peter began.

But Papa cleared his throat loudly. "What did I tell you?"

"It's a surprise," Peter replied mournfully. Papa nodded curtly.

I stood up, and Peter ran off, screaming, "Bun-bun! Bun-bun!"

Papa was talking to Mama, so I crept over to the phone and dialed a number.

"Stella's Spectacular Sewing, Eleanor speaking, how can I help you," Ellie's voice said dully into the phone.

"It's me, Ellie," I whispered.

Ellie's voice lit up at once. "Sarah? What is it?"

"Papa's home. You're coming over for dinner with your mama and papa." I nibbled on my fingernail.

"Really? Yes! We set our plan into action tonight, Sarah. The candy store is open till nine." There was a click, silence, and I knew she was gone. *She probably hung up to keep me from arguing,* I thought, chuckling.

I knew that Mama wasn't going to want me in the kitchen while she cooked, so I snuck out the back door and entered the dusty barn. This was my happy place, in case you hadn't noticed already. It was quiet as I sidled up to the horse pen, opened it, and sat down next to Daisy, who was lying on the floor. She huffed and let me rest my head on her. The barn door creaked again, and Papa appeared. He looked around, but couldn't see me from where I was on the floor, so he left, and the door creaked shut. I sighed and pulled a small book out of my pocket. The cover read *Great Expectations* in worn letters. I opened it and started to read until they came to get me.

•••

"Welcome, welcome. I'm Charles Lynn." Papa took Mr. Norfit's hand and shook it firmly twice.

"Zach Norfit," Ellie's dad replied.

"Stella Norfit," Mrs. Norfit beamed, shaking Papa's hand. "This is Eleanor."

Ellie grunted as Mama took Mr. Norfit's hand.

"This is Peter," Papa said, pushing him forward a little bit. Peter buried his face in Papa's dress pants. Mr. and Mrs. Norfit laughed. Ellie shot me a dark glance.

"Let us eat." Mama grinned and showed the guests to the dining room with many "after you"(s) and not "y'alls".

My family sat on one side of the table, the Norfits on the other. Mama cut up the pork, dished out the black and pinto beans and corn, surprise rolls, and sat. Papa asked God to bless dinner, and we ate.

"So, Charles," Mr. Norfit began. "I hear you struck it rich a week or so ago. That true?"

"Yes," Papa replied smugly.

"Don't get smart with me," Mr. Norfit warned, opening his jacket to reveal a police badge. I stared at Ellie, and she shrugged.

"I'll get smart with anyone who threatens me in my own home," Papa shot back.

Mr. Norfit stood up and had his hand on his belt, where I knew was the classic pistol all policemen carried. Papa stood up as well, and they glared at each other.

I couldn't take it.

"Stop!" I shouted, standing up. "Papa, don't deny it."

Papa turned to me, a shocked look on his face. "How did you know?" he whispered.

"What about our plan?" Ellie wailed.

"We don't need a plan," I replied, not looking at her. My eyes were locked on Papa. "All the clues lead up to this. Papa somehow made it up here, probably by stealing. He's a good thief because he's got quick fingers. Then he got into the bank and stole the money. He knew it would look like he didn't do it, because he's just an innocent man with his son. But he's not."

"Sarah," Papa whispered.

"It's not right for me to do this to my own father. But I would rather live in a home without him right now than with him. Officer Norfit, I know he did it. There's no other way."

Officer Norfit pulled handcuffs out of his belt and glanced at me. "Are you sure you want to do this?" he asked. "If he's proven guilty, you'll most likely have to come to the prison to see him."

"I know," I replied.

"I'm proud of you, Sarah," Papa told me as Officer Norfit clipped the cuffs on his wrists. "Very angry, but proud. You were smart enough to find all the tracks and brave enough to turn me in. It's incredible you figured it out in a few hours."

I gave a small smile. The room was silent as Officer Norfit led Papa outside, got into their wagon, and left for the police station.

Belle, Ellie, and I were up in the rafters of the barn. We recounted the story for Belle when she came over the next day with a small cake.

"Do you feel okay that you did it?" Belle asked, eyes wide. "I mean, he's your papa. I couldn't do that to my papa, no matter how bad the crime."

"I don't feel that bad," I replied. "I did the right thing."

"You did good," Ellie said, grinning.

"Yeah," I replied.

"You don't think you did something, do you," Belle murmured.

"No," I sighed. "I don't."

"Your Papa did that to himself. All you did was let him see the effects. No one needs money that badly that they should rob a bank."

I nodded. "Thanks, you guys."

They smiled. "Anytime."

**Megan Sutherland** is a twelve-year-old from Lake Linden-Hubbell Schools. She loves to read, write, draw, listen to music, go outside, and type. She also likes playing basketball and volleyball, as well as riding her bike and walking her dogs. She wants to be an environmental scientist or author when she grows up.

# Crucify and Burn

## by May Amelia Shapton (1st Place Senior Div.)

◆❖◆

Confined in my body are only ten colors, but when the light dances over me it might as well be ten thousand. All those brilliant shades of red and blue, green and purple, pink and orange, each shape bound by black metal, they come from within my soul, given life by the light that scatters them on the floor below. I am a window, seven hundred years old. I have seen two hundred and fifty thousand sunrises.

Below me people pass. On one side they bustle, trade, love and travel, on the other, they walk in silence, cry, kneel, and pray. They are beautiful though, no matter what age, for the fact they can do these things at all. Even the pigeons that have their wings do not love or cry; they can't even talk. But I hear the voices proclaiming their faith at all hours, and the confessions of faceless people meant only for the priest, I hear those too. And when they have left I hear the strange, melancholy ramblings of the priest who is just as lost as those he tries to help. It's all so

wonderful it makes me wish I knew what it was like to have tears come from within. I've heard that crying hurts, but I wouldn't mind because I've had my share of pain. No one hears my confession, my plea to the heavens each morning. Today is no different.

One child I've watched since he was only just born is getting scolded for using his phone and not paying attention. The guest speaker is nervous even though he's been here before, while a stranger in the back tries not to be noticed because they haven't. Laughter is floating around and it seems I could almost see it if only I looked a little closer. I am trying to distract myself. A fly buzzes around the chandelier. Seven hundred years has not made me any better at waiti. . . No no no no no! AAAAAAHHHHHH!!!

•••

Or at least, you know, that's what I would say if I had vocal chords. Every bloody day! Why does it have to be like this? All the peo-

*reek of Car Ferry No 4. at Manistique*

Shipwreck train car ferry AAR4 manistique

ple are gone now. I never get to see them leave. Has it been an hour? Two? Five? I don't know. But each day I live in fear of that time when the sun clears the edge of my pane, for it is in that moment, when the light comes streaming through in all its unfettered glory, that I am crucified by heavenly fire. Every inch of my being burns with agony. I last only long enough to see the pulpit become illuminated by the light of my sacrifice, to see a radiant spotlight fall on the faces of the people I've watched, to see the priest tilt his head and smile up at me. Then it all becomes too much and I wake up only after the sun has passed.

It's that smile. I know it is. It's what confuses me, and angers me, and pleases me all at once. They've all done it through the ages, not just this one, and I want to know what it is they see in me. I want to know. But I can't because in that smile is also the truth. The truth that he smiles because he sees my beauty and not my pain, and the truth that he can leave and have free will to ask

another being for help if he needs it. That smile mocks me and makes me hate people even though I love them, which just makes me hate myself. Yet nothing changes. I want to speak and to see, but every time it's the same, crucify and burn, crucify and burn. Crucify and burn!

•••

I'm tired of this cycle, tired of this fear. The soft moonlight filters in and soothes my pain now. The silver light reflects off of me instead of burning through me. Yes, the moon has always been my friend. Two hundred and fifty thousand sun rises is also two hundred and fifty thousand moons. One side facing in to feelings I don't want to face, the other facing out only to be beaten by rain and wind and ice. Who am I to ask for what I want? I, who try to love, but secretly despise. Empires have changed hands and names around me, but I am still here. Crucify. . . and burn. . .

•••

The stranger from this morning has returned. It's very dark now. Perhaps they want to ask the priest a question about their faith? Perhaps that is why they were uncomfortable this morning. Because they are thinking of converting, but aren't sure yet? This morning they sat too far back so the angle was wrong and I couldn't see them properly, but I see now from their slight frame that they are a woman. A thick black cloak hides her movements and a hood covers her head. She walks along the edge of the wall until she is almost parallel with the center shrine, then turns and walks out into the middle of the room where she kneels. I don't understand. I've never seen anyone act like this. She seems to have some reason for being here, but is scared of something. I think. And now from the shadows within the side of the cloak she has been keeping against the wall, she withdraws her last hope of not getting caught. It's clear now why she's been so cautious, so uncomfortable. There is a black bag next to her on the floor, and inside it is a bomb.

Her hands shake as she takes it out and sets it on the ancient stone floor. And then she takes off her hood. To help her see, perhaps? I don't know and it doesn't matter. She is the most beautiful creature I have ever seen in all my two hundred and fifty thousand days. The moonbeams filter through me and illuminate her face as she turns to look up at me. For a moment in time we are connected by the light and I could swear she knows what I'm thinking. Her skin glows gently and I see tears in her eyes. They shine like pearls as they slide down her cheeks. I was right after all. She is scared, scared of life and death, of pain and responsibility, of failure, rejection, knowledge and ignorance, and most of all she is scared of whatever has brought her to this place tonight. She is terrified of everything and it has broken her. She is like me. She understands what I've seen, what I've been through. We acknowledge each other in silence, but it feels we have spoken a thousand volumes.

She shakes as she stands, and I watch my reflection tremble in her dark, hopeless eyes. Then the world shatters into ten thousand colors and there is nothing but pain unlike anything I've ever known.

Falling Falling Falling Falling Falling Falling Falling Falling Falling Falling Falling Falling Falling Falling Falling Falling

Hundreds of versions of me are plummeting toward the ground. Tiny fragments and huge jagged shards, once a single entity, now free at last. And onto all of us, over and over as we fall around her, is reflected the face of the beautiful woman lying now almost dead.

There is smoke, flames and chaos all around us when at last I pierce her chest. I feel as her heart tries to beat around me, feel her blood well up at my edges. I know that for the first time in many, many years, perhaps her whole life even, she is happy. Somehow, I think I finally understand what the priests saw in me all those years, the Divine beauty of things beyond control or understanding.

Then the other bits of my former self come crashing down and a hundred glass knives slam into her body, killing her instantly and pinning her to the floor where she lies. The tears in her eyes, knocked free, mix red and run to the floor. They might as well be mine though, for I feel them as my own, and that ability to cry that I had so coveted is finally mine in my last moments before the shock wears off, and the pain of my body being shattered, and of my splintered soul that can no longer keep its light becomes oblivion. The fire caused by the bomb engulfs us and there is nothing more to tell. Only crucify and burn.

**May Amelia Shapton** is a senior at Lake Linden-Hubbell High School. She enjoys traveling, and cross-stitching, and her love of reading spans all genres. She also loves cats, the sound of rain on a roof and the smell of a book. Her after school time is mainly spent working, playing in her school drumline, and captaining her school robotics team. In her opinion, the best things in life are good food, bad laughs and nice friends.

# Thief of Hearts

## by Cora Mueller (2nd Place Senior Div.)

◆❖◆

The dream was a languid thought, one that I couldn't quite place my finger on. The whole point of a dream is to send you spiraling toward another dimension that reflects your own, only slightly more realistic world.

It was wintertime in Blaksin. You wouldn't know it, though. Pyirmas had passed without a second glance, with no decorations, happiness, or good times to send it on its way. The New Year had come once again, but no one was celebrating. The Bridge Street Massacre was on our tails, the politician Maka's murder only a few months previous. A cold sweat soon came upon me, but it was freezing in the dream. I brushed it all off, as one can in sleep, and continued staring down at my freezing world.

Why was I dreaming of a freezing world? Blaksin didn't get snow in wintertime — Jack Frost hadn't darkened our doorstep in years. This was the point in which I knew I would wake up; reality's chilling hands were grasping for my mind, pulling me back with logic. The cold sweat didn't stop; it dripped down me, in swaths of slush, and froze where it held to me. I wasn't watching a freezing world.

I was freezing. I tried to move, but the ice wouldn't let me. It had grabbed onto the snow and held me there, stuck in one place, as I grew more chilled. I felt like a pig stuck in a freezer, my only hope that the butcher would come to get me. Well, my only hope I'd wake up soon. The logic had come, and when logic comes, dreams fall behind pathetically and become distant memories. Sweat dripped from my forehead — aha! This time, it was warm. Reality was coming in fast.

Reality would not have an easy battle.

For the next eternity of waking up, I fought what I felt was a sickness that had entered my body and dream at that moment to break out of this newly deemed nightmare. The sweat came in waves, the cold freezing it up immediately and me becoming slicker and sicker and painfully stuck to the ground. The cold was trying to reach my brain through my ears, and as it froze its way through, I saw a breaking point. For me, and for the dream. It was wake up or be in here forever more.

So I did what I had to do.

Sleep left me immediately, and as I looked up at the ceiling, my hands sticky and wet, the chills rolled over and away from me. The fear receded, as did the vicious fictional frostbite and immobility, and all that was left from the nightmare was a cold feeling embedded deep in me. I struggled to remove the thick blanket and lay on the barren mattress, feeling deflated. It was at that moment I realized the coldness hadn't left for the dream landscape yet, and I realized something was terribly wrong. Within me, I knew there was something missing.

It was the dreadful feeling that I'd forgotten something, but I didn't know what. I leaped out of bed, fearful of intruders, fearful of the unknown entity that could be hiding in the other room, and that's when I knew it.

Someone had stolen my heart.

A thought so odd had to have been made up. It was fiction, a lie I told myself because of my overactive imagination and adrenaline to explain the emptiness. But then I paused for a moment and shakily drew my hand to my chest. I waited for a second, and then another, and then pressed my palm harder. I moved it down, up, left and right, but it was gone. My pulse had disappeared overnight. It occurred to me that this could be a dream as well and that I was now stuck in an infinite parade of dreams which I would wake from to another dream. But logic, which had rescued me from the frozen nightmare, deemed that I was not in my head but in the real world. My heart was gone, but I was still there, still breathing, so my only other choice was to accept it. This was reality, this was a world where a heart could be stolen away at midnight, and my balcony door was open.

I stumbled toward it, my limbs drowsy from sleep and my body not accustomed to giving itself orders this early in the morning. The wicker door was flung open to the night and the elements, and the frosty nightmare suddenly made sense. It was frigid in the room, something I had been too distracted to notice before, and with a second thought I pulled

the heavy blanket off the floor and dragged it with me.

I lived in a cramped apartment on the top floor of a crumbling building, and the best part about it was the balcony. I had planned to put up greenery of some sort, but that plan fell through as soon as autumn came. No plants want to grow in Blaksin's autumn. No plants can. But the balcony was still a spot to smile at the happenings on the street below — the hustle of merchants in the early morning and street urchins vying to make a quick buck — and had a great view of the waterfront, which looked its best during the dawn's light.

At that moment, I chose not to look fondly at my neighbors, but to direct wary gazes at each and every corner I could imagine a thief would be lurking. And there were many. It seemed as if during the night, darkness reigned over the city, and all crevices conspicuous to the human eye were now hidden in black masses.

I searched, dread hanging over me like the thick blanket clinging to my back with feverish hands. Avail refused me. My breath hitched, and for a second, I thought I would cry. But I only collapsed onto the floor. Without my heart, I was nothing. I was an empty shell of clammy hands and an excavated chest left with a shard of coldness.

It was quite coincidental when I noticed through the bars of my balcony fence a pair of eyes I could not previously see. And those cat eyes I knew belonged to a wretch of a man, a brutal and vigilante pirate whom I had had a few run-ins with in the past.

Chapman Wright, you son of a gun.

Without a second thought, I launched myself off the balcony to reclaim my heart.

The drop would have killed me if I had not aimed for the ledge across the way. From there I scrambled to the balcony he had perched on, but by then he was gone. I twisted the quilt around the iron bars and swung down to the second-floor terrace, keeping my eyes out for any sign of him. There was no flurry of movement in the night, but I knew he was smarter than to just run for it. I held my breath and focused on the sounds of the night. There were no padding footsteps, no flutter of ill-fitting clothes, nothing — save for a quiet breath.

I turned my gaze slowly around, staring into the eyes of the criminal. Wright sat there, shrouded in darkness and crouched upon the iron railing. He raised a silent eyebrow, and without a second thought jumped off. He landed like a cat and met my eyes again. He stood there, lazy confidence the only armor he wore, before backing away with a smirk. In his right hand lay a parcel wrapped in newspaper, and he taunted me with it, holding it up to let the sliver of moonlight bounce off it.

It was a challenge someone of his ilk would present, and it was a challenge I was ever willing to take. I grappled the brick and mortar building and slid down, chasing him into the nipping night.

Wright kept to the pavement, darting through alleyways and skirting bridges, and it made it wholly difficult for me to determine where he was heading. On the Blaksin streets, everywhere headed to everywhere. Confusion may have not been his goal, but mine was what consumed my every thought, and so I, steadfast, continued hunting him down. A heart is not something to take for granted, especially when it can be stolen so easily out from under you.

The shadows were his friends. Wright flashed in my vision, a disappearing act that kept reappearing just in time for me to follow. There was a rhythm to it, one I didn't know — a dance he had perfected long before I stepped upon the floor. Left at the Collins' Bakery, dead-on until the Wellside Bridge came into view, then a right toward the harbor. At some point, I realized that he had led me in a circle — six lefts around the same block — and I stopped to catch my breath. My was body racked with the icy air, the cold clamping down in my chest and my throat sore from the frigid breeze.

When I heaved myself upward, again, expecting to be alone and having to hunt him down once again, he was leaning against a doorframe. He was fiddling with something, but when he noticed me, his smile grew into a shark's grin. He took a few dramatic steps out, twirling and his clothes swirling about

him, before taking off again. I tried to feel resentment, and I could taste the beginnings of it, but it dissipated and all that was left was the cold feeling clinging to me.

I needed my heart once more, or I would be left to freeze.

Our chase throughout town led to a luxurious building overlooking the river waterfront: the Merchant's Manor. For a man so devoted to the Almighty, he didn't mind boasting his wealth for all eyes to see and then parading it around. The house, if you could call it that, sat on its own little island in the waterway with its own little gate and its own little bridge. Wright was right now dancing on that bridge, weaving his way through the shadows and odd spots toward the sparkling marble mansion of the Merchant.

I hid behind the stone wall that railed the bridge and observed Wright stride up to the iron-wrought fence gate. He peered back at me over his shoulder, but I was hidden by the shadows. If he couldn't see me, I would consider it luck in this horrible, frozen darkness. A guard came, stiff and grumpy, muttering something to Wright that I couldn't hear even in the silent night. Then the guard became clearer in his own, gruff way. "You sure you weren't followed? We've had some problems with... our publicity lately."

"I can assure you, she didn't so much as wake up." There were a few more grumbles, but I was too busy grinding my teeth in frosty pain. There were no sounds after that other than the padding of footsteps and the small clanking of the gate being locked.

I crept toward the bridge, shivering and shaking with every brush of wind. The waterfront brought more cold air, and cold air apparently felt like sharp, stabbing pains whenever it touched oneself. I neared the gate, and with all the strength I could muster from my run, grasped the bars. I winced and stumbled backward, the chill of ice burning my hands. And then I collapsed. It was not because of the frigid blaze of the bars, nor the bleak weather, but because the coldness inside had lurched outward. The icy illness had taken root and was growing, filling more of my empty body with its numbness.

I needed my heart.

With a vigor I previously lacked, I clambered up the fence and tumbled onto the ground below. The cement would have broken my fall if it had been there; instead, a large flower pot full of exotic flowers softened the blow to an abrupt crack. I rolled off the pink blossoms and mumbled something crass before ripping myself off the ground. The ground moved beneath me as I lunged forward towards the large horse, my bare feet digging into the soil and clinging to the earth. The house had a gilded entrance, but the gold was a mere distraction. The door would not do.

To the left, I saw a small servant's entry. My legs were cold upon the hard cement, but I forced myself to keep walking, my only solace the idea of a warm hearth awaiting me inside. I prayed and pushed on the door, and to the little luck I had left, it opened. Inside the mansion, the walls were as marble as they were outside. Luxury dripped from everything I saw, though I was surrounded by what could only be a side hallway for staff. I crept along the path, leaving a trail of wet dirt that I did not care about until I heard the sound of voices. The halls looked all the same, but I followed the echoes until they were loud enough that I knew exactly where I was.

A small wooden door stood before me, and beyond it lay the Merchant and Wright. I stood as close as I dared, but I could not understand any of the words passing between them. That left me no other option than to cautiously push the door open, and I peered out into the lamp-lit space of arches and pillars the Merchant called his parlor. Everyone else knew that it was a throne room, and even though years had passed by since I had last been in its presence, I remembered its splendor. One cannot help but agree after seeing the marble beauty the Merchant sat at.

It only took a moment to locate the two; they stood in the center of the large room, separated only by the dais the alabaster throne stood on. For what it was worth, the Merchant gave off the appearance of a kindly old man. However, his image was worth a wanted poster in every city outside the country. He had special ties with the government.

The Merchant's spindly hands reached out to grab something from Wright, a parcel the contents of which were not needed to describe, and then Wright turned on his heel and went on his merry old way. My eyes followed the Merchant's movements like the desperate person I was. If he locked it up somewhere I could find it. I would find it. If I didn't, I would die.

It was as if my body had been following my thinking; for the moment I thought the words, I convulsed in cold pain. The frost inside wasn't spreading outward anymore — it was ripping the rest of my body into the empty space, trying to build a new heart wrought of ice and organs. I crumpled to the floor, the thump of my body echoing around the cavernous room, and in my delirium, I noticed the guards storming toward me. I was caught like a rat in a trap. I could only writhe in their grasp as they strode forward as one.

The agony of freezing inside ripped through my body as a single, unending wave of numbing pain. It would not stop, not when I was thrown against the cold ground, nor when the Merchant cuffed my head back with his shoe. It grabbed hold of my entirety as the Merchant glared down at me, and as he spoke, but by the second sentence the torment had died down to a dull ache in my soul.

"And how terrible it was that you woke up. We will have to talk to Mr. Wright about that, will we not, gentlemen?" The Merchant spoke with an air of sophistication and malice. He was disgusted. "What do you have to say for yourself, madame?" I gurgled out a reply, still nursing my frostbitten body.

"Yes, yes, you want your heart back. Like they all do, I suppose, though... getting here to reclaim it is something to behold." He stepped back onto his marble throne with a terrible smile and the energy of a man much younger than himself. There I lay in the few seconds of silence, the subsiding pain growing more distant with each passing breath.

"Shall we get rid of the body, sir?" One of the brutes asked, vexation demolishing the last of my misery. I struggled up off the ground, my limbs fragile and torpid, and turned to meet his iron gaze.

"What body?" I hissed, for that was all I could muster. I slowly faced the Merchant once again. I eyed the throne, worry building in me as I didn't spot the parcel. He must have hidden it while I was a convulsing glacier on the floor.

"No. Leave her. It might do her well to watch." The guards backed away, tucked into the marble pillars that sprouted from the room. The Merchant's sharp-toothed smile returned and he snapped his fingers twice before speaking. "You will die by morning, so I suppose that I should explain to you in detail what I will do with your heart." He chuckled ruthlessly as a servant, permanently bent over in a bow, glided toward him with a metal platter.

The coldness in my chest surged again, but this time it was battling against a warmth. The silver was the only separation between me and my heart, and if I could muster up the last dredges of my strength, I would be able to close that distance to nothing at all. I eyed it with the bloodthirst of a tiger stalking its prey, success within my grasp. It was then that I forgot of the old man drowned in decadence and the cat-eyed thief who had ripped my heart from me.

It was my mistake.

It took only seconds. My body crumpled as the parcel was unwrapped, open and willing to allow my heart back in. But it didn't. It pulsed and beat in his claws, but its subtle glow was pulled farther away from me and closer toward him. His jaw unhinged, his razor teeth gleaming in the firelight, and for a few moments the only truth I knew was that my heart would be gone, in the gullet of this monstrosity, and that the minute it was gone, I would rip him by his skin and hair into shredded pieces of upper class and fine wines. And then I would die, but revenge would be mine, and I could die happy with that.

With this thought, my body closed itself in its willingness and I rose, preparing to launch a counterattack and stab his eyes out. It would be a bloody mess, but a righteous one, and even if I was torn limb from limb by his no doubt loyal guards, I could die happy. My heart, once gently beating beneath his fingertips, was now throbbing and convulsing. Adrenaline came to me, a great rush of dangerous courage and a bloodthirst. It flung itself from his greedy maw and fell at my feet.

Chippewa woman · making birch bark canoe

At once, a multitude of things happened. I grabbed for it, and it beat harder, and I felt my blood pumping, and the frost melted from my insides out too quickly. There were the sounds of guards moving, and the Merchant pushed himself off his pedestal with an evil grin.

"My child, what success your heart will bring me! Thank you for revealing its true power. You will die, of course, immediately, but it will be painless, I promise!

And then, before I could answer such a convoluted phrasing, a gunshot rounded the Merchant's parlor. Blood spurted from his head, decorating the marble around him with its scarlet droplets, and he fell gracelessly to the floor. No one moved, not the guards, not the servant, and certainly not the man now dead.

I took the only chance I knew I'd have and I *ran*. I blasted through the nearest exit — a small window my physique only barely allowed me passage through. I hit the ground hard, and then crumpled to the ground. Trouble was coming. There was the pounding of guards' feet, the sound of their weapons clanking and guns reloading — thank god both barrels had been fired — and, by the looks of things, someone was running across the roof.

But I had my heart back. The numbness that had flooded through me, the feeling of absolute pain and the death breathing over my shoulder, they all dissipated the moment I had placed my hands on it.

It was, admittedly, slightly disturbing to see your raw, beating heart outside of your body. I ignored that, and it was much easier for me to do so in the dark night. I was tempted to hop over the nearest wall and into the river, but then I reasoned that I couldn't swim, so there was no point in drowning.

I turned toward the back of the building, hoping that there was some way to get across the river — a servant's bridge or something to connect it to the other side of town — and there it was! An old, rickety, trodden on wooden bridge that had missed the redecoration. It looked flimsy enough to be swept away by a gust of wind, but it had stayed upright somehow, so I wouldn't judge it too harshly.

I kept to the walls. There was a feeling of rejuvenation holding the heart, and my near-death experience was long forgotten by my lungs, my legs, my nerves. Being whole again really helped running away from a vengeful horde of guards.

I ran when I figured that the sound of footsteps were getting far too close, and was at the bridge with gunshots at my heels. Crossing it wasn't the issue, I could see then. The problem would be beating up the ten city guards who had been alerted of the murder of some poor old citizen, and were presently standing at the other side.

The Merchant's guards were storming toward me, and I realized that, well, I *was* going to die tonight, whether it be in the city's cell, or tormented by whoever took over the Merchant's criminal business, or stabbed through the gut, or drowned in the river.

I had really come to terms with death in the past few hours, so I took the least painful route. I walked to the middle of the bridge; someone shot a warning at me, and the oncoming guards stopped and huddled around the other side.

I then realized that the heart was far more valuable than I could have previously assumed, and that it could easily be a bargaining tool. Too bad that I seemed to require it

to keep on living, but as I might die within the next few minutes anyway...

No. I wasn't going to trade death for a very cold last few hours. I was going to scare them, though. So much so, and then I'd jump, of course, and hopefully be carried somewhere warm enough that I wouldn't die of hypothermia. Or, hopefully, Atlantis lived in the harbor and I could just wallow down there instead of drowning.

"Gentlemen, we are certainly at a predicament, aren't we?" I said darkly. I knew how to be vindictive when I felt like it. I gently removed my heart from its position wrapped tightly next to my stomach and held it over the water. Half the guards began to freak out, but the minute one of them took a step, I snickered.

"I wouldn't do that if I were you. See, my hand is getting tired, but it gets more tired the closer you come to me." For threatening speeches, it wasn't any good, but I was on a time crunch, coming to terms with my imminent death, and tired. It had been a night. Mentally, of course, since I felt all the better with my heart in my hands.

It seemed to realize the betrayal I was putting it through, however, and a gut-wrenching pain filled my empty chest. I almost dropped it. The pain subsided, but the fear in my enemies' eyes only grew. I could taste the way they'd regret ever stealing my heart.

Well, Chapman Wright did the dirty work, but that would only be another thing on the list that this entire night would make. I'd go out with a bang. A cold, hard splash into the river, and then I would be gone. I'd like that. I preferred it over death in a cell.

And then I saw the rowboat. It was creeping toward me, following the river's direction into the harbor, and on it sat a peculiar old man. He was whistling some foreign tune, and waved peacefully at us as if we weren't in the middle of a standoff.

Oh, *no*. Not an old man. Chapman Wright, continuing his spree of crimes, had stolen a boat from the Merchant's docks. I wished I'd thought of it first.

And then I realized something.

The boat would be under the bridge for a few seconds.

And I could make that jump.

I inched closer to the edge, garnering the attention of every one of those hounds the Merchant had called, and I really needed to stop referring to the Merchant as some alive person, but it seemed too difficult to fathom that he was actually dead. And as the boat slid underneath, I hurled myself off in the most dramatic and haphazard fashion I could, and fell the twenty feet to the bottom of the hull.

I'd had my unfair share of drops from a range of heights, and at least half had ended up worse than this. My heart was beating a bit faster now, but thankfully I'd absorbed most of the impact with my back.

Wright seemed surprised with the sudden off-balance, but he kept rowing and whistling, and as I looked up in sheer delight I realized that the group of frothing, vicious guards standing on top of the bridge would be hunting me down in a matter of moments, and that I had absolutely nowhere to go.

Wright seemed to read my mind.

"You need a ride?"

"Out of town, as quickly as possible, thank you very much."

"I've got a boat."

"You don't suppose we'll be able to row to another country in this?"

"I mean, if you want to put in a bit of effort."

I stopped, gathered my thoughts, and then slapped him.

"Why did you steal my heart? Wait, let me rephrase that. Why did you rip my heart out from my chest using some satanic ritual?"

"To kill the Merchant, of course. I let you follow me, didn't I?" So I was a distraction.

"That's what that chase was for?"

"Of course. If I didn't want you following me, you wouldn't have been able to."

"I sincerely doubt that." We were silent for a moment, with nothing but the jeers of the Merchant's guards running through the city behind us.

"How big is the boat?"

"Big enough to get us to Maverick, if you wanted."

"How much do I need to pay you?" At this he paused, and then turned to me.

"I expect at least ten gold." That wasn't even enough to buy a decent meal.

"Woah, what a rip-off."

"And you'll help me find this prophet in Sicaro."

"A prophet? No, wait, you stole my heart, I deserve to be put on a desert island." At this he looked icily back at me.

"You want to be carrying around that heart for the rest of your life?" I paused and took a few breaths.

"You can't put back a heart."

"I would never do something I couldn't undo." I felt the urge to slap him again, and wished that I'd kept my righteous aggression for right then.

"I heavily disagree with the fact that you think you can put back a heart."

"But the prophet in Sicaro can."

"You want my help to find a *prophet*? You know how dangerous that is, right? You know how we can die? I've come this close to death way too many times for a single night, and I'm not in the mood to guarantee mine once again."

"Well, you didn't die from any of those."

"That's terrible logic." And we continued bickering for the rest of the boat ride right up until we had to hide under a bridge from the guards who were swarming the area. By sunrise, we had snuck to the harbor and were making our way to his ship from the underside. Above were the footsteps of angry guards and neither of us wanted to get into trouble with them after we'd survived that night.

I was heading to Sicaro to find a prophet to put back my heart, I mused as we swung onto the outer hull of his ship. And to think that it could only ever be *easy* for me.

**Cora Mueller** is a freshman at Houghton High School. She usually passes the time by reading, sketching, or singing along to her favorite musicals. She loves the science fiction genre, but rarely expresses it in her writing. She has been telling stories since she was a child and finds herself often daydreaming of far off worlds.

# Attention

## by Fenwood Tolonen (3rd Place Senior Div.)

◆ ❖ ◆

I was walking around the house again, bored and lonely. I picked up Teddy along the way to the living room. Mommy and Daddy still weren't home yet. They used to tell me that they went to a place called work. I wonder what they do there and what it is like. I really wanted to have someone listen to what I have to say, so I sat Teddy down and talked to him.

"It's OK, Claire, they will listen to you soon," Teddy told me. He always knows what to say!

Mommy and Daddy don't listen to me anymore. They always look sad...I wonder why. I think that mommies and daddies should listen to their four-year-olds. We have a lot to say, you know. I could hear sounds coming from the door, which meant Mommy and Daddy were home. When they opened the door, I waved but they didn't wave back. They still looked sad—Mommy looked like she was crying, so I wanted to make them food. Everyone likes food. I went over to the other room and opened the fridge. It was really cold, but I have been cold all the time now for some reason...this time it made me shake. I grabbed a box filled with eggs. I know what

they are since Mommy has always told me to hold on tight, so I made sure to. I looked over to see mommy and daddy staring at me. I waved to see if they will finally pay attention to me, but nothing.

I went over to the table and tried to put the eggs on it, but it was tall, probably made for mommies and daddies, not four-year-olds. I tried to reach, but the eggs fell and broke, causing a runny, yellow yolk to come out.

"What the hell was that?" I heard Daddy yell. I covered my ears; Mommy does not like me hearing words like that. I looked over at Mommy and Daddy to see if they were mad, but they did not seem mad or sad...yet, they were not happy. They looked just like I do when something scares me. *Why?*

I left the eggs there since Mommy would come pick them up. I walked over to her and grabbed her shirt and pulled. She looked down, but not at me, with a sad and scared look in her eyes. *How can I get her to look at me?*

"Did you feel that?" I heard Mommy ask Daddy, but neither looked at me.

Sault Ste Marie -- stuck in snow

Daddy replied, a bit annoyed with wide eyes, "I didn't feel anything, don't say stuff like that."

I sat down and started to cry. *That will make them look at me.* I threw Teddy to show how mad I was, but they only looked at Teddy and not me. I cried even more. *How can they just let me be like this*?

They are not very good mommies and daddies. I got up and I kicked the chair they sat on; I was really mad.

"Did you do that?" Mommy asked. She sounded a bit upset. *Why?*

"I assumed you did that," Daddy's voice was softer since I walked away but he also sounded upset.

I walked around the home and kicked all the doors. *If I cannot get them to look at me by being nice and sad, they have to look at me when I'm being bad*! I heard Mommy and Daddy get up, I started to jump up and down. They looked at the doors; Mommy looked scared while Daddy looked mad and scared. I took Teddy and sat down. Mommy and Daddy got up and started to put their shoes on. *They are going somewhere.* I ran over to them and tried to put my shoes on, but it was hard. I ran between them so I could go with them too.

I jumped in the car and was singing a song. I was a pretty good singer; Mommy told me so. Or at least she used to tell me so. The car ride was taking a long time and they didn't bring me any toys. When the car stopped, Mommy and Daddy slowly walked out.

We were at a place where the dead people sleep. It was cold and dark with a lot of stone blocks coming out of the ground. I have been here a couple of times before but I hated this place. I walked with them and saw Grandma and Grandpa. I waved and yelled but even they didn't look at me. They stood at a block of stone. Someone dead must sleep here. I walked up closer and was able to make out two words: Claire May. That was my name, but I'm not sleeping! I looked at Mommy and Daddy and they were crying. *Why?*

"It's a shame that she didn't make it," I heard Grandma say, but who didn't make it? Mommy said that her little girl was gone. *But I'm right here.* All of a sudden, it hit me. Like when I kicked the doors.

I am dead. I am the person sleeping here.

**Fenwood Tolonen** is a freshman at Lake Linden-Hubbell High School.

# *Young Writers Encouraged to Submit to 2020 Dandelion Cottage Short Story Contest.*

◆❖◆

**Contest Rules**

- Each teacher may nominate up to two short stories to represent their school.
- Home-schooled students may submit stories through their local school.
- Home-school co-ops representing more than ten students will be treated as a school.
- Maximum length: 5,000 words.
- Authors must attend or be home-schooled in an Upper Peninsula School District.
- Teachers, parents, and others may offer suggestions and comments, but all writing must be the work of the author. In the real literary world, editors will offer suggestions. This is to be a learning experience.
- Short stories must be submitted electronically in MS Word (preferred) or PDF format prior to January 31st.

- Authors will retain the copyright to their work, but UPPAA reserves first publishing rights for eighteen months after submission. Winning entries will be published in the annual U.P. Reader. . Selected works may also appear in a "Best of U.P. Reader" edition to mark our 10th anniversary.

**Recognition**

- First place winner will receive $250.
- Second place winner will receive $100.
- Third place winner will receive $50.
- Winning school will receive a trophy for display during the coming year.
- Only one prize ($150) will be awarded for the best middle-school entry.

**Please visit www.DandelionCottage.org for more details on how to submit your stories.**

# Help Sell
# The U.P. Reader!

## The popularity of the *U.P. Reader* is growing, but we need it to grow more.

Help us sell the *U.P. Reader* by selling the Reader alongside your other books. The *U.P. Reader* at its wholesale price allows those who wish to carry it to make a nice profit on the sales. Bookstores and individuals can all benefit from helping the U.P. Reader grow.

**If you have writing that has been published in the *U.P. Reader*, you should be selling copies of the Reader alongside your other work.** This not only helps get exposure for your writing but for all the others that were accepted alongside yours. Part of the mission of the *U.P. Reader* is to get the many voices of the writers of the UPPAA in a single publication so that readers would have a place to find and sample the incredible talent that makes up the authors and poets of the Upper Peninsula.

**Taking a few Readers to an event can make the difference in selling.** Those who have been selling the U.P. Reader have seen good sales and considerable interest in the publication from readers and customers. Many customers ask the seller if they have a piece in the book to sign it. As the U.P. Reader is helping you as a writer, you can be helping the *U.P. Reader.*

**Do you have local booksellers in your area?** Encourage them to stock the *U.P. Reader.* Bookstores that are selling the Reader are seeing brisk sales. Many of the bookstores have restocked their issues several times and are saying how much they enjoy them. They are profitable and returnable. The *U.P. Reader* is a win-win situation for bookstores.

**Take a copy of the U.P. Reader to your child's English or Language Arts teacher.** The Dandelion Cottage Award is open to all children in U.P. schools and homeschool. There is never a fee to participate!

**Back issues of the *U.P. Reader* are also still available.** They can still be ordered right alongside the new issue and can be combined to sell as a set. There are many who still haven't discovered the U.P. Reader yet, and a package set is a nice way to introduce them to the joys reading a Reader. These can still be purchased wholesale just like the current issue.

There are hardcover versions of the *U.P. Reader* as well. These are beautiful bound versions of the *U.P. Reader* that are a wonderful keepsake for the real *U.P. Reader* fan. Again, these can be ordered wholesale and sold right alongside the paperback versions.

To order, go to UPReader.org/publications on the web and put in your order. Contributing authors will be emailed a discount code and their orders will be discounted to the wholesale price (50% Off!).

Please help us, help you make the *U.P. Reader* a success!

# Come join
# UPPAA Online!

The UPPAA maintains an online presence on several social media areas. To get the most out of your UPPAA membership, be sure to visit, "like," and share these destinations and posts whenever possible!

## Web Sites
- **www.UPPAA.org**: learn about meetings, publicity opportunities, publicize your own author events, add your book to the catalog page, read newsletter archive.
- **www.UPReader.org**: complete details about deadlines, submission guidelines, how to place a print advertisement, where to buy U.P. Reader locally, and more.

## Facebook Pages
- **UPPAA**: www.facebook.com/UPSISU/ —OR—type in **@UPSISU** into the Facebook "search" bar
- **UP Reader**: www.facebook.com/upreaders/ —OR— type in **@UPreader** into the Facebook "search" bar

## Twitter
- Message to **@UP_Authors** or visit https://twitter.com/UP_Authors

# U.P. Reader — Volume #1 (2017)

Ask your local bookseller or visit www.UPReader.org to order

ISBN 978-1-61599-336-9

# U.P. Reader — Volume #2 (2018)

Ask your local bookseller or visit www.UPReader.org to order

ISBN 978-1-61599-384-0

# U.P. Reader — Volume #3 (2019)

*Featuring*

"The Purloined Pasty" and "The Amorous Spotted Slug" by Larry Buege

"Grand Island for a Grand Time" by Mikel B. Classen

"#2 Pencils" by Deborah K. Frontiera

"The Rolls K'Nardly"

"Seeds of Change" and "The Lovers, the Dreamers,and Me" by Amy Klco

"The Best Trout I Never Ate" and "Pirates, Gypsies and Lumberjacks" by David Lehto

"Cut Me" and "The Demise of Christian Vicar" by Sharon Kennedy

"Warmth" by Bobby Mack

"Welcome to Texas, Heikki Lunta!" by Becky Ross Michael

"Aiding and Abetting" By T. Sanders

"Three Roads" by Donna Searight Simons and Frank Searight

"Trouble with Terrans" by Emma Locknane

"Stellae" by Lucy Woods

"Free" by Kaitlin Ambuehl

"becoming zen" and "good life" by T. Kilgore Splake

"Catching Flies by Aric Sundquist"

"You Are Beautiful" and "The Snake Charmer" by Ninie G. Syarikin

"Summer of the Yellow Jackets" by Tyler R. Tichelaar

Ask your local bookseller or visit www.UPReader.org to order
ISBN 978-1-61599-447-2

# U.P. Reader — Volume #4 (2020)

*Featuring*

Ask your local bookseller or visit www.UPReader.org to order

ISBN 978-1-61599-508-0

CPSIA information can be obtained
at www.ICGtesting.com
Printed in the USA
BVHW011917271221
624949BV00003B/179